Advances in Natural Language Generation

COMMUNICATION IN ARTIFICIAL INTELLIGENCE SERIES

Artificial Intelligence (AI) is a central aspect of Fifth Generation computing, and it is now increasingly recognized that a particularly important element of AI is communication. This series addresses current issues, emphasizing generation as well as comprehension in AI communication. It covers communication of three types: at the human–computer interface; in computer–computer communication that simulates human interaction; and in the use of computers for machine translation to assist human–human communication. The series also gives a place to research that extends beyond language to consider other systems of communication that humans employ such as pointing, and even in due course, facial expression, body posture, etc.

Communication in Artificial Intelligence Series Editors:
Robin P. Fawcett, Computational Linguistics Unit, University of Wales Institute of Science and Technology
Erich H. Steiner, IAI EUROTRA-D and University of the Saarland

From Syntax to Semantics: Insights from Machine Translation, eds: E. H. Steiner, P. Schmidt and C. Zelinsky-Wibbelt

Advances in Natural Language Generation: An Interdisciplinary Perspective, Volume II eds: Michael Zock and Gérard Sabah

Further titles are in preparation

Advances in Natural Language Generation

An Interdisciplinary Perspective

Volume 1

Edited by
Michael Zock and Gérard Sabah

Ablex Publishing Corporation
Norwood, New Jersey 07648

Printed in Great Britain

Library of Congress Cataloging-in-Publication Data
Advances in natural language generation: an interdisciplinary
  perspective/edited by Michael Zock and Gerard Sabah.
      p.   cm.–(Communication in artificial intelligence)
    Includes bibliographies and indexes.
    ISBN 0-89391-527-0 (v. 1). ISBN 0-89391-537-8 (v.2)
    1. Computational linguistics.   2. Natural language processing
(Computer science)   I. Zock, Michael.   II. Sabah, Gerard.
  III. Series.
P98.A35 1988
410'.28'55133–dc19   88-17820
                                                           CIP

Ablex Publishing Corporation
355 Chestnut Street
Norwood, New Jersey 07648

Contents

Volume 1

Foreword
D. McDonald   ix

Introduction
Michael Zock and Gérard Sabah   xiii

Part I   State of the art   1

 1 Language generation and explanation
   K. McKeown and W. R. Swartout   1

**Part II   Linguistic approaches: in defence of a particular
          theory–formalism**

 2 Can a 'parsing grammar' be used for natural language
   generation? The negative example of LFG
   R. Block   53

 3 The application of unification for syntactic generation in
   German *H. Horacek*   63

 4 Concerning the logical component of a natural language
   generator *S. C. Dik*   73

Part III   Implementational issues

 5 Two approaches to natural language generation
   G. Adorni   93

 6 The production of spoken dialogue
   G. Houghton and M. Pearson   112

 7 Natural language generation from plans
   C. Mellish   131

8 An approach for creating structured text
   N. Simonin   146

Part IV   Psychological issues
   9 Automatic and executive processing in semantic and syntactic
     planning: a dual process model of speech production
     T. A. Harley   161

  10 Incremental production of referential noun-phrases by human
     speakers
     H. Schriefers and T. Pechmann   172

Part V   Educational applications
  11 Natural languages are flexible tools: that's what makes them
     hard to explain, to learn and to use
     M. Zock   181

Index to Volume I   197

Volume 2

Foreword
D. McDonald   ix

Introduction
Michael Zock and Gérard Sabah   xiii

Part I   Linguistic Approaches: in defence of a
         particular theory–formalism
   1 Discontinuous Phrase-Structure Grammar and its use in
     sentence generation
     H. Bunt   1

   2 Language generation as choice in social interaction
     R. P. Fawcett   27

Part II   Implementational issues
   3 A lexically distributed word ordering component
     D. Parisi and A. Giorgi   51

   4 The generation of subsequent referring expressions in
     structured discourse
     R. Dale   58

5 Generating referring phrases in a dynamic environment
   H. Novak   76

6 The generation system of the SEMSYN project: towards a
   task-independent generator for German
   D. Rösner   86

7 Natural language generation: one individual implementer's
   experience
   T. L. Kwee   98

Part III   Psychological issues
8 Discourse planning and production: an outline of the process
   and some variables
   V. Zammuner   121

9 The effect of the macro-control of information on the temporal
   characteristics of text production
   A. Piolat and F. Farioli   144

Part IV   Educational applications
10 Building a sentence generator for teaching linguistics
   D. Bakker, B. van der Korst and G. van Schaaik   159

Index to Volume 2   175

Foreword

Natural language generation is a young field, probably only five or six years old. True, there have been isolated efforts to make computers speak human languages in a principled way since the very first computers were developed, but the work of these early pioneers largely fell on deaf ears. Building on other people's work was the exception rather than the rule, and there was no community to provide support. Nearly all of the first people in the field soon went on to other projects where their work was better received. The problem was that their work was before its time: there can be no community without an appreciation of a common set of demands and problems, and until the early 1980s this simply did not exist. Why this has happened has a combination of several factors, not the least of which is exemplified by this book.

One factor contributing to generation's youth has been the lack, until recently, of any need for it. The people who study generation are trying to understand the human capacity to use language—with all its subtleties of nuance, and the complexity, even arbitrariness, of its motivations. They develop large and elaborate theories, with equally large programs to instantiate and test them, as befits the subject they are studying. Computers, on the other hand, do not think very subtle thoughts: indeed, their programs, even artificial intelligence programs, inevitably leave out rationales and goals behind the instructions for their behaviour, and certainly none of them (with the exception of a few programs written specifically to drive generation systems) has any emotional or even rhetorical attitudes towards the people who are using them. Without the richness of information, perspective and intentions that humans bring to what they say, computers have no basis for making the decisions that go into natural utterances—it makes no sense to include a natural language generator in one's computer system if there is no way to drive it.

But while computers have not had the knowledge that it takes properly to motivate the content and style of what they might say, they nevertheless have had strong demands placed on them to communicate—for the AI program to explain the reasoning behind its decisions or the machine tutor to interact with its students—and this invariably means using natural language. For some of these tasks, artfully combined 'canned' texts—strings of words in print statements—have been sufficient. In the past they were certainly a better technique than the cumbersome and grammatically brittle generators that were available. But those days are rapidly coming to an end, and with that comes the realization that a true generation capacity will soon be a requirement, not a luxury.

A modern generator permits computer application programs to distance themselves from language in ways that print statements cannot permit. This distance makes it possible to increase dramatically the quality of the texts that are produced by allowing independent influences to enter into the process and their constraints and contributions combined. There are of course technicalities: the generator takes care of making the number of subject and verb agree and gets the right case on the pronouns. The more important contribution of a generator, however, is that it provides a framework that makes the process of assembling and couching the message a text conveys exceptionally flexible.

An applications program, on its own, may select the individual references and propositions that should be composed to form the complex sentences of, say, an explanation to a specific, specialized audience. (Though note that much of the organization in a text has to come from its position in the ongoing discourse and must accommodate the syntactic peculiarities of the wording that is used—all of which requires linguistic knowledge that will reside in the generator.) A grammatically sophisticated generator will annotate these conceptual units according to the different ways they could be combined and realized, and will establish a set of decision criteria—rhetorical, semantic and pragmatic—which govern what actually happens. The process invariably then goes through a series of stages and representational levels, each with its own capabilities and specializations, and with its own opportunities for independent influences to have their effect. This stratification and differentiation sharpens and clarifies our sense of what it is that makes an utterance effective, and makes research on generation tractable and additive.

The generators actually available right now of course have their limitations and rough spots—a great many of them. This motivates research into alternative theories of grammar, alternative control flows, experiments with particular decompositions of the process into modules, and especially the study of language itself: how goals are actually achieved, nuances expressed, the intricacies of grammatical constructions and references dealt with, and so on. Such research is the subject of this volume.

Research does not flourish without a community to nourish it. This brings us to the other principal factor—the key to the emergence of generation as a field—the international workshops on natural language generation. The first workshop was in Germany in 1983, riding on the coat-tails of an international AI meeting; the second at Stanford the next year; and the third in Holland in 1986. The most recent meeting is the subject of this book: the European workshop in January of 1987 at the Abbey of Royaumont in France.

These workshops have established generation as a field: they have set its (rather wide) boundaries, promulgated a common sense of the state of the art, identified the central questions. Even more important, they have provided the means for the individuals in the field to come to know each other, to become more than just anonymous names in papers, to meet new people and learn about the range of work that they are doing. This process has created a sense of community: people who share the same concerns, puzzle over the same problems, react to the same odd things that they hear while talking over dinner. The pioneers have gained colleagues; the newcomers have been inducted into a strong, if thinly populated, tradition.

Part of this tradition is a diversity of views and backgrounds. Unlike some schools within the field of natural language understanding (easily twenty years older), generation research embraces not just computational linguistics and artificial intelligence—its core discipline—but also 'conventional' linguistics and psycholinguistics. Perhaps youth brings with it a lack of bias; on the other hand, simply making the effort to bring these diverse groups together to a single place for several days allows the common elements and goals within their work to be recognized. This interdisciplinary group is well represented in this European workshop, as it was in the one before, continuing the cross-connection and exposition that was established there.

Language generation is not a simple process. It is not language understanding in reverse, and it challenges many of the established ideas within linguistic theory. It has its own subtleties and depths, with surprises waiting for those who explore them. Its study has created a new field with enormous vigour and infectious enthusiasm. More so than any of its complementary fields, generation will provide a real 'window into the mind', since it alone forces one to synthesize actual mental models—the conceptual sources of what the generators say—before any other work is possible, models that can be tested just by looking at the utterances they lead to and seeing how reasonable they are. It is research that is fun to do, and challenging, and it promises to change the way we think about language and ourselves.

David D. McDonald
Northampton, Massachusetts
November 1987

Introduction*

Text production is decision-making under specific social, pragmatic and psychological constraints. It consists of determining, organizing and expressing thoughts in order to achieve some goal.

Despite its youth, the modelling of text production, language generation has become a rapidly growing field. In the last decade, several international workshops have been held, special sessions have been scheduled at major AI conferences, and more than a dozen books have appeared (see bibliography). The chapters in this volume are the result of one of these workshops. More precisely they are the revised versions of chapters presented at the First European Workshop on Language Generation at Royaumont Abbey in France. These chapters are a good reflection of the kind of problems researchers are currently struggling with.

We start this book with a chapter by Kathleen McKeown and William Swartout, two prominent American scientists who survey the literature on text generation. This review is useful in various respects: it defines the problems of text generation, it provides a general framework within which the different contributions can be located, and it describes the techniques developed by researchers. As this chapter is primarily concerned with work done in American institutions, it provides a good setting for the rest of the chapters presented in this volume, which come mainly from European researchers.

The work presented here is grouped into four sections: grammar formalisms, psychological issues, implementations and educational applications.

* We are greatly indebted to ARI Communication and the German French Programm of the CNRS who sponsored this workshop.

Grammar formalisms

Russell Block analyses the suitability of LFG as a formalism for parsing and generation. On linguistic grounds, he comes to the conclusion that separate formalisms are necessary. While a non-transformational theory like LFG might be perfectly adapted for parsing, it seems to be inadequate for generation. A Standard Theory Transformational Grammar seems to be a better candidate.

Harry Bunt is also concerned with the problem of designing a single grammar formalism for analysis and synthesis. His formalism, a semantically and pragmatically augmented phrase structure grammar, is capable of generating discontinuous constituent structures, a notorious problem in language generation.

Helmut Horacek disagrees with Block's conclusion. The research group he works in uses LFG both for parsing and generation. The author shows in his chapter how unification grammars can be adapted to overcome some of the shortcomings, in particular backtracking and handling of free word order.

Starting from the premise that linguistic well-formedness is a necessary but not sufficient condition for communicative adequacy, Simon Dik suggests linking the linguistic component to a knowledge base and to a reasoning component. The task of the latter is to draw conclusions on the basis of existing or incoming information. As we have three components, we are faced with the problem of how to represent knowledge in each of them so as to allow for communication. An optimal solution would be the use of a unique representation language. According to the author, functional grammars are particularly well suited to solving this problem.

Robin Fawcett describes the theoretical underpinnings of COMMU-NAL, a project he is currently conducting. The acronym of the system stands for Convivial Man–Machine Understanding through Natural Language. Its goal is to enable ordinary people to interact naturally with knowledge-based systems. Discussing some of the basic decisions which must be made before starting to build such a system, he argues, in particular, for the use of meaning-based or systemic functional grammars.

Psychological issues

H. Schriefers and Thomas Pechmann argue that planning and expressing content are done in parallel. They even claim partial parallelism to be a prerequisite to account for the fluency and speed of human performance.

While the idea of incremental processing is appealing, at least on intuitive grounds, little empirical evidence has been gathered up to now. These authors try to back up their claims by providing such evidence.

Trevor Harley suggests that normal speech production uses two types of mechanisms. One is fast, most probably parallel, and not prone to interference from the contents of working memory: this mechanism is called AUTOMATIC. EXECUTIVE PROCESSING, on the other hand, is slow, serial and prone to interference from working memory. The advantage of this slower mechanism is that it provides the speech production system with a flexibility that it would otherwise not have. The author provides empirical data to substantiate his claims.

Annie Piolat and Fernand Farioli present a system which assists students in text planning (composition). Their system is also a research tool. Keeping a trace of various aspects of human performance—for example, the time taken for a specific operation: text planning, wording and so on—the psychologist may draw on these facts in order to elaborate his theory. The authors' goal is to provide empirical evidence of the inter-relationship of the planning-, composing- and revising processes.

Vanda Zammuner presents an empirically motivated model of discourse planning and production. She analyses the different knowledge sources and shows how these components interrelate. Viewing discourse production as a special case of problem-solving, she is particularly concerned with strategic planning, i.e. how to be efficient given a set of constraints.

Implementation issues: sentence-, discourse- and text generation

Giovanni Adorni discusses two methods of converting a deep structure into a surface string. The first starts from conceptual dependency networks, using a transformational grammar. The second uses logical predicates as input. The task is divided into a lexicalization and linearization procedures. The former produces an unordered set of words composing the final sentence; the latter integrates these elements into a syntactic structure. The author claims a quasi-universal status for the underlying meaning representation, while the linearization procedure is language-specific.

An interesting feature of the first system is the fact that it only knows about syntax. What conceptual primitives or relationships are necessary to build the surface structure, or how those conceptual primitives are mapped on lexical items are learned by the system.

Domenico Parisi and Alessandra Giorgi present a lexically-driven word-ordering component. This approach is interesting in that it contrasts with the traditional philosophy of syntax, i.e. structure-driven processing. As far as the role of the lexicon is concerned, there seems to be convergence between psychological and various recent linguistic theories. All of them emphasize the role of the lexicon as an important aspect of structure building.

George Houghton and Mark Pearson are concerned with the production of dialogues. The communication setting is composed of two 'actors' (robots) which try to solve practical problems in a microworld. The user of the program determines the actors' goals as well as the physical arrangement of the elements composing this microworld. The actors attempt to make plans to achieve their goals. Whenever they lack knowledge to form or execute a plan, they engage in dialogue, querying the other participant for help. The output from this system is synthesized speech.

Robert Dale is concerned with the generation of referring expressions in structured discourse. As successful reference implies adequate description of a referent in order to allow its discrimination from a set of alternatives, the question arises of how to reduce the set of possible candidates (the search space). Examining Grosz's and Sidner's approach, he concludes that their model is inadequate in several respects; however, a revised version could be good candidate.

Chris Mellish's goal is to organize large amounts of data in order to generate smooth readable text. Rejecting the 'hill climbing' method as too expensive he presents another technique of generating text from plans. Critically analysing the shortcomings of his method, he suggests a series of improvements.

Nathalie Simonin's chapter deals with the task of structuring an unordered set of information and converting this set of messages into coherent text. Starting from a knowledge base, her system produces short summaries of the agricultural, economic and political situation of various countries. The process is decomposed into different tasks: extraction of relevant information, dynamic building of the text plan by grouping the information according to some point of view (for example, topic), elimination of redundancies, determination of linear order of the messages, generation of inter-sentence links, sentence generation. It should be noted that her system is bi-directional (top–down and bottom–up). There is constant interaction between choices concerning content and the choice of textual structure. Another interesting feature of this system is the fact that the various levels all use the same representation mechanism, namely functional descriptions.

A striking feature of Hans Joachim Novak's system is the fact that it takes visual data as input. His system generates coherent text describing an image sequence of a traffic situation. As the hearer cannot see the scene, the system has to describe it in terms which allow the hearer to imagine it, i.e., build a corresponding visual representation of the scene. In order to achieve this goal, particular attention is necessary so as adequately to describe the objects and to specify their relative position in the scene.

Dietmar Roesner sketches the evolution of his system from a machine translation system (SEMSYN) to a full-fledged top–down driven text generator (SEMTEX). The former translates titles of scientific papers on computer science from Japanese into German, whereas the latter produces newspaper stories about job market development. GEOTEXT, a more recent application, produces descriptive texts from a set of commands given by a student, expressing what the latter is doing while solving a geometry problem.

Kwee Tjoe Liong discusses the linguistic and computational problems he encountered when trying to extend the grammar of a very well-known system, TEXT. He also raises the problem of conflicting interests between the goals of computer scientists and linguists. While the former are concerned with optimization, concrete results and performance, the latter are more concerned with long-term issues, possible generalizations. Every system designer is faced with the problem of where to draw the border line, while trying to reconcile these two conflicting goals.

Application

Dik Bakker, Bieke van der Korst and Gerjan van Schaaik's system teaches students the basics of a specific linguistic theory, namely functional grammar. The system helps the students to specify what they want to say, translating this message into linguistic form. While the user expresses the content, the systems checks for syntactic and semantic consistencies and provides feedback in case of error. The major processing steps may be traced, thus showing what grammar component is activated at any given moment. This facility is useful in that it may give the user some insight into the overall organization of the grammar at work.

Michael Zock starts by analysing why natural languages are so hard to explain, to learn, or to use. Coming to the conclusion that the difficulties are caused by the interaction of the various constraints, he presents the outline of a system whose task is to disentangle these intricate dependencies. The purpose of his system is to assist a student in expressing content. By allowing the user to test the outcome of his choices, he should learn what the choices are, what they depend upon, and how they interrelate. The author lays particular emphasis on this last point. Being concerned with the temporal aspects of the process, he tries to provide a means to visualize the interaction of conceptual, textual and linguistic choices.

Conclusion

Language generation is a complex task; consequently it does not pertain to one sole domain. The meeting at Royaumont was an attempt to bring together people from various backgrounds in order to have them look at the same object from different perspectives.

Text generation is also a real challenge both because of its complexities and its potential impact (social, cultural and scientific). It is a fascinating and youthful discipline. In the past a great deal of effort has been devoted to investigating the structure of sentences and more recently to the structure of text. Surprisingly little is known about the processes put to use in order to produce these structures. This is about to change, because studying text structures amounts to study products of thought, while studying dynamic text production amounts to studying the process of thought, that is to say thought in action.

Michael Zock and Gérard Sabah
LIMSI/Orsay

Bibliography

Aitchinson, J. (1976), *The Articulate Mammal*, London, Hutchinson & Co.

Appelt, D. (1985), *Planning English Sentences*, Cambridge, Cambridge University Press.

de Beaugrande, R. (1984), *Text Production: Towards a Science of Composition*, New Jersey, Ablex.

Butterworth, B. (ed.) (1980), *Language Production*, vols 1 and 2, London, Academic Press.

Danlos, L. (1987), *The Linguistic Basis of Text Generation*, Cambridge, Cambridge University Press.

Davey, A. (1979), *Discourse Production*, Edinburgh, Edinburgh University Press.

Deese, J. (1984), *Thought and Speech*, Englewood Cliffs, NJ, Prentice Hall.

Kempen, G. (ed.) (1987), *Natural Language Generation: New Results in Artificial Intelligence, Psychology and Linguistics*, Dordrecht, Martinus Nijhoff Publisher.

Leont'ev, A. (1975), *Psycholinguistische Einheiten und die Erzeugung sprachlicher Äusserungen*, Munich, Heuber.

Levelt, W. (1988), *Speaking: From Intention to Articulation*, Cambridge, Mass., MIT Press.

McKeown, K. (1985), *Text Generation: Using Discourse Strategies and Focus Constraints to Generate Natural Language Text*, Cambridge, Cambridge University Press.

Meehan, J. (1980), *The Metanovel: Writing Stories by Computer*.

Patten, T. (1988), *Text Generation*, Cambridge, Cambridge University Press.

Popov, E. (1982), *Talking with Computers in Natural Language*, Berlin, Springer Verlag.

Rosenberg, S. (ed.) (1978), *Sentence Production: Developments in Research and Theory*, Hillsdale, NJ, Lawrence Erlbaum Associates.

Schlesinger, I. (1977), *Production and Comprehension of Utterances*, Hillsdale, NJ, Lawrence Erlbaum Associates.

Zammuner, V. (1981), *Speech Production*, Hamburg, Buske Verlag.

Part I State of the art

1 Language generation and explanation*

KATHLEEN R. McKEOWN†
WILLIAM R. SWARTOUT‡

1.0 Introduction

Researchers in language generation and explanations are concerned with developing methods that will allow a computer system to respond to their users in natural language. Responses include a wide variety of ways a system may be required to communicate. Language generation can aim to produce short answers, paragraph-length responses to specific types of isolated questions (e.g. explanations in expert systems), or descriptions and summaries of an internal information store.

Explanation is a subtype of language generation—i.e. generation for the purpose of explaining an expert system's reasoning. Because of the success and pervasiveness of expert systems, explanation is a particularly important form of generation. In this chapter, we focus on the problem of language generation in general; within this framework, we describe how explanation differs from the general case. Since problems in explanation are often similar to those in language generation, much of our discussion of the two issues is merged.

In the remainder of this section, we characterize the main problem of language generation and explanation as one of choice, describe the range of

* Reproduced with permission from the Annual Review of Computer Science, Volume 2, © 1987 by Annual Reviews Inc. The authors acknowledge the generous support of the following funding agencies during the writing of this chapter: DARPA grant N00039-84-C-0165 to Columbia University, ONR grant N00014-82-K-0256 to Columbia University, NSF grant IST-84-51438 to Columbia University and DARPA Grant MGA 903-81-C-0335 to Information Sciences Institute. We also than Barbara Grosz, Michael Lebowitz, William Mann, Kathleen McCoy, Cecile Paris and Ursula Wolz for their helpful comments on various drafts of the chapter.

† *Department of Computer Science, Columbia University, New York, USA.*
‡ *USC/Information Sciences, Marina del Rey, California, USA.*

system organizations and solutions used, identify applications for which generation systems have been built, and, finally, outline some ways in which explanation differs from language generation in general.

1.0.1 *Generation as choice*

In the process of generating natural language—whether responses to user questions, summaries, or explanation—a generation system must be able to decide what to say and how to present its message effectively. To construct textual content, all appropriate information must be represented in or derivable from its knowledge base. It must then be able to disregard information not specific to the task at hand and integrate pertinent information into a coherent unit. It must determine how to start the text appropriately, how to order its elements, and how to close it. In order to present effectively the information it will include in its text, a generation system must also determine what words to use and how to group them into sentences.

To illustrate these choices, consider the two-sentence text shown in Example 1, below. In determining content, a generator must decide that it should write about 'this article' and that of all it knows about the article it will include information about the authors and topic. In determining organization a generator must decide, at one level, that it is better first to introduce the authors and then the topic and not vice versa,[1] and at another level must decide that two separate sentences are more appropriate than a single complex sentence (e.g. *This article is written by Kathy McKeown and Bill Swartout and is a survey of research in language generation and explanation*.).

In determining how to express selected information in language, a generator must be able to select appropriate words and syntactic structure from a variety of options. To produce the first sentence of Example 1, a generator must decide that although both the active and passive are possible (the active would result in *Kathy McKeown and Bill Swartout wrote this article*), for the full text it wishes to produce the passive is better than the active. In deciding between possible lexical choices, it may deliberate between the verb *to write* and the phrase *The authors of this article are*. It also must consider why to use the pronoun *it* in sentence 2 in place of the definite noun phrase *this article*.

Example 1
1. This article was written by Kathy McKeown and Bill Swartout.
2. It is a survey of research in language generation and explanation.

Furthermore, for choices like those just illustrated the generator must have a principled reason for making a decision, which it can use in all similar cases. If it has no reason for making choices, the best a generation system can do is either always select the same option or randomly select among options. Both of these approaches will result in some cases in awkward, unnatural text. For example, some early generation systems always used simple active sentences with no pronouns. Replacing *it* in 2 by *The article* illustrates how awkward the approach can be. On the other hand, random selection between options not only creates awkward text, but also may convey inaccurate information. For example, if pronouns are randomly selected to replace proper names, ambiguity can be introduced in the resulting text.

Researchers in language generation have investigated a variety of factors that can influence the choices a generator makes. They have drawn upon research in linguistics for constraints on choice of words and syntactic structure of the generated text, relying on identification of function in language (e.g. Halliday 1969) to determine why particular words or syntax should be selected. Non-linguistic factors are also crucial; in particular, the purpose for which text is being generated has a pervasive influence. Text is written (and utterances are spoken) to accomplish speaker goals; the speaker INTENDS to affect the hearer through communication (e.g. cause the hearer to perform an action or understand an explanation). Researchers have accounted for this influence upon a language generator's choice in a variety of ways. Some explicitly represent and reason about speaker and hearer beliefs. Others have focused on specific purposes for producing text (e.g. generating descriptions), identifying techniques suitable for those purposes alone.

1.0.2 *Approaches*

The fact that a generator must face choices involving the content and organization of produced text in addition to choices involving its surface form has led to a common separation of processing into two stages. In the first stage, termed DEEP GENERATION, the content and organization of the text are determined. An ordered message is produced and passed on to the second stage, termed SURFACE GENERATION, where the words and syntactic structures of the text are determined. The actual natural language text is produced at this stage. Figure 1.1 shows a typical language generator using these two stages.

Most early work on computer generation of language focused on problems in surface generation. Problems ranged from issues in the direct translation of an underlying formal representation (e.g. Simmons & Slocum 1972; Chester 1976), to the development of grammars and mechanisms for using those grammars to produce language (e.g. McDonald 1980; Kay 1979), and the development and representation of

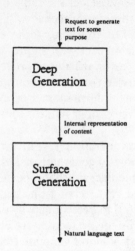

Figure 1.1 Organization of a language generator

criteria for making decisions and vocabulary (e.g. Goldman 1975; McDonald 1980). Recent work continues to develop formalisms for surface generation (e.g. Patten & Ritchie 1986; Joshi 1986) as well as comprehensive grammars to make available eventually as portable components (e.g. Mann & Mathiessen 1983).

Less work has been done on deep generation. Earlier work in this area addressed two main issues: planning to determine an appropriate speech act (e.g. Cohen 1978), and textual organization (e.g. Mann & Moore 1981; Weiner 1980). Recent work examines three main influences on determining content: strategies for text organization (Mann 1984; McKeown 1985), the audience for whom text is generated (Hovy 1985; McCoy 1985; Paris 1985), and the use of planning formations (Appelt 1985a; Pollock 1986).

This separation of the two processes has made it convenient to address problems in one stage independently of the other and thus has been adopted by many researchers (e.g. Mann 1984; McDonald 1980; McKeown 1985). Recently, however, a number of investigators (e.g. Appelt 1985a; Danlos 1984; Hovy 1985) have noted problems with pipelining the processes to require that all deep generation decisions be made before surface generation begins. Such strong separation prevents options and limitations in word choice and syntactic structure from influencing the determination of textual content and organization, an influence that certainly plays a role in many types of language production, particularly when editing can occur. Thus one emphasis in language generation is on investigation of the extent and type of interaction that should occur between the two processes.

In determining what information is appropriate to include in a text, researchers often found that information was not available in the underlying system. A system that is to produce natural language must have available the information needed to produce good text. Systems with sufficient knowledge for problem-solving may still be incapable of producing understandable text. Thus, an adequate knowledge representation is a prerequisite to later processes in text generation. Much work has already been done on knowledge representation for generation (e.g. Clancey 1983a,b; Meehan 1977; Swartout 1983b), and investigation of this issue continues to be a main thrust of generation research.

1.0.3 *Language generation applications*

The purpose for which language is produced naturally influences the type of generation required. The generator may be required to provide answers as part of an interactive system. Alternatively, a system may produce text that can be read by one or more users at a later date.

One common interactive application for language generation is answering questions about an underlying data base or knowledge base through short answer or paragraph-length text. A generator can be used to phrase the content of a short-answer response to a question in English when another component of the system determines content. Such single-sentence generation has been addressed by the NYU question-answering system (Grishman 1979), by a project focusing on generation from semantic networks (e.g. Simmons & Slocum 1972), and by researchers using different grammatical formalisms (e.g. Shapiro 1982; Kay 1979).

For questions requiring paragraph-length responses, a generator must be able to determine content as well as phrasing. Typically, the data base or knowledge base contains an excessive amount of potentially relevant, complex information and the generation system must sort out what could reasonably be part of an appropriate response. Generation systems designed specifically to produce paragraph-length responses include TEXT (McKeown 1982, 1985) and TAILOR (Paris 1985). A generator must also be able to determine content of a response when addressing a questioner's misconceptions (McCoy 1985) or when anticipating a user's reactions to a response (Busemann 1984; Jameson 1983).

Intelligent computer-aided instruction (ICAI) is another interactive environment where language generation is necessary. For the most part, ICAI systems have used relatively unsophisticated techniques for language generation, although there has been work on language generation as part of a tutorial system for the English language aimed at people with language-delaying handicaps (Bates & Ingria 1981), as well as a system for managing discourse in a tutorial environment (Woolf 1984). Clancey's (1983a,b) work on a tutorial component for medical consultation should also be noted. The ICAI environment provides an excellent environment for generation issues. Help systems are another potential environment for language generation in which relatively little work has been done (but see Jacobs 1985).

Non-interactive applications where generation is required include knowledge-base description, summarization or abstracting, scene description, game commentary, machine translation, and story generation. Knowledge-base description can be used as a debugging tool for a learning system or a parsing system. A generator can be used to verify that the knowledge base was updated correctly. Although it was not designed specifically for a parser or learner, Mann & Moore (1981) built a generator for this purpose called KDS (Knowledge Description System) which produced a description from an underlying knowledge base stating what to do in case of a fire alarm. Scene description, another application, requires input from an underlying vision system, but in other respects it resembles knowledge-base description; of course the type of language that will be produced differs (e.g. for scene description the choice of spatial prepositions is important). Summaries can be generated of stories (Lehnert 1983; Danlos 1984), technical articles, or other activities (e.g. see Kukich (1983) on summary of stock market activity; Swartout (1983a) on summary of results of dynamic simulation of a program specification). A number of generation systems have produced commentary on current activity. PROTEUS (Davey 1979), for example, produced descriptions of tic-tac-toe games; both MUMBLE (McDonald 1980) and Chester's generator (Chester 1976) produced descriptions of logical proofs. Of non-interactive applications, story generation is probably the most demanding, involving problems in content determination, plot and character development, organization, and phrasing. Few story generation systems have actually been developed (but see Meehan 1977; Lebowitz 1985b).

1.0.4 *Explanation*

Another important application of generation systems is explanation for the expert system domain. Because explanation serves a specific purpose within an expert system, a number of constraints apply to its generation process that are not found in other language generation systems.

Explanation has proved crucial to the success of expert systems for several reasons. First, designers must spare expert system users the effort of understanding internal program structures. Users of medical expert systems, for example, are doctors and medical students who have no need to understand production systems. Natural language is a mode of communication that provides such users with responses stated in their terms.

While not experts in the programming methodology of expert systems, users are often knowledgeable in the domain of the system. Again, doctors fit this characterization. Their purpose in using the system is often for consultation: to gain advice on a case or to confirm their own diagnosis. In order to evaluate the advice provided and to determine whether to accept it or not, such users need to understand how and why the system came up with its advice.

Explanation is also helpful for builders and maintainers of the expert systems who might use it to identify errors in the underlying inference process. Often a trace of the inference process itself can be so lengthy (for example, in ACE (e.g. Stolfo & Vesonder 1982) a single recommendation may invoke up to 15,000 individual production rules) that errors are difficult to detect. Often a system is constructed incrementally by a number of different researchers who may not consistently follow the conventions used previously. In such cases, explanation facilities have been shown to point out even such simple discrepancies as errors due to roundoff that had previously gone undetected (e.g. Kukich 1984).

To assure that the explanations a system produces accurately reflect how it works, most expert systems produce explanations by paraphrasing in natural language the internal structures used for reasoning. Problems that are particular to explanation and not language generation in general have to do primarily with the use of these internal structures as the basis for content. Often the detail in inference rules that is needed to arrive at a correct solution is not needed as part of an explanation. Similarly, the kind of information that is helpful for human readers of explanation may not be available in the inference trace. One major focus of explanation research has been on the type of additional knowledge needed to provide good explanations. Note that this problem echoes the general problem of deciding what information to include in a text and how to organize it. Finally, since expert system explanation generation uses relatively simple techniques to produce the actual wording, problems in surface generation have not been addressed in this environment.

1.0.5 *Organizational preview*

In the remainder of this chapter, we discuss the problems of deep generation and surface generation. Our treatment of deep generation includes an identification of techniques for determining the content and organization of the text as well as an examination of the kind of information needed in a knowledge base to support useful explanations. We then turn to surface generation, discussing techniques developed for determining words and syntactic structures. Finally, we identify current directions in language generation and explanation.

1.1 Deep generation

To produce a text, a generation system must be able to determine which information to include from all the information represented in its knowledge base and how to organize it into text. In determining content, a generator must decide what information is relevant for the purpose of the text, what the audience (or user) needs to know, and how much detail about an object or event to include. In organizing its materials, a generator must choose a linear order for the information selected, specifying how to aggregate the information (i.e. where to form paragraph and sentence boundaries). It must produce a COHERENT text—one in which sentences are related to the preceding or succeeding sentences. The determination of textual content and organization can place demands on design of the underlying knowledge base as well. A knowledge base designed for purposes other than language generation may not contain the information needed to produce good text.

Problems in deep generation were not well recognized until people gained experience with surface generation of single sentences. Originally, generation system designers assumed that the content of the generated text would be predetermined by some other component of an application system in the process of performing some other task. In this simplistic view, for example, the content of a response in a natural language data base system was determined by a search of the data base. Similarly, in an expert system, the content of an explanation was determined by the inferencing component. While this assumption was for the most part adequate when predetermined content could be generated as a single sentence, attempts to generate multi-sentence texts revealed problems with this approach. Researchers found that language issues also play a role in determining the content and organization of a text. A component designed for some other task may produce inappropriate content or the wrong amount of detail for a human reader. Similarly, while the organization of information may be perfectly appropriate for the system task, reorganization may be needed for the human reader. Both of these problems hold for explanation production in expert systems. Finally, the underlying component necessary for production of the content of certain types of texts may not be available.

This is, for instance, the case for meta-level questions in natural language data bases.

Articulation of these problems led to the development of four main areas of research. Discourse strategies, representing common textual organizations found in naturally occurring texts, are used by a generation system to decide what information to include at each point in the text. Other systems make use of information about the intended reader of the generated text, often in conjunction with discourse strategies, in determining what to say. A third approach focuses on the use of planning and reasoning about speaker and hearer beliefs to produce a text. These three approaches all address the problem of determining content at the point when language must be produced. But in identifying problems with using predetermined content for text generation, a more fundamental problem with generation systems emerged. Often the knowledge base of existing systems did not contain the information needed to produce good texts. A fourth area of research deals with the development and design of knowledge bases to meet the needs of generation systems. This area is concerned with the representation of content to support generation before the process of generation begins.

1.1.1 *Discourse strategies*

One approach to determining the content and organization of generated text has been to use a model of discourse structure. This approach is based on the observation that people generally follow standard patterns of organization when producing texts. For example, a narrative commonly begins with a description of setting (e.g. scene, characters, or time-frame) and then follows a temporal sequence of events (Rumelhart 1975). If these patterns are captured formally, they can guide a generation system in its decisions about what to say next.

In this section we discuss three systems that make use of a model of discourse structure as part of the deep generation component. We focus on TEXT (McKeown 1982, 1985), a system that uses discourse strategies to generate responses to meta-level questions as part of a natural language data base system. As background, however, we briefly describe BLAH (Weiner 1980), an earlier system that uses an EXPLANATION GRAMMAR to produce explanations of income tax returns. Finally, we turn to Rhetorical Structure Theory (Mann 1984), which embodies a set of rhetorical schemata for a wide variety of purposes, but does not currently produce text using the schemata.

BLAH BLAH (Weiner 1980) was developed to provide explanations of why certain deductions were taken on income tax returns. Weiner formulated his method for explanation generation on the basis of an analysis of naturally occurring explanations given by tax return filers (Goguen *et al*. 1982). This analysis yielded an explanation grammar which dictates the possible orderings of propositions in an explanation. Each proposition is classified as one of four types: (a) statement of fact or of an action taken; (b) reason why a fact holds for an action taken; (c) example that supports a statement; and (d) alternatives to a statement, all of which will be shown to be inadequate except the statement.

Weiner also uses a number of subordinators to connect the propositions such as *and/or* and *if/then*. Since explanations are frequently embedded, a statement followed by a reason may in turn function as a reason for another statement. To account for this, Weiner's grammar generates tree structures, which may in turn be manipulated by transformations to generate the hierarchical structure of the final text. An explanation generated by BLAH is shown in Example 2.

Example 2
Peter is a dependent of Harry's because, first of all, Peter makes less than 750 dollars because Peter does not work, and second of all, because Harry supports Peter because Harry provides more than one half of Peter's support.

Weiner's work is seminal to other work on discourse structure in that it demonstrates the value of using naturally occurring text as a basis for formulating models of text organization. The explanation of grammar resulting from the analysis, however, is quite limited. Because of its simple structure and the small number of proposition types, BLAH can only produce a restricted range of texts.

TEXT TEXT (McKeown 1982, 1985) was developed to provide paragraph-length responses to meta-level questions about the structure of an underlying data base. TEXT's data base contained information about military vehicles and weapons. It could generate responses to three classes of questions: (a) requests to define a concept; (b) requests to compare two objects; and (c) requests to describe available information.

To develop the system, McKeown analysed naturally occurring texts written for three corresponding discourse purposes: DEFINE, COMPARE and DESCRIBE. Her corpus of texts came from a variety of sources, including dictionaries and technical texts, and included a total of fifty-six paragraphs. Each clause in a paragraph was classified as one of a set of ten possible rhetorical predicates. By factoring out common patterns, McKeown identified four discourse strategies that together accounted for the structure of the paragraphs. These were termed the CONSTITUENCY, IDENTIFICATION, ATTRIBUTIVE and COMPARE AND CONTRAST strategies. Each strategy is associated with one or more discourse purposes.

One of the strategies formalized for TEXT is the CONSTITUENCY strategy. It can be used for two discourse purposes: DEFINE and DESCRIBE. It is characterized by four main steps:

1. identify the item as a member of some generic class or present attributive information about it;
2. present the constituents of the item to be defined;
3. present characteristic information about each constituent in turn;
4. present attributive or analogy information about the item to be defined.

This strategy is formalized in TEXT as a SCHEMA using a graph representation. The CONSTITUENCY schema is shown in Figure 1.2. Each arc of the graph represents one of the steps above and is labelled by a predicate that characterizes the type of information required. The graph begins with the IDENTIFICATION predicate, indicating identification of the generic class is required. The ATTRIBUTIVE predicate is an alternative that will only be taken if the discourse goal is DESCRIBE.[2] The arc labelled CONSTITUENCY indicates that the constituents, or subclasses, of the item should be included next.

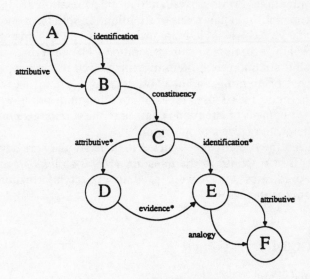

* These arcs are traversed for each constituent

Figure 1.2 The CONSTITUENCY schema

Step 3 is represented by the two arcs emanating from the state C and the arc from state D. These arcs are taken for each constituent. They indicate that identificational or attributive (attributes of an object) information and EVIDENCE (e.g. attributes supporting an object's classification in the data base) are to be provided next. The two arcs from state E represent step 4 and indicate that attributive or ANALOGY information is to be provided.

To generate the content of a response, TEXT traverses the schema graph. Each predicate in the schema has a function associated with it which retrieves information matching the predicate from the underlying knowledge base. For example, the identification predicate has an associated function that takes as input the object to be identified and returns a PROPOSITION that includes the object to be identified, its superordinate and any defining attributes. This is TEXT's definition of what it means to identify an object and is based on the definition of the identification predicate used in the analysis of texts. The information extracted for a single predicate will eventually be translated to a single sentence. As TEXT traverses an arc, it extracts information from the underlying knowledge base using the function associated with the predicate labelling the arc.

Where there are alternatives in the schema (several arcs emanate from a single state), TEXT uses constraints from FOCUS OF ATTENTION to select the alternative that ties in best with the text it has already generated. Focus of attention identifies the item in a proposition on which the writer is centering attention. Previous research in interpretation (Sidner 1979) identified constraints on how focus of attention can shift from one sentence to the next. McKeown added an ordering on these constraints that indicates which is preferable for generation. The ordering causes the system to shift attention to an item just introduced if possible, otherwise maintain focus of attention, and in all other cases return to an earlier focus of attention. Since TEXT uses focus of attention in deciding what to say next, a record of focus of attention is passed to the surface generator to use in deciding how to realize a proposition.

TEXT used the constituency schema to generate the paragraph shown in Example 3 in response to the question *What is a guided projectile?* The numbered predicates shown were used to extract information for the corresponding sentences.

Example 3
(definition GUIDED)
;
;What is a guided projectile?
;
Schema selected: constituency

1. identification: guided projectile
2. constituency: guided projectile
3. identification: missile
4. identification: torpedo
5. evidence: missile
6. evidence: torpedo
7. attributive: guided projectile

Message through dictionary. Entering tactical component

1. A guided projectile is a projectile that is self-propelled. 2. There are 2 types of guided projectiles in the ONR data base: torpedoes and missiles. 3. The missile has a target location in the air or on the earth's surface. 4. The torpedo has an underwater target location. 5. The missile's target location is indicated by the DB attribute DESCRIPTION and the missile's flight capabilities are provided by the DB attribute ALTITUDE. 6. The torpedo's underwater capabilities are provided by the DB attributes under DEPTH (for example, MAXIMUM OPERATING DEPTH). 7. The guided projectile has DB attributes TIME TO TARGET & UNITS, HORZ RANGE & UNITS and NAME.

TEXT is able to generate a far greater variety of discourse structure, and consequently texts, than is BLAH. Since a single discourse purpose may be achieved by more than one strategy (e.g. the discourse purpose DEFINE can be carried out by using either the IDENTIFICATION or the CONSTITUENCY strategy),[3] the structure of a generated text will differ depending upon the strategy selected. Second, since any single strategy has a number of alternatives, the resultant text will be different depending upon which alternative was taken. Finally, because of the greater number of predicates, the structure of its generated text is significantly more complex. The approach to discourse stategies taken in TEXT is limited in that it does not taken into account constraints from the user of the system (see the section on taking the reader into account, below). The large number of alternatives in a single strategy means that the strategy does not totally restrict text content, and the semantics of the rhetorical predicates hold only for the data base domain.

Rhetorical Structure Theory   The aim of Rhetorical Structure Theory (RST) (Mann 1984) is the development of a comprehensive theory of text organization that can eventually be used as part of a text generation system. To this end, Mann's group[4] have analysed a diverse collection of short texts.[5] At this point, their theory is DESCRIPTIVE; it captures structures of the analysed texts, but they have not yet shown how it can be used to produce text.

RST consists of a set of schemata (currently twenty-five), each of which indicates how a unit of text structure can be decomposed into smaller units.

Mann terms such units TEXT SPANS. A schema consists of a NUCLEUS and zero or more SATELLITES whose function, in most cases, is to support the nucleus in some way. In addition, there is a RELATION between each satellite and the nucleus indicating how the satellite provides support. The schemata are unordered (satellite and nucleus can appear in any order in the text) and are recursive. A text span serving as the satellite of one schema may be decomposed into a nucleus and satellite of its own using another schema. As an example, consider the REQUEST schema shown in Figure 1.3. It consists of a nucleus REQUEST and a satellite that either MOTIVATES or ENABLES the request. Since the satellite is both optional and repeatable, there may be no motivation or enablement in any given text or there may be any number of one, the other, or both.

Several differences between Mann's approach and earlier work appear in the nature of the schemata. They tend to be smaller and less constraining than McKeown's (or than McCoy's or Paris's, which are discussed below). As a result, many apply to the same text. While in theory more than one schema can apply to a single text in McKeown's work using recursion, a single schema tends to dominate the structure of a generated text. The combination of many smaller schemata within a single structure should give a generation system using this approach the ability to produce a wider variety of texts and text structures, since it can vary smaller portions of the text by switching schemata.

On the other hand, because of the open-ended nature of the schemata (i.e. optionality and repetition are possible for every satellite, and any schema can be expanded by any other at any point), it is unclear how they will be used as part of a generation system. Before they can be used to generate content and structure, control strategies must be developed that dictate when a satellite should appear, when not, how many times it should occur, and when it should be expanded as some other schema. Mann & Thompson (1986) suggest that goal-pursuit techniques will be used to choose between the wide variety of options available within this approach,

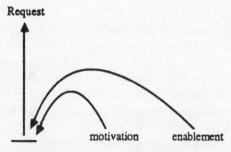

Figure 1.3 The REQUEST schema

but a great deal of work remains to be done specifying constraints on the options the goal pursuit techniques can use.

1.1.2 *Taking the intended reader into account*

Human writers take into account the intended audience of their text when deciding what to say. Choice of information and of the way it is expressed or structured depends upon the beliefs, background and goals of the participants in the interaction. If they are to achieve the quality of human generated text, computer generation systems too must take into account the intended audience when determining content.

In this section we survey three language generation systems that make use of information about the intended readers of their generated text when determining what to say. Since the intended reader is in most cases the system user, we henceforth refer to the reader as the 'user'. We focus on work by McCoy (1986) which identifies how to respond to different user misconceptions (i.e. incorrect user beliefs) by making use of discourse strategies. We then turn to two very recent projects where the main emphasis is the influence of the user on generation. Paris (1985) identifies and uses different discourse strategies to produce descriptions of physical objects to users who fall along a spectrum from domain novice to domain expert. Hovy (1985, 1986) shows how information about the reader can influence the style of generated text, both in its emphasis (i.e. what is included or left out) and phrasing. We conclude the section by pointing to other work which considers the system user when determining content.

ROMPER Responding to Object-related Misconceptions using PERspective (ROMPER) (McCoy 1985, 1986) was developed to generate responses to user misconceptions, which McCoy defines as discrepancies between what the system believes and what the user believes. McCoy's contributions lie in three areas: the classification of misconceptions that can occur in relation to a knowledge base containing an object taxonomy and information about objects' attributes and values; the development of a notion of object perspective; and the identification and formalization of discourse strategies that can be used to respond to different misconception types.

McCoy identifies two main classes of misconceptions: those concerning an object's classification in the object taxonomy (misclassifications) and those involving an object's attributes (misattributions). She further subdivides misclassifications into (a) cases where the user has posited an incorrect superordinate of an object because the user thinks the object is similar to the posited superordinate (e.g. classified a whale as a fish because whales are similar to fish); (b) cases where the misclassification occurs because the user has posited a similarity between a descendant of the incorrect superordinate of an object and the object (e.g. classified a whale as a fish because of its similarity to sharks); and (c) all other misclassifications. Similarly, she subdivides misattributions into (a) cases where the user has posited an incorrect object that happens to share certain attributes with the correct object (e.g. positing the interest rate of stocks instead of bonds); (b) cases where the user has posited incorrect attributes for a given object (e.g. positing the interest rate of a stock instead of the dividend); and (c) all other cases.

Based on a transcript analysis, McCoy identified a response strategy that could correct each misconception type. In this regard, her work is similar to the work on discourse strategies, discussed above. ROMPER embodies six different strategies, corresponding to the six misconception types. Unlike other strategies, McCoy's encode two types of information: a domain-independent specification of the content of each proposition, and information about the 'communicative role' of the proposition. This separation of content and communicative function is one of the distinguishing features of McCoy's work.

As an example, consider the strategy shown in Example 4.

Example 4
((deny (classification OBJECT POSITED))
(state (classification OBJECT REAL))
(concede (share-attributes OBJECT POSITED ATTRIBUTES1))
(override (share attributes—POSITED ATTRIBUTES2))
(override (share-attributes OBJECT REAL ATTRIBUTES3)))

This schema is called the 'like-super' schema and is used when the user mistakenly classifies some OBJECT as a POSITED superordinate, thinking OBJECT is similar to POSITED. This schema dictates that the misclassification should be denied, the correct classification stated, the attributes the two objects share conceded, and finally the distinguishing attributes pointed out. The communicative role is indicated by predicates such as *deny*, *state*, or *concede*, while content is determined by predicates such as *classification* or *share-attributes*. The response shown in Example 5 was generated by using the like-super schema; the user misclassified bankers' acceptances as US government securities. Note that McCoy's schemata generate a much narrower range of texts than Weiner's, McKeown's or Mann's, since they contain no optionality or repetition.

Example 5
Bankers' acceptances are not US-government-securities. They are bank securities. It is true that they are like US-government-securities because both have a high

safety and a high liquidity. However, they differ from US-government-securities in that, on the one hand, US-government-securities have a safety which is greater than all other investments, a low yield, and have a yield which is less than other money market securities. In contrast, bankers' acceptances are issued at face-value, have their yield set by the issuer, have a fixed return, are taxed at a federal level, a state level, and a local level, are purchased from a commercial bank, and are issued by a commercial bank.[6]

In order to determine which response to generate, McCoy developed the notion of object perspective. She represents a number of possible perspectives that can be taken on a domain separately from the object taxonomy. A perspective identifies attributes that are highlighted and attributes that are suppressed when an object is viewed from that perspective. McCoy assumes that one perspective is active at any point in the discourse and that the active perspective could be determined from preceding discourse, although she does not give an algorithm for this. Perspective is used to provide a measure for finding an object that is similar to the incorrect object posited in the user model, thereby determining the type of misconception that occurred.

By separating the representation of perspective from the domain representation, McCoy has gained a clear advantage over previous treatments that included perspective as part of the domain, using multiple inheritance. Her approach allows for domain information to be modified independently of perspective. By classifying types of misconceptions that can occur, McCoy provides a more general method for misconception correction than did previous efforts, which required an a priori enumeration of all specific misconceptions that could occur (e.g. Brown & Burton 1978). Note, however, that an a priori classification of misconception types must be done to extend coverage beyond misclassifications and misattributions, which are relevant only to knowledge bases consisting of object taxonomies and attributes. Thus, further classifications would have to be made for knowledge bases including procedural, cause–effect, or temporal information, among others. In regard to discourse strategies, McCoy's strategies appear to be more limited than earlier work since they allow for no variation. Her formalism, however, is more sophisticated because of its separation of communicative function and content.

TAILOR   TAILOR (Paris 1985, 1987) is part of a question-answering system developed for RESEARCHER (Lebowitz 1985a). RESEARCHER contains a complex knowledge base of information about physical objects. Its question-answering component must be able to respond to requests for descriptions of the objects, and this is TAILOR's focus. Since there is too much information represented about each object to include in a single description, TAILOR must determine what information to include. One constraint on determining content for a description of a physical object is information about the user's knowledge of the domain. Paris's work shows how to generate a range of descriptions to users whose domain knowledge falls along a naïve-expert continuum.

To determine the kind of information that should be included in responses for users with different domain expertise, Paris (1985) analysed encyclopaedia entries for various physical objects, using entries for the same object from adult and junior encyclopaedias. (She assumed the adult to have more domain expertise in any given domain than the child.) Rather than provide more detail for the naïve reader and less for the expert (or vice versa), an approach taken previously in natural language generation (Wallis & Shortliffe 1982), the encyclopaedias offered different kinds of detail to the two kinds of readers: experts, having knowledge about many objects and how they function, were given details about parts, while novices were given details about how each object functions.

Paris captured this difference in detail through two different discourse strategies. The structure of descriptions for domain experts could be captured by McKeown's (1985) CONSTITUENCY schema described above, while Paris formalized the PROCESS schema indicating how the system should trace causal relations in the underlying knowledge base, for descriptions for domain novices. Furthermore, rather than restricting the system to two static classes of users, Paris shows how to mix the strategies in producing a single text for users who might fall between the extremes of expert and novice. Since she represents level of domain expertise by the objects and parts the user knows about in the domain, the CONSTITUENCY schema or PROCESS schema can be invoked separately in an object description depending upon whether the user knows about a particular object subpart. Given a request for a telephone, TAILOR produces a response for an expert with no knowledge about transmitters, as shown in Example 6. In this text, the CONSTITUENCY schema is used for the overall structure, but when the transmitter is introduced, TAILOR provides process information. By mixing strategies Paris shows how to produce a large range of different descriptions of a single object tailored to a user's background. One difficulty with this sort of approach is verifying that the text produced for one user is more effective for that user than other descriptions.

Example 6
The telephone has a housing that has various shapes and various colors, a transmitter that changes soundwaves into current, a curly-shaped cord, a line, a receiver to change current into soundwaves, and a dialing-mechanism. The transmitter is a microphone. A person speaking into the microphone causes the soundwaves to hit the diaphragm of the microphone. The soundwaves hitting the diaphragm causes

the diaphragm to vibrate. The vibration of the diaphragm causes the current to vary. The current varies, like the intensity varies. The receiver is a loudspeaker with a small aluminum diaphragm. The housing contains the transmitter. The housing contains the receiver. The housing is connected to the dialing-mechanism by the cord. The line connects the dialing-mechanism to the wall.

PAULINE   PAULINE (Hovy 1985, 1986) was developed to produce different descriptions of the same situation depending upon various characteristics of the speaker modelled by PAULINE and the designated hearer. Hovy's approach is unique in that it takes into account the social relationship between speaker and hearer, the social background of the speaker as well as the hearer, and the effect the speaker wants to achieve through the production of text. These factors are treated as input parameters that influence the style of the generated text, determining what information is included or left out as well as the wording. In this section, we describe how PAULINE determines content based on these factors.

Hovy's work is best illustrated by PAULINE's description of an event in three different scenarios shown in Example 7 below. PAULINE is describing the outcome of a hypothetical primary election between Carter and Kennedy in which Kennedy narrowed Carter's lead.

Example 7

Scenario 1: (Parameters—PAULINE: pro-Kennedy; Hearer: pro-Carter, PAULINE's friend, not expert; Time: a lot)

Kennedy diminished Carter's lead by getting all of 2185 votes in the primary in Michigan. In a similar case, Carter decreased Udall's lead in a primary in 1976, and he easily trounced Udall to be nominated by 2600 delegates. I am real glad that Kennedy is now closer to getting the nomination than before.

Scenario 2: (Parameters—PAULINE: pro-Kennedy; Hearer: pro-Carter, PAULINE's sibling, expert; Time: unspecified)

Well, so Carter lost the primary to Kennedy by 335 votes.

Scenario 3: (Parameters—PAULINE: pro-Carter; Hearer: pro-Kennedy, PAULINE's boss; Time: rushed)

PAULINE says nothing . . .

PAULINE determines the style of the generated text through the use of eighteen RHETORICAL GOALS (RGs). For example, the RG DETAIL, which can take on values along a scale from facts to interpretations, influences the content of the text. PAULINE uses a large number of rules, such as the one shown in Example 8, to set RG values. In Scenario 1, PAULINE sets RG detail to all, indicating it should include both situation facts and interpretations of the facts since the hearer is no expert. In contrast, it decides to include just facts and not interpretations in Scenario 2 since the hearer is an expert. The time available to produce the text also influences content. In Scenario 1, PAULINE has a lot of time for planning the text and is able to make analogies to other situations that support its argument (e.g. the Udall primary). In Scenario 3, however, it does not have the time to choose appropriate wording for a boss and so says nothing.

Example 8
One rule to set RG *detail*:
    If hearer's knowledge level = expert or
    hearer's interest level = high
    Set RG:DETAIL to facts

Hovy addresses an important issue in language generation in noting influences such as speaker–hearer relationship on content, and PAULINE is capable of producing a range of impressive output. However, Hovy attempts to show the effect of such influences on far too many decisions in the generation process. As a consequence, he is unable to do a thorough analysis of the effect of these parameters on choice. He provides few satisfactory rationales for how his input parameters influence generation decisions. As a result, his values for RGs and his rules for setting them sometimes appear arbitrary.

Other work There are a number of systems that take the intended reader into account when producing text, although space precludes providing details. In the ADVISOR system (McKeown *et al.*, 1985), a user's domain goals, derived from the preceding discourse, influence content of the explanation produced. In particular, McKeown *et al.* show how the domain goals determine what facts should be taken into consideration by the underlying inference engine, thus determining the justifications provided for the advice produced. Chin (1986) shows how to use a set of dual stereotypes to decide what kind of responses to provide as part of a UNIX help system (Wilensky *et al.* 1984). He classifies both users and commands into four categories (naïve, beginner, intermediate, expert), and this determines what help is provided. Jameson (1983) has developed a generator that, given explicit assumptions about the hearer's standards and prior expectations, will select additional comments for a response based on their anticipated impact on the hearer. Finally, a considerable amount of work on user modelling and generation has been done as part of the HAM-ANS project, including overanswering of yes–no questions (Wahlster *et al.* 1983) and generation of responses to avoid negative reactions using stereotypes (Morik 1986).

1.1.3 *The use of planning formalisms for language generation*

The previous section showed a number of diverse ways in which information about the intended reader of the text can influence generation of text. In this section, we turn to work that is also based on the necessity of reasoning about the intended reader's beliefs when generating language. Unlike work just presented, however, it proposes a single-principled technique for making use of that information. It features use of a logical representation of speaker and hearer beliefs, an adaption of the planning formalism for the generation process, and a sound method of reasoning about plans and beliefs. Its contributions are twofold: first, in its characterization of language generation as a planning activity, and, second, in the development of a formal mechanism, relatively different from other generation systems, for the production of language. We focus on Appelt's (1985a) development of KAMP as paradigmatic of this approach and turn briefly to work by Kronfeld (1986) and Pollack (1986) which uses similar formalisms.

KAMP Appelt (1981, 1985a) was the first to use a model of hearer beliefs as part of a system that generates natural language utterances.[7] His system, KAMP, embodies a formal representation of speaker and hearer mutual beliefs using possible-world semantics[8] (Moore 1981) and a formal axiomatization scheme to plan and produce utterances. KAMP was developed within a task domain for the purpose of producing utterances an expert might produce to aid an apprentice in assembling a piece of equipment. Appelt's work successfully shows how a system can plan to fulfil multiple-speaker goals in a single utterance, how to apply an AI planning paradigm (Sacerdoti 1977) to the generation problem, how to reason about speaker and hearer beliefs, and how to allow for interaction between decisions about content and decisions about expression. In this survey, we demonstrate how Appelt's approach works for production of noun phrases that refer to, or denote, some object in the world (termed REFERRING EXPRESSIONS).

Appelt uses an axiomatization of operators in terms of relations over possible worlds to allow the system to reason about the knowledge of the speaker and hearer and how it would change as different actions (such as the generation of utterances by the system) are performed. The utterance is produced by a planning mechanism based on a NOAH-like hierarchical planner (Sacerdoti 1977). Actions available to the planner are also axiomatized using possible-world semantics, although simplified action summaries are used to produce the plans and the axioms themselves used to verify that the plan is correct. Planning proceeds on four levels of abstraction. At the highest level, the system plans a rough characterization of speech actions that need to be carried out to satisfy a goal. For example, if the system, as expert, has the goal for the novice user to remove a pump from a platform, it may plan to request the user to remove the pump from the platform and to inform the user that a specific wrench should be used. At the next level, the system plans the overall syntactic structure of a speech action. For example, it may decide to employ an imperative sentence to request the user to remove the pump. At the third level, the content of each speech action is determined. Here, for example, the system may determine that if the user already knows the pump is attached to a platform, it need not actually mention the platform in requesting the user to remove the pump. At the lowest level, words and their surface order in the sentence are planned. After planning to use an imperative sentence to request the user to remove the pump, the lowest level might determine that the syntactic structure of the generated sentence should be a verb followed by two noun phrases. Note that Appelt's division of levels and use of a uniform planning mechanism for each level make KAMP's organization considerably different from the two-stage generation process we have assumed so far.

One important feature of KAMP is the use of procedures, termed CRITICS, which look for interactions between plans produced by different levels of the planner and propose modifications. If the system has created two plans, one to request removal of the pump and one to inform the user that a specific wrench be used, the system may determine that the specific wrench can be specified as modifier of the request, and that the two planned sentences can thereby be collapsed into one. This planning sequence results in the final generated utterance *Remove the pump with the wrench in the toolbox*. The use of critics is another way in which KAMP provides for interaction between decisions about content and wording.

Among generation systems, KAMP provides the most thorough account of the mechanisms needed to produce referring descriptions. For this particular task, representation and use of mutual belief are crucial, as the hearer will not correctly identify the referent of a description if its terms are not understood. Appelt's formalism also shows how a system can satisfy multiple-speaker goals in a single utterance. KAMP uses its critics to determine when two-speaker plans, such as requesting and informing in the example given, can be combined into a single utterance. Finally, the procedure proposed by Appelt demonstrates how knowledge about expression can influence the planning of organization and content.

While the formal approach taken by Appelt allows for a sound and complete method of inferencing to produce plans, the formalism seems unnecessarily complex. In KAMP's limited task domain, it is possible to use a detailed model of speaker and hearer beliefs and determine through theorem proving whether the hearer has the information needed to carry out a task. In less well-defined domains such as tutoring or explanation production, it may be difficult to enumerate all relevant speaker and hearer beliefs and to formalize in detail the plans required to produce texts. These points raise the question of whether Appelt's model for reasoning about belief (in particular, the use of a theorem prover) is the best approach. Finally, Appelt's use of the planning formalism for the planning of utterance actions is problematic. In early versions of KAMP, grammatical information was not modularized as part of a grammar but spread throughout the system in procedures and critics of the planner. Use of a grammar would make utterance planning both more compatible with linguistic theory and more transportable. Such modularization is an approach Appelt clearly favours, as indicated by the development and incorporation of TELEGRAM (Appelt 1983) as part of KAMP.

BERTRAND   Kronfeld's (1986) work aims at production of referring expressions (definite noun phrases) that accurately reflect certain distinctions in speaker intentions and the effect of the expression on the hearer. His thorough analysis of the use of referential expressions also aims at explaining philosophical work (e.g. Donellan 1966). Although his contributions are more theoretical than practical at this point, he develops a computational model for generating definite descriptions. The model is currently being implemented as part of BERTRAND, a system that will ultimately produce definite noun phrases.

Kronfeld identifies three dichotomies that distinguish different uses of definite descriptions: whether the speaker knows what object an expression denotes (the EPISTEMIC distinction), whether the speaker intends the referring expression to pick out a unique object (the MODAL distinction), and whether the semantic denotation of the referring expression coincides with the intended referent (the SPEECH ACT distinction). In this section, we show how the modal distinction and the speech act distinction allow for the generation of different types of noun phrases.

In Kronfeld's model, production of a definite noun description relies upon an underlying representation where each object is represented to a speaker (or system) by the maximal set of terms, called an INDIVIDUATING SET, all believed by the speaker to denote the same object. For example, for some speakers the terms {Shakespeare, the author of *Othello*} would be an individuating set for Shakespeare. How a definite description is produced depends in part on the speaker's referential intentions. A speaker may intend the hearer to identify some particular aspect of the object and in that case will choose a particular term specifying the aspect from the set. In other cases, the speaker may only intend that the hearer be able to identify the object and will pick a term from the set that allows identification to occur (often a proper name, but also possibly a description). Thus in sentence 1 of Example 9 below, the speaker intends that the hearer think of Shakespeare as the author of *Othello*, while in 2 only intends that the hearer make a connection between the name *Shakespeare* and the referent. Kronfeld notes that this decision, the modal distinction, must be made by the planner of a generation system since it requires reasoning about speaker intentions.

Example 9
1. The author of *Othello* wrote the best play about jealousy.
2. Shakespeare was born in Stratford-upon-Avon.

Once the planner has determined the referring intentions, decisions regarding the speech act decision are made. Kronfeld notes that a definite description may not semantically describe an object but may still successfully allow the hearer to pick out the intended referent. For example, the definite description *the man over there drinking the champagne* may still allow the hearer to identify the man the speaker has in mind even if he happens to be drinking ginger ale. On the other hand, a definite description of an object may be semantically correct but may not be appropriate in the given conversation. For example, the definite description *The city hosting the Russian Ballet* may do just as well as the description *New York* in allowing the hearer to pick out the intended city (if New York is, in fact, hosting the Russian Ballet). However, it is not just an acceptable substitute for *New York* in the sentence *New York needs more policemen*, as it would imply something untrue (namely that New York needs more policemen because it is sponsoring the Russian Ballet). Kronfeld's work identifies the information needed by an utterance generator in order to make the choice of appropriate definite description.

The value of Kronfeld's work for generation lies in his very thorough analysis of distinctions that occur in definite descriptions and in identifying the information needed to make such decisions when producing definite descriptions. Although he has a preliminary implementation of individuating sets in BERTRAND, this program does not yet produce definite descriptions. As a result, it is too early to evaluate how well his analysis will work as part of a system.

SPIRIT   Pollack (1986) develops a representation that allows for the generation of appropriate responses to certain types of questions. In particular, she notes that a question may request information needed to carry out a domain plan but the questioner's plan may be invalid. As a prerequisite to responding to invalidities, Pollack presents a model of plan inference that distinguishes between the beliefs of the questioner and of the respondent, demonstrating, like Appelt and Kronfeld, the importance of formally representing and reasoning about beliefs. Her model of inference has been implemented as part of SPIRIT.[9]

Pollack's work is in reaction to earlier work on plan inference (Allen & Perrault 1980) which used an inferred questioner plan to respond with more information than was actually requested but which was needed to carry out the inferred plan. While it is an important part of producing co-operative responses, Pollack notes that their approach can only infer and address valid plans. But Example 10 (from Pollack 1986) illustrates that R must infer a plan that is no longer valid (calling Kathy at the hospital) to provide an appropriate response. By representing plans as mental concepts, separating out beliefs of the questioner and respondent about plans, Pollack's model can infer invalid plans as well. In the inference model, the respondent reasons about his beliefs about the questioner, not about the actual plan. Furthermore, she encodes different relationships between actions than does Allen, as well as beliefs about them. This representation allows her to infer four types of invalidities: plans that contain unexecutable actions, ill-formed plans (e.g. the questioner's beliefs about conditions for executing an action may be false), interactions between unexecutable actions and ill-formedness, and queries where the inferred plan does not make sense. Since each type of invalidity may arise in a number of ways, Pollack's approach allows for the generation of different responses that address the reason for the invalidity. Since Pollack's emphasis is on plan inference, more work is needed on the generation of both content and wording of the response using the results of inferencing. Her work is important in showing how an underlying representation can influence the possibility of generating different types of responses. This leads to the next section, where we discuss the influence of the underlying knowledge base in producing appropriate explanations.

Example 10
Q: What is Kathy's phone number at the hospital?
R: Kathy is no longer at the hospital. Her home phone number is xxx-xxxx.

1.1.4 *Knowledge representation*

Before a generation system can produce text, the knowledge to be conveyed must be represented somewhere. Two issues arise when considering knowledge representation from the standpoint of generation. The first, GENERATIONAL ADEQUACY, concerns the content of a knowledge base. An ADEQUATE knowledge base represents the knowledge needed to support the generation of the kinds of text we want. ADEQUACY is the issue of whether or not the system knows what it is talking about. The second issue concerns the FORM of the knowledge representation formalism. Two central questions are (a) how 'close' the knowledge representation is to natural language (see Hawkinson 1980; Martin 1981; Szolovits *et al*. 1977; Schank *et al*. 1973); and (b) whether its structure makes distinctions that are necessary for generation.

In many natural language generation systems, generational adequacy is achieved by constructing the knowledge base especially to support generation. Adequacy becomes an issue when we try to generate natural language from a knowledge base that was designed for some other purpose. The problems that arise when this is done have been most extensively explored in the context of producing natural language explanations of expert system behaviour.

In building an expert system, the initial focus is representing the knowledge needed to produce expert problem-solving behaviour. At one time, it was thought that if knowledge was represented in a sufficiently declarative form it would be relatively easy to produce explanations of the system's behaviour by paraphrasing it into natural language. This is a seductive suggestion. The fact that the expert system exhibited the same behaviour as the expert was evidence that the expert's knowledge had been captured, so it was thought that explanation would only require parroting back the knowledge base to the user in a palatable form.

This explanation-by-paraphrasing approach could give reasonable explanations of HOW the system's problem-solving methods worked or were applied to a particular problem. However, the problem was that the range of questions that people may reasonably ask of an expert (human or machine) goes beyond questions about how a solution was obtained. For example, most expert systems cannot adequately justify their actions or define the terminology they use. Providing such explanations requires additional knowledge over and above the knowledge needed to produce the solution. Requirements for explanation must be taken into account while a system is being designed. Attempting to add an explanation capability to an existing system will usually result in inadequate explanations.

If a system is to offer good explanations of its reasoning, certain fundamental requirements must be met in system structure and design. The three main requirements are separation of different kinds of knowledge, statement of knowledge at a more explicit and abstract level, and explicit modelling and recording of the process of system creation.[10] The quality of the explanations a system provides indicates how well the requirements were satisfied.

- SEPARATION OF KNOWLEDGE: Separation of different kinds of knowledge allows an explanation facility to isolate the knowledge needed to answer a user's question. The explanation can thus be made free of superfluous material.
- ABSTRACT REPRESENTATION: Representation of knowledge at a more abstract level makes it possible to produce explanations of general problem solving strategies (Hasling 1984; Swartout 1983b), and also opens up the possibility of knowledge reuse.
- CAPTURING SYSTEM CREATION: To justify an expert system's actions or recommendations, an explanation facility needs access not only to the system itself, but also to the design decisions that UNDERLIE the system. Explicitly modelling and recording the process of creating the system captures the rationale behind the system and makes it possible to give justifications.

To illustrate these points, we will present examples from several expert systems. MYCIN (Shortliffe 1976) was the first expert system to provide explanations. These were produced by paraphrasing its rules or traces of their execution. NEOMYCIN (Clancey 1983c) improved MYCIN's explanations by providing an abstract representation for problem-solving knowledge. The Digitalis Therapy Advisor (Swartout 1977) represented its knowledge in a formalism that was based on linguistic principles, facilitating the paraphrasing process. Finally, XPLAIN (Swartout 1983b) and its successor, the Explainable Expert Systems (EES) framework (Neches *et al.* 1985), make additional kinds of explanation possible by providing explicit means for separating different kinds of knowledge and recording the design decisions that underlie an expert system.

MYCIN's internal knowledge representation was neither close in form to natural language nor based on linguistic principles. To provide explanations, templates were associated with all the clinical parameters, domain objects, and functions in MYCIN's knowledge base. These templates were usually short English phrases. The templates for functions could contain blanks associated with the functions arguments. When the function was paraphrased, the blanks would be filled in by the paraphrase for the associated argument.

Consider an example of MYCIN's explanations. Suppose a user was interested in finding out when it would be appropriate to conclude that a patient's infection was caused by *E. coli*. MYCIN could tell the user which rules concluded about *E. coli* infections. A typical example is RULE543 (shown in its internal form in Example 11).

Example 11
RULE543

   PREMISE: ($AND (SAME CNTXT TREATINF MENINGITIS)
                 ($OR (NOTSAME CNTXT EXAMSTAIN)
                      (NOTSAME CNTXT SPECSTAIN))
                 (SAME CNTXT TYPE BACTERIAL)
                 (SAME CNTXT STEROIDS)
                 (NOTSAME CNTXT DIAGNOSES LYMPHOMA)
                 (NOTSAME CNTXT DIAGNOSES LEUKEMIA))
   ACTION: [CONCLUDE* CNTXT COVERFOR TALLY '((E COLI
                 400)
                 (LISTERIA 200)
                 (KLEBSIELLA-PNEUMONIAE 200)
                 (PSEUDOMONAS-AERUGINOSA 100)]

   The system could display the rule to the user by producing a direct paraphrase (such as that in Example 12).

Example 12
If:
1) The infection which requires therapy is meningitis,
2) A: A smear of the culture was not examined, or
   B: Organisms were not seen on the stain of the culture,
3) The type of infection is bacterial,
4) The patient has received corticosteroids just prior to or during his infection,
5) Lymphoma is not one of the diagnoses of the patient, and
6) Leukemia is not one of the diagnoses of the patient

Then:

There is evidence that the organisms (other than those seen on cultures or smears) which might be causing the infection is e.coli (.4), listeria (.2), klebsiella-pneumoniae (.2) or pseudomonas-aeruginosa (.1)

MYCIN's explanations are limited by the fact that the only knowledge available for explanation is the knowledge that had to be in the system for it to PERFORM correctly. Knowledge needed to develop the system rules is not represented and is hence unavailable. For example, if the user wanted to know how the administration of corticosteroids was involved in the diagnosis of an *E. coli* infection (clause 4, Example 12), the system would be unable to generate an explanation since that knowledge is not represented in MYCIN. This knowledge was used in creation of the system but did not have to be represented explicitly in the system for it to perform properly. The straightforward paraphrase, therefore, does not tell the user what the relation between corticosteroid administration and *E. coli* is. Does it cause *E. coli* infections directly? Does it create conditions favourable for infection by *E. coli*? Does it tend to be associated with *E. coli* infections without a causal link? Answers to these questions cannot be included in the explanation because MYCIN's rule representation does not draw these distinctions. Clancey points out that for an explanation the system needs to represent the support knowledge that underlies this rule. With this support knowledge the system would know and could explain that *E. coli* is a likely agent of the infection because corticosteroid administration weakens the immune system, allowing organisms normally found in the body, such as *E. coli*, to proliferate.

Example 12 reveals additional ways that MYCIN's representation foils explanation. Because MYCIN represents rule clauses uniformly, it prevents the explanation routines from drawing any distinctions among them. The clauses in this rule perform very different functions. For example, while clauses 3 and 4 capture the medical association between infection by organisms like *E. coli* and corticosteroid administration, clauses 1 and 2 establish the context in which the rule should be applied, namely, when the disease is meningitis and when hard evidence about the infection is not available. Because these various concerns are lumped together in one rule, it is difficult to identify in an explanation the overall diagnostic strategy MYCIN uses. The explanations of individual rules often seem clear, but it is hard to get a general picture of what is going on. That fact made it difficult to use MYCIN's rule base for tutoring medical students about diagnosis (Clancey 1983a,b).

To provide a more explicit representation of problem-solving knowledge, Clancey created the NEOMYCIN system (Clancey 1983c), which explicitly represented its problem-solving knowledge in the form of meta-rules (Davis 1980). NEOMYCIN used techniques similar to those employed in MYCIN to produce explanations (Hasling *et al*. 1983, 1984; Hasling 1983); but because its explanations were based on a more explicit representation, it was possible to produce much better explications of the system's problem-solving strategy (as shown in Example 13).

Example 13
17)Has Mary been hospitalized recently?
**WHY
.
.
.
**HOW 25.0
[i.e. HOW are we trying to develop the differential using basic history and pertinent physical exam?].

We did the following:
[26.1] Got a general idea of the problem: categorized it into one of several pathogenic classes or disease loci, or both.
[26.2] Confirmed and refined the differential diagnosis through specific questions. We are now:
[26.3] Rounding out the diagnostic information by looking generally into past medical history and by reviewing systems.
[back to question 17 . . .]
**NO

XPLAIN and Explainable Expert Systems (EES)　NEOMYCIN was an important advance over MYCIN, but the technique it used was inadequate to support important classes of explanations, such as justifications of behaviour and definitions of terms. To show that, we outline some of the limitations of a version of the Digitalis Therapy Advisor (Silverman 1975; Gorry *et al*. 1978), which produced explanations using the paraphrase-the-code approach (Swartout 1977).[11] That system represented its problem-solving knowledge in explicit plans, so its explanations did benefit from the sort of problem-solving knowledge advocated in NEOMYCIN (although NEOMYCIN allows a more abstract representation of problem-solving knowledge than was supported in the Digitalis Advisor). The Digitalis Advisor also employed a knowledge representation that was close to natural language (see Szolovits *et al*. 1977). That made it possible to produce paraphrases directly from the same representation that were used for problem-solving, and obviated the need for paraphrasing templates. Even so inadequacies resulting from missing knowledge became apparent. Consider the explanation in Example 14.

Example 14
WHAT IS THE LEVEL OF SERUM CALCIUM?

ENTER NUMERICAL VALUE ⇒ why?
The user types "why?" indicating that he questions why he is being asked to supply the value of serum calcium.

MY TOP GOAL IS TO BEGIN THERAPY. ONE STEP IN DOING THAT IS TO CHECK SENSITIVITIES. I AM NOW TRYING TO CHECK SENSITIVITY DUE TO CALCIUM.

Here the user has been asked to enter the level of serum calcium the system needs in order to determine whether or not this patient is overly sensitive to digitalis. The user does not understand the purpose of the question, asks why, and is provided with an explanation. While this explanation does hint that an abnormal level of serum calcium is a sensitizing factor for digitalis, a user might want an elaboration of this explanation. But the system cannot provide such elaborations as:

1. Justification: if the user wanted an explanation of why serum calcium is involved in sensitivity to digitalis, it could not be given. None of the causal information required to produce such explanations is represented explicitly in the system. Although that information was needed to design the system, it is not needed at runtime.
2. Descriptions of general problem-solving methods: these could not be offered because all the system's problem-solving knowledge is represented at a specific level.
3. Definition of terms: a definition of the term SENSITIVITY could not be provided. Again, this knowledge is not represented.

XPLAIN (Swartout 1983b) and its successor, Explainable Expert Systems (EES) (Neches *et al.* 1985), were developed to permit these elaborations. They both provide frameworks to capture the knowledge that is needed to construct the expert system but that is not represented as part of it. XPLAIN captured the knowledge necessary for the first two types of elaborations; EES also captures knowledge for the third.[12] XPLAIN and EES are based on the observation that the PROGRAMMER of an expert system can usually provide good explanations of how and why it works by remembering the design decisions behind the code.

The approach in both XPLAIN and EES was to replace the human system builder with an automatic programmer that would synthesize the desired expert system from a SPECIFICATION consisting mainly of abstract knowledge about how the domain worked, how problems were solved in that domain, and (in the case of EES) domain terminology. During the program-writing process, the design decisions made by the automatic programmer were recorded in a DEVELOPMENT HISTORY. This history provided explanation routines with the (normally missing) knowledge needed to produce richer explanations and justifications, as shown in Example 15.

Example 15

Please enter the value of serum potassium: why?

The system is anticipating digitalis toxicity. Decreased serum potassium causes increased automaticity, which may cause a change to ventricular fibrillation. Increased digitalis also causes increased automaticity. Thus, if the system observes decreased serum potassium, it reduces the dose of digitalis due to decreased serum potassium.

Please enter the value of serum potassium: 3.7

Please enter the value of serum calcium: why?

[The system produces a shortened explanation, reflecting the fact that it has already explained several of the causal relationships in the previous explanation. Also, since the system remembers that it has already told the user about serum potassium, and because it knows that the same domain problem-solving knowledge was used to generate the code for both serum potassium and serum calcium, it points out the analogy between the two. This is a case where making use of analogy, which is powerful but usually difficult to recognize, is greatly facilitated by having the appropriate underlying representation.]

The system is anticipating digitalis toxicity. Increased serum calcium also causes increased automaticity. Thus (as with decreased serum potassium), if the system observes increased serum calcium, it reduces the dose of digitalis due to increased serum calcium.

The quest to provide better explanations has attracted increasing research interest (see Chandrasekaran & Josephson (1986) and Chandrasekaran (1986) for recent efforts). The major result in this area has been the realization that if a system is to provide explanations, then explanation concerns must be taken into account AT THE TIME THE SYSTEM IS DESIGNED. Adding an explanation facility to an already existing system severely limits the quality and range of explanations that can be offered. The major focus of research has been on providing representations that separate and abstract the knowledge that underlies a system and recording the process by which that knowledge is incorporated into a working system.

So far, expert system explanation facilities have employed relatively simple natural language generators. The improvements that have been realized in explanation quality stem from the use of better knowledge bases, rather than from the use of more sophisticated generators. However, we are now finding that those relatively simple generators are less appropriate, in part due to the progress we have made in building more complex knowledge bases. Because current knowledge bases separate out different kinds of knowledge and represent knowledge at different levels of abstraction, they confront generators with a range of choices concerning what to present and how to present it that never arose with simpler knowledge bases. Thus, as a consequence of providing richer knowledge bases, it now makes sense to employ more sophisticated and linguistically motivated generators for expert system explanation.

1.2 Surface generation

A surface generator is the component of a language generation system that is responsible for realizing determined content in language. It receives as input from the deep generator an internal representation of what is to be said (expressed, for example, in logical form as a subset of a frame-based knowledge representation). It must select words to refer to portions of the internal representation, and arrange the words in linear order to form one or more sentences that conform to the syntax of the language.

Current surface generators[13] typically contain two knowledge sources, a dictionary and a grammar (see Figure 1.4). The selection of words (LEXICAL CHOICE) is made by the dictionary. Words for a sentence may be selected before the grammar is invoked, or the dictionary may be assessed from the grammar when words are needed. The grammar is used for constructing the syntactic structure of the sentence to be produced. In so doing, it must select between possible syntactic choices (for example, between active and passive voice) and ensure that the resulting sentence is grammatical (for example, that the verb agrees in person and number with the sentence subject).

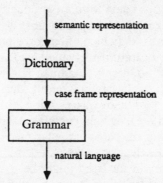

Figure 1.4 Components of a typical surface generator

Input to the surface generator is one or more propositions. Usually a surface generator produces one sentence per proposition, but some systems are able to combine two or more propositions in a single complex sentence (Appelt 1981, 1985a; Derr & McKeown 1984; McDonald & Pustejovsky 1985).

Our discussion of modern surface generators is divided into two main sections. In the first we discuss lexical choice and then focus on the use of grammars within generation systems.

1.2.1 *Lexical choice*

The problem of lexical choice for generation can be seen as the reverse of lexical disambiguation for parsing. For parsing, a system is given a word (in the context of a sentence) and must determine what that word refers to in its knowledge base. A generator must determine a word or phrase that can be used to refer to a given concept in the underlying knowledge base. A generation system must be able to determine which of several synonyms best suits the given context.

One major aspect of generation research has been to identify the constraints on a system's choices. After identifying a constraint and determining how it restricts the choice of words, the system must represent the constraint so that it can be used computationally by a program. In this section we first discuss constraints upon word choice. Within this context, we present Goldman's early work in the MARGIE system, upon which the dictionaries of many later generation systems have been based. We then present several implementations of lexical choice.

Constraints   Words are typically selected for tokens in an input proposition. Some constraints thus come from the proposition itself. Recall that a proposition will be realized as a sentence in most systems. The proposition usually consists of a predicate (which often corresponds to the verb in the resulting sentence) and its arguments (which get mapped to the case roles of the verb and various modifiers). Goldman (1975) noted that semantic features of predicate arguments can influence lexical choice for a predicate of a proposition. Since Goldman was working with Conceptual Dependency (Schank *et al*. 1973), which contains a small set of language-independent primitives for the verbs of the language but not for the nouns, Goldman focused on the selection of verbs.

As an example, the predicate *ingest* might be translated as *to eat* if the object ingested is solid, as 'to drink' if the object is liquid, or as *to inhale* if the object is gaseous. Rather than determining a single verb, however, each of these constraints actually suggests a class of verbs that can be further refined by taking into account semantic features of other arguments. Goldman represented these constraints using a discrimination net. Tests at each branch of the net determine which class of verbs is taken. At the leaves of the net are the possible verbs. Thus if the object is liquid, we obtain a class of verbs that includes *to drink*. If the agent is not human, we obtain one set of verbs, including *to lap*. If the agent is human, we obtain a second set. If we take into account a third argument, perhaps *manner*, we can refine our choice further. If manner is *normal*, we might choose the verb *to drink*, but if it indicates *quickly* we might choose the verb *to guzzle*.

McDonald (1980) noted that lexical choice may depend not only on the semantic features of arguments, but also on the actual choice of words for other arguments. In particular, the choice of verb can dictate what syntactic role other arguments will play, which in turn will dictate what words are selected to represent those arguments. Some verbs take a noun phrase as object, others an adjective, and yet others a gerund. As an example, consider the process of lexical choice for the logical formula 'Human $(x) \rightarrow$ mortal (x)'. The translation of the connective $(\rightarrow)$ determines the syntactic role, and in turn, word choice, for the left- and right-hand sides of the formula. If the connective is translated using the sentential connectives *if . . . then . . .*, then the left- and right-hand sides must each be realized as a sentence. This choice might result in the generation of sentence 1, Example 16. If the connective is realized as the verb *to imply*, however, the left- and right-hand sides must be clauses, and sentence 2 might be generated. But the connective could also be realized as the verb *to be*, in which case the agent will be a quantified noun phrase, the object an adjective, and the result might be sentence 3.

Example 16
1. If any thing is a man, then it is mortal.
2. Being a man implies being mortal.
3. All men are mortal.

Pronominalization also crucially depends on earlier word choice and not simply on the underlying representation. Word choice makes available different discourse entities for later pronominalization. Depending on how the logical formula was translated, later reference to different entities can be pronominalized. In sentence 1, Example 16, *it* was selected to refer to *any thing*. If sentence 2 were produced, the sentence *It also implies being subject to supply-side economics* could follow, where *it* co-refers to *being a man*. A sentence such as *They are also egotists* could follow sentence 3, where *they* co-refers to *All men*.

Appelt (1981, 1985a) showed how knowledge about the hearer's beliefs can influence the lexical choice. If the hearer knows what a wheelpuller is, then the utterance *Use the wheelpuller next* is fine. If not, a description using distinguishing physical attributes such as *Use the red tool on the table next* is more appropriate. In recent work, Appelt (1985b) proposes a set of actions underlying the production of noun phrases that provide an account of how the mutual beliefs of speaker and hearer affect the generation of definite and indefinite noun phrases.

Danlos (1984) notes that a variety of influences on lexical choice interact in unpredictable ways. Furthermore, she claims that influences on both conceptual (deep generation) and surface decisions also interact unpredictably. For example, Danlos shows that lexical choice (a surface decision) influences the possible ordering of two consecutive sentences (a conceptual decision) and vice versa. If a particular word is desired, then this may determine the order in which its sentence and surrounding sentences should occur. If a particular ordering is desired, this may preclude use of a given word. Since there are many such choices and interactions involved in the generation process, this leads to a combinatorial explosion of possibilities for expression. According to Danlos, it is impossible to predict which combinations are awkward. In each case, interactions among constraints are specific to the words involved.

Implementation of constraints   Several implementations of lexical choice have been based on Goldman's (1975) system. McDonald (1980) represented choice routines within separate entries in a dictionary, each entry keyed by the internal concept for which a word or phrase must be chosen. While the routines are actually programs to be executed, they are based on Goldman's discrimination-net representation. The dictionaries produce underlying syntactic structure, which gets attached to the syntactic tree of the sentence being produced. The dictionary is accessed from the grammar in the process of building syntactic structure. TEXT's (McKeown 1982) dictionary is based on McDonald's design, but all necessary entries are accessed and choices made before the grammar is invoked.

Danlos's (1984) approach to lexical choice is considerably different from Goldman's. Her analysis of interactions between constraints on lexical choice and other decisions leads her to conclude that no general principles specify interaction between conceptual and surface decisions. Rather, for each new domain a new ordering must be developed. Danlos develops a method that works for her domain. She makes use of a DISCOURSE GRAMMAR that identifies possible discourse organizations along with the lexical choices that can be used for each organization. Thus lexical choice and order of information are decided simultaneously before other decisions (e.g. syntactic decisions) are made. The discourse grammar amounts to a sophisticated form of template, since it spells out surface strings. Since slots contain syntactic markers and can be manipulated later by a syntactic grammar, they are slightly more general. Although Danlos's observations of interactions and influences on lexical choice are intriguing, her solutions are not, as they require a new design and implementation of a generator for each new domain. Furthermore, the use of discourse grammars containing surface strings is a brittle mechanism, requiring a tremendous effort in hand-enumeration of possibilities. The value of Danlos's work lies in the challenge it poses to future researchers to identify general principles that can account for the examples she has presented.

Other researchers advocate folding the lexicon into the knowledge representation. One variation of this approach is presented by Matthiessen (1981) who represents the semantic structure of the lexicon as intensional concepts in a KL-ONE (Brachman 1979)-style knowledge base. His approach provides for links between the syntactic structure of the lexicon and the semantic structure, showing how, for example, the semantic role of AGENT might function as the syntactic role ACTOR, if the semantic concept for SELL were lexicalized using the verb *to sell*. While Matthiessen's approach demonstrates how complex semantic structure can be used in a lexicon without duplicating information in the underlying knowledge base, he does not show how to choose between synonyms for the same intensional concept. In later work (Mann & Matthiessen 1983), it is apparent that the lexicon is only accessed after the grammar has completed its task. Sets of semantic features are used where lexical items would occur and are sufficient for making syntactic choices. After all syntactic choices have been made, the lexicon is accessed to replace each set of features with a lexical item.

Other systems use word-based lexicons (e.g. Appelt 1981, 1985a; Bates & Ingria 1981) similar to parser lexicons, while another class of systems (Kukich 1983; Jacobs 1985) uses dictionaries that are closer to Danlos's approach in that they select whole phrases and leave structures unindicated.

Other than Goldman, Danlos and Matthiessen, the researchers mentioned here have not focused primarily on the problem of lexical choice. Thus most approaches simply provide engineering tools that allow their systems to make lexical choice in a reasonable, if relatively unsophisticated, way. By current criteria, none of these approaches far surpasses the others; most seem successful to some degree.[14] On the other hand, a truly satisfactory theoretical approach to lexical choice has yet to be developed, and this area of language generation appears promising for future research.

1.2.2 *Grammars for generation*

Using a grammar to produce appropriate surface strings is close to being the reverse of parsing. A generation grammar[15] typically accepts either a semantic representation or a deep-structure representation of the sentence to be generated. In the former case words have not yet been selected, while in the latter they have. The key tasks in this component include arranging the words (a process governed by syntactic constraints), producing the correct morphological endings on words (e.g. verb tense and number must be taken into account to produce the correct verb ending), and selecting among syntactic alternatives where they exist (verb voice is one such alternative; another would be modification using a relative clause for a prepositional phrase).

More language generation work has been done in this area than in any of the others we have surveyed so far. In order to present enough detail, we focus here on one approach: that of McDonald in the MUMBLE system. While many approaches would also have been suitable, MUMBLE is one of the first of the more sophisticated surface generators to be used robustly in a variety of applications. Furthermore, surface generation is McDonald's primary concern. We then turn briefly to systemic and functional grammars for generation, and finally to PHRED (Jacobs 1985), a system that proposes an alternative to the use of a grammar for surface generation.

MUMBLE   MUMBLE was developed as part of McDonald's dissertation work (McDonald 1980) and has since been significantly extended and changed. We base our description on the 1985 version of the system (McDonald & Pustejovsky 1985; McDonald 1984). McDonald has sought to develop a computationally efficient, transportable linguistic component. He aims to provide large coverage of the language and to develop a module that can be used with a variety of deep generators. MUMBLE has three main characteristics.

1. It is DESCRIPTION-DIRECTED. The input, or semantic representation of the text, controls the generation process. This contrasts with most other linguistic components, where flow of control is determined by the grammar, not the input.
2. It is an INDELIBLE process. Once a decision has been made, it cannot be retracted. This is equivalent to Marcus's (1980) notion of determinism in parsing and means that there is no parallelism or backtracking in the generator.
3. It is PSYCHOLOGICALLY MOTIVATED. McDonald hopes to model the human language-production process. Because of the principle of indelibility, MUMBLE models a speaker rather than a writer of human language. McDonald, who has spent time studying human speech errors, claims that his program will produce errors only in instances where humans would also have made errors.

As input, MUMBLE receives a rhetorically annotated plan specifying what information is to be included in the text. The generation process consists of three subprocesses: Attachment, Realization and Phrase Structure Execution (PSE). While these levels are organized as separate modules, they are not strictly ordered in the overall process. They can be viewed, rather, as interleaved processes that pass information and partially refined structures between themselves. Flow of control is in part dictated by the input plan and in part by programmed knowledge dictating when to invoke the next component. All processes build and refine the surface structure of the text to be generated. McDonald carefully points out that this is the only linguistic structure to be constructed. MUMBLE does not use or construct a deep-structure representation of the text.

Attachment is responsible for assigning plan units to positions within the surface structure. At any point in the process, the surface structure contains 'attachment points' to which new structures can be added. Initially, the first plan unit is assigned to the only available attachment point, the node dominating the first sentence. At later points in the process the system may have to decide among several possible attachment points.

Attachment is interleaved with Phrase Structure Execution (PSE). All plan units are not attached at once. As soon as a partial tree is constructed. PSE takes over. The generation process is primarily driven by PSE, which does a depth-first traversal of the tree. PSE may invoke procedures to perform certain transformations or enforce constraints indicated by the labels of the tree. During this process words undergo morphological analysis and are output when the leaves of the tree are reached. If any points in the tree are encountered where additional syntactic structures can be attached, Attachment is called again to determine if there are any new structures that should be attached. If any plan units are found in the tree, the Realization process is called to determine how to realize the units as language.

Realization is responsible for all of the choices that have to be made during language generation. It has the task of selecting an appropriate word or phrase to 'realize' a plan unit. Classes are divided into two types: domain-dependent classes, which serve as dictionary entries as described in the section on lexical choice (above), and linguistic classes, which identify transformation families for a particular syntactic constituent. For example, McDonald defines a linguistic realization class for 'transitive latinate verbs forming nominalization' which identifies seven syntactic choices for realizing any verb of this class: active (e.g. *Petruchio tamed the shrew*), passive (e.g. *The shrew was tamed by Petruchio*), gerundive with subject (e.g. *Petruchio taming the shrew . . .*), gerundive passive with subject (e.g. *The shrew being tamed by Petruchio . . .*), nominalization (e.g. *The taming of the shrew . . .*), nominalization with subject (e.g. *Taming of the shrew by Petruchio . . .*), and definite nominalization with subject (e.g. *The taming of the shrew by Petruchio . . .*). In addition to identifying the choices, the class includes a test for each choice which must succeed in order for that choice to be selected. For example, one test may select the passive if *the shrew* is in focus. Grammatical information is therefore divided between realization classes, which make syntactic choice, and procedures, which enforce syntactic constraints and are invoked by tree labels.

To summarize, flow of control begins with Attachment, which assigns the first plan unit to a position in the surface structure. For example, if producing English for the plan unit (head (tame P1 S1)), the first step would be to position it in a skeletal tree as in Figure 1.5. Control then passes to PSE, which traverses the partial tree and invokes Realization whenever a plan unit is encountered. In the example, Realization would be invoked on encountering the starred node in Figure 1.5. PSE continues when a new structure is added to the tree by Realization. Note that Realization may only partially realize a plan unit at any point and therefore may be reinvoked after PSE. For example, Realization may first select the verb *to tame* for the token *tame* by using a domain-dependent realization class; Realization may determinine that *to tame* should appear in the active voice using the linguistic class for transitive latinate verbs given above. The tree might then appear as in Figure 1.6.[16] PSE would continue its depth-first traversal and would invoke Realization when P1 and S1 were encountered. Realization could make use of the linguistic context in deciding how to refer to them (i.e. the fact that P1 will appear as subject of a transitive verb and S1 as object). Attachment is reinvoked when a plan unit has been fully realized (i.e. when the tree has been fully constructed) or at any point in the tree traversal when other syntactic structures can be attached (e.g. at the end of any noun phrase).

In sum, McDonald has achieved efficiency in MUMBLE by constraining it to be deterministic. MUMBLE also has extremely good coverage of the language, in part because it has been developed and extended over a long period of time, and in part because McDonald has maintained close interaction with linguists in developing the grammar. Finally, MUMBLE

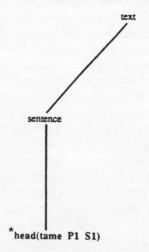

Figure 1.5 Initial surface tree

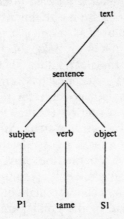

Figure 1.6   Partially expanded tree

has been used by researchers at the University of Massachusetts for a number of different domains. That it has been ported to the University of Pennsylvania and interfaced with TEXT by Rubinoff (1986)[17] indicates some degree of transportability.

MUMBLE's main disadvantage is its use of a procedural grammar. This affects the clarity of the system. Since grammatical information is encoded in arbitrary LISP procedures as opposed to a formal declarative grammar, only extensive consultation and documentation will enable an outsider to add new information. Furthermore, grammatical information appears in two separate places in the system: syntactic choices are made by realization classes, and syntactic constraints are enforced by procedures that are invoked by labels in the surface tree. McDonald (1986) notes that there is no distinct grammar in MUMBLE as there is, for example, in syntactic parsers. Since syntactic information is split between several places it is more difficult to examine and modify. Because grammatical information is represented and used differently than in other systems, adaptation of the system can be more difficult.

Systemic and functional grammars   Many other surface language generators do make use of a distinct grammar, many of them derived from the functionalist tradition (Halliday 1969). Two primary classes of grammars have been used: SYSTEMIC GRAMMAR and FUNCTIONAL UNIFICATION GRAMMAR. Both types allow functional and semantic information to be used as a basis for choice.

NIGEL, developed by Mann & Matthiessen (1983) and intended by them to be a large and linguistically justified generation system, makes use of a systemic grammar. They have focused intensively on achieving wide coverage of the language, consulting with linguists for this purpose. At this point, NIGEL has not been used as part of a larger application for generation, although Mann has plans to make the system available to other researchers for testing in the near future. The grammar consists of a number of different 'systems', one for each type of constituent. Each system represents the different choices possible for that type of syntactic constituent. The choice made by one system may form the input for another independent system. Thus a set of systems form a hierarchy, and each branch in the hierarchy represents a possible choice point. A 'chooser' is located at each branch and queries the outside world for information needed to make the syntactic choice. For example, to choose between an indefinite and definite article, a chooser might query the knowledge base to determine whether the head of the noun phrase refers to a generic or individual concept and might query the discourse model to determine whether the object has been previously mentioned. A chooser is encoded as a LISP function, and its output indicates which branch to take. Flow of control in this type of system is determined by the grammar. Generation begins by entering the grammar at the sentence system (if a sentence is to be produced). Here, for example, choice between active and passive voice would be made. Flow of control begins at the top of the hierarchy, and the system traverses the network by invoking the chooser at each branch point, continuing down the branch indicated by the chooser. Other systems would be invoked for subconstituents of the sentence.

Use of the systemic approach is intuitively appealing for generation because it allows for extensive interaction between the syntactic component and other aspects of the system when making syntactic choice. On the other hand, the large number of queries that must be designed and then executed for a single grammar (in NIGEL, the grammar contains 200–300 choosers) has led Patten & Ritchie (1986) to design a system that can infer responses to some choices based on responses to earlier choices. In their approach, the left-to-right sweeping through the network is abandoned and the system makes consecutive back and forth sweeps until all choices have either been posed as queries or deduced.

In some ways similar to systemic grammar, functional unification grammar (FUG), designed by Kay (1979), was first adapted as part of an application for generation by McKeown (1982, 1985) for TEXT.[18] FUG has two main attractive qualities. First is the ability to encode functional information directly in the grammar. A grammar, or functional description, consists primarily of attribute value pairs, where a value can also be a functional description. Functional categories, such as topic, comment or focus, can also appear as attributes and values. As there has been quite a bit of linguistic research on the relation between functional information and syntactic construction, these categories can be used in FUG to constrain syntactic choice. One main thrust of McKeown's work has been the use of focus of attention to constrain choices such as active/passive, or simple versus complex sentences (McKeown 1983; Derr & McKeown 1984). A second main advantage is the use of unification. Unification allows for the input to the grammar to be specified in simplified form. Syntactic details are filled in by unifying the input (which is in the same formalism as the grammar) with the grammar. Unification also allows for simplification of the grammar, since constraints on choice can be expressed as meta-constraints as opposed to being expressed separately for each applicable grammar rule.

Unification also leads to the major disadvantage of the system, however. Given that unification is a non-deterministic process, a straightforward implementation of FUG is not particularly efficient. Some attempts have been made to improve performance by allowing for interaction between the grammar and the deep generation component. Appelt (1983) developed TELEGRAM, which modified FUG by allowing the planner to be reinvoked at each choice point in the grammar, to guide the unification process. This approach had some success. Nevertheless, Ritchie (1986) shows that the computational properties of FUGs make general operations NP-complete. Despite these points, McKeown & Paris (1987) are able to achieve processing times similar to that of McDonald's (1980) MUMBLE in a reimplementation of FUG.

PHRED   A different approach was taken by Jacobs (1985). Jacobs's primary concern was capturing linguistic generalizations in a domain-independent way, but not by ignoring the semantic idiosyncracies of many words in the language. To do this, Jacobs uses a knowledge base of pattern-concept (PC) pairs, representing both specialized phrasal knowledge and general syntactic rules. A PC pair associates a pattern, including a word or phrase and parameters that will occur with it in a sentence, with a concept from the underlying knowledge base. For example, it may associate the word *remove* with the concept 'state-change' when the change in location is from inside a container. The pattern's parameters include agent, object and a 'from' prepositional phrase. Ordering patterns, representing general syntactic rules, specify possible orderings of constituents in sentences and are similar to transformations of transformational grammar or patterns of functional unification grammar.

A sentence is generated in three stages: FETCHING, RESTRICTION and INTER-PRETATION. Fetching retrieves appropriate PC pairs from the knowledge base, given a semantic input. Restricting verifies that the PC pairs meet given constraints. For example, it unifies variables between patterns and concepts and combines properties of the constituents between PC pairs and ordering patterns. Interpretation produces the output words from the restricted pattern, recursively invoking the fetch and restriction cycle for patterns that are not yet specialized enough for output.

PHRED has been used successfully to produce responses to questions as part of the UNIX Consultant System (Wilensky *et al.* 1984), to paraphrase semantic input, and to produce foreign language responses. It also addresses the problem of co-ordinating idiomatic and non-idiomatic language use. However, the non-standard approach taken by Jacobs is not clearly better than previous approaches. It will make transportability difficult, requiring a compatible knowledge base and extensive documentation for writing new PC pairs.

1.3 Current directions

In this chapter, we assume a model for language generation that divides processing into two stages—deep and surface generation. As is indicated by the approaches taken by several researchers, notably Appelt and Danlos, this separation of processing does not account for the influence of lexical and syntactic choice on conceptual decisions. One major direction in current generation research is investigation into the nature of the interaction that must occur between these components.

Danlos stands at one extreme in this line of work, touting a totally integrated treatment of the two components. (In Danlos's view, if there is to be separation and ordering, then it must be dependent on domain.) Total integration, however, means that we lose the usual benefits of modularization in computer systems. In particular, we lose the separate expression of grammar based on linguistic research that can be ported as a separate module from one domain to another. While Appelt's early work in KAMP also integrated knowledge about deep and surface generation, he seems to support the notion of separate interacting components by adopting a module for syntactic processing in the development of TELEGRAM. Current work looks more closely at the type of interaction that must occur and specifies precisely when in the course of processing it should happen. Hovy's (1985) work is one example of this trend. He specifies five points of interaction between conceptual and linguistic decisions; processing is controlled primarily by the linguistic component. As there currently appears to be no consensus on the nature of interaction, we expect this to continue to be a focus of generation research.

In the area of deep generation, discourse strategies continue to be used as a major tool for determining content and organization of texts. The technique is often incorporated into generation systems as a practical means to achieve the end of determining content. New results are promised by Mann's work on rhetorical structure theory, which may provide insights into the interaction between speaker goals and strategies. Criticisms of the use of discourse strategies centre around the nature of rhetorical relations, indicating that the range of relations may be too broad (Grosz & Sidner 1986). The lack of definitions for relations makes identifying them in text a subjective task, and inconsistency in labelling text sentences with relations by different researchers has been noted (P. Cohen, personal communication). While this criticism points to the need for more formal definitions and careful screening of relations to include only those that are structural in nature, the use of organizational strategies composed of structural relations continues to be an extremely useful tool for generating textual content. This is evidenced by the large numbers of systems that have adopted the use of strategies (e.g. McCoy 1985; Paris 1985; Kukich 1984; Hovy 1985; Danlos 1984; Kittredge *et al*. 1986).

Research incorporating the effect of the reader on text generation is still in early stages as indicated by the lack of a unified approach to the problem. Furthermore, the systems surveyed dealt primarily with the effect of the user on selection of content, yet one would expect that how one chooses to word a text would be influenced by the expected audience as well. The influence of a user model on lexical and syntactic choice is one area ready for further development. In fact, two recent works touch on this topic and promise future results: Appelt (1985b) in detailing the influence of mutual beliefs on the production of noun phrases, and Hovy (1985) in noting the influence of the speaker–hearer relations (which Hovy aptly terms 'speaker affect') on overall textual style. Another advance in user modelling may come from the consideration of generation within the context of an ongoing dialogue. This will allow the user to provide feedback indicating how well text has been understood.

In the area of explanation, researchers continue to search for better underlying representations for expert systems so that better explanations can be produced. Progress has been made in this area. Explanation research may now seek to improve the quality of the explanation generators themselves by employing more linguistically motivated text generators.

Finally, in the area of surface generation, the problem of lexical choice appears to be a major open area for new research. Danlos's examples and claims have already prompted a number of researchers to investigate new approaches to the problem. A second problem that continues to undergo scrutiny is the choice of grammatical formalism. While some formalisms offer benefits in clarity, others offer benefits in efficiency. There does not, as yet, appear to be any consensus on the best choice of formalism for generation problems (although note that most researchers have selected a formalism that stems from the functionalist tradition) and thus we expect to see more research in this area.

In sum, language generation and explanation is a young but rapidly maturing field. For practitioners in natural language processing, a set of tools and approaches is available for practical application across the spectrum of knowledge representation, deep generation and surface generation. For researchers in natural language processing, the field of generation and explanation offers a range of challenging open problems ready for further exploration.

Notes

1. Note that what is better will change in different circumstances.
2. This is represented as a test on the attributive arc and is not shown in the figure.
3. The strategy is selected based on the information available about the object in question in the knowledge base.
4. The group includes Sandra Thompson, Christian Matthiessen and Barbara Fox.
5. As of 1984, their corpus included 100 short texts.
6. The responses given here are actually generated from ROMPER's output using the MUMBLE system (McDonald 1980) and a dictionary and grammar written by Robin Karlin (Karlin 1985).
7. Appelt's work derives from and extends Cohen's (1978) system, which used an explicit representation of speaker and hearer beliefs to generate speech acts (e.g. to choose between an inform or request act). Appelt extended Cohen's approach to apply to all levels of the generation process, including sentence construction.
8. Possible-world semantics allows for the formal representation of hypothetical and future states. The current situation is represented as one possible world. Actions denote a change from the world in which the action was performed to another in which the effects of the action are encoded.
9. System for Plan Inference that Reasons about Invalidities Too.
10. Although these requirements may be imposed to meet explanation goals, they also improve organization of the system itself, making it easier to maintain and evolve.
11. Digitalis is a drug given to many patients with cardiac disease. It makes the heart work more effectively as a pump, and it helps to counteract abnormal heartbeats.
12. Explanation routines are currently being constructed for EES that will allow it to answer questions about terminology.
13. One early method of surface generation was 'direct translation'. It relies on a

direct correspondence between pieces of the underlying representation (in expert systems, the inference trace) and strings of the surface language. Although heavily used in expert systems, it is a simplistic method of generation, relying primarily on hand-encoded templates. We omit discussion of this method and move immediately to more sophisticated language generators.

14. An in-depth overview of generation dictionaries can be found in Cummings (1986).

15. Although 'generator' is sometimes used to refer to the process of generating sentences from a grammar, we have used that term here to refer to a much wider range of processes. Since there does not appear to be a standard term to refer to the process of generating from a grammer, we adopt 'generation grammar' as a shorthand notation.

16. For illustrative purposes, we are using a considerably simplified version of the tree structure. McDonald's tree would be augumented by labels that indicate syntactic constraints.

17. TEXT was initially developed using functional unification grammar (see the following section).

18. Bossie (1982) implemented the grammar and unification system for TEXT based on Kay's design.

Bibliography

Allen, J. F. & Perrault, C. R. (1980), 'Analyzing intention in utterances', *Artif. Intell.*, vol. 15, no. 3.

Appelt, D. E. (1981), 'Planning natural language utterances to satisfy multiple goals', Ph.D. thesis, Stanford University.

— (1983), 'TELEGRAM: a grammar formalism for language planning', in *Proc. 8th IJCAI*, Karlsruhe, August, pp. 595–9.

— (1985a), 'Planning English sentences', in Joshi (ed.), *Studies in Natural Language*, Cambridge, Cambridge University Press.

— (1985b), 'Some pragmatic issues in the planning of definite and indefinite noun phrases', in *Proc. 23rd Ann. Meet. Assoc. Comput. Ling.*, Chicago, Ill., July, pp. 198–203.

Bates, M. & Ingria, R. (1981), 'Controlled transformational sentence generation', *Proc. 19th Ann. Meet. Assoc. Comput. Ling.*, Stanford, Calif., June, pp. 153–8.

Bossie, S. (1982), 'A tactical model for text generation: sentence generation using a functional grammar', University of Pennsylvania Tech. Rep., Philadelphia, Pa.

Brachman, R. (1979), 'On the epistemological status of semantic networks', in *Associative Networks: Representation and Use of Knowledge by Computer*, N. Findler (ed.), New York, Academic.

Brown, J. S. & Burton R. R. (1978), 'Diagnostic models for procedural bugs in basic mathematical skills', *Cognit. Sci.*, vol. 2, no. 2, 155–92.

Busemann, S. (1984), 'Topicalization and pronominalisation: extending a natural language generation system', *Proc. 6th ECAI*, Pisa, pp. 221–4.

Chester, D. (1976), 'The translation of formal proofs into English', *Artif. Intell.*, vol. 7, 261–75.

Chin, D. N. (1986), 'User modelling in UC, the UNIX Consultant', *Proc. CHI'86*, Boston, Mass., April, pp. 24–6.

Clancey, W. J. (1983a), 'Overview of GUIDON', *J. Comput.-Based Instruct*, vol. 10, nos 1 & 2, 8–15.

—— (1983b), 'The epistemology of a rule-based expert system: a framework for explanation', *Artif. Intell.*, vol. 20, no. 3, 215–51.

—— (1983c), 'The advantages of abstract control knowledge in expert system design', *Proc. Am. Assoc. Artif. Intell.*, pp. 740–78.

Cohen, P. (1978), 'On knowing what to say: planning speech acts', University of Toronto, Tech. Rep. No. 118.

Cummings, S. (1986), 'The lexicon in text generation', presented at the Workshop on Automating the Lexicon, Pisa, May.

Danlos, L. (1984), 'Conceptual and linguistic decisions in generation', *Proc. 10th Int. Conf. Comput., Ling.*, Stanford, Calif., July, pp. 319–25.

Davey, A. (1979), *Discourse Production*, Edinburgh, Edinburgh University Press.

Davis, R. (1980), 'Meta-rules: reasoning about control', *Artif. Intell.* vol. 15, 179–222.

Derr, M. A. & McKeown, K. R. (1984), 'Using focus to generate complex and simple sentences', in *Proc. 10th Int. Conf. Comput. Ling.*, Stanford, Calif., pp. 501–4.

Donellan, K. S. (1966), 'Reference and definite description', *Philos. Rev.*, vol. 75, 281–304.

Goguen, J. A., Linde, C. & Weiner, J. L. (1982), 'Reasoning and natural explanation', unpublished proceedings of ISI Workshop on Explanation.

Goldman, N. M. (1975), 'Conceptual generation', in R. C. Schank (ed.) *Conceptual Information Processing*, Amsterdam, North-Holland.

Gorry, G. A., Silverman, G. & Pauker, S. G. (1978), 'Capturing clinical expertise: a computer program that considers clinical responses to digitalis', *Am. J. Med.*, vol. 64, 452–60.

Grishman, R. (1979), 'Response generation in question-answering systems', *Proc. 17th Ann. Meet. ACL*, La Jolla, Calif., August, pp. 99–102.

Grosz, B. J. (1977), 'The representation and use of focus in dialogue understanding', Tech. Note 151, Stanford Res. Inst., Menlo Park, Calif.

Grosz, B. J., Sidner & C. L. (1986), 'Attention, intentions, and the structures of discourse', *Am. J. Comput. Ling.*, vol. 12, no. 3, 175–204.

Halliday, M. A. K. (1969), 'Options and functions in the English clause', *Brno Stud. Engl.*, vol. 8, 82–8.

Hasling, D. W. (1983), 'Abstract explanations of strategy in a diagnostic consultation system', *Proc. Natl. Conf. Artif. Intell.*, pp. 157–61.

Hasling, D. W., Clancey, W. J. & Rennels, G. (1984), 'Strategic explanations in consultation', *Int. J. Man—Machine Stud.*, vol. 20, 3–19.

Hawkinson, L. (1980), 'XLMS: a linguistic memory system', Tech. Rep. TM-173 MIT Lab. Comput. Sci.

Hovy, E. H. (1985), 'Integrating text planning and production in generation', *Proc. Ninth Int. Joint. Conf. Artif. Intell.*, Los Angeles. Calif., August, pp. 848–51.

—— (1986), 'Some pragmatic decision criteria in generation', presented at the

Third Int. Workshop on Nat. Lang. Generation, August, Nijmegen, The Netherlands.

Jacobs, P. S. (1985), 'A knowledge-based approach to language production', Ph.D. thesis, University of California, Berkeley.

Jameson, A. (1983), 'Impression monitoring in evaluation-oriented dialog: the role of the listener's assumed expectations and values in the generation of informative statements', *Proc. Eighth Int. Joint Conf. Artif. Intell.*, Karlsruhe, W. Germany, August, pp. 616–20.

Joshi, A. K. (1986), 'Tree adjoining grammars and their relevance to generation', presented at Third Int., Lang. Generation Workshop, Nijmegen, Holland, August.

Kay, M. (1979), 'Functional grammar', in *Proc. 5th Ann. Meet. Berkeley Ling. Soc.*

Kittredge, R., Polguere, A. & Goldberg, E. (1986), 'Synthesizing weather forecasts from formatted data', *Proc. 11th Int. Conf. Comput. Ling.*, Bonn, W. Germany, August, pp. 563–5.

Kronfeld, A. (1986), 'Donnellan's distinction and a computational model of reference', *Proc. 24th Ann. Meet. Assoc. Comput. Ling.*, New York, June, pp. 186–91.

Kukich, K. (1983), 'Design of a knowledge-based report generator', *Proc. 21st Ann. Meet. Assoc. Comput. Ling.*, Boston, Mass.

—— (1984), 'Knowledge-based explanation generation', presented at Second Ann. Lang. Generation Workshop, Stanford University, 8–10 July.

Lebowitz, M. (1985a), 'RESEARCHER: an experimental intelligent information system', *Proc. Ninth Int. Joint Conf. Artif. Intell.*, Los Angeles, Calif., August, pp. 858–62.

—— (1985b), 'Story-telling as planning and learning', *Poetics*, vol. 14, 483–502.

Lehnert, W. G. (1983), 'Narrative complexity based on summarization algorithms', *Proc. Eighth Int. Joint Conf., Artif. Intell.*, Karlsruhe, W. Germany, August, pp. 713–16.

McCoy K. F. (1985), 'The role of perspective in responding to property misconceptions', *Proc. Ninth Int. Joint Conf. Artif. Intell.*, Los Angeles, Calif., August, pp. 791–3.

—— (1986), 'The ROMPER system: responding to object-related misconceptions using perspective', *Proc. 24th Ann. Meet. Assoc. Comput. Ling.*, New York, NY., June, pp. 97–105.

McDonald, D. D. (1980), 'Natural language production as a process of decision making under constraint', Ph.D. thesis, Cambridge, Mass., MIT Press.

—— (1984), 'Description directed control: its implications for natural language generation', in N. J. Cercone (ed.) *Computational Linguistics*, New York, Pergamon, pp. 111–30.

—— (1986), 'Natural language generation: complexities and techniques', in S. Niremburg (ed.) *Theoretical and Methodological Issues in Machine Translation*, Cambridge, Cambridge University Press.

McDonald, D. D. & Pustejovsky, J. D. (1985), 'Description-directed natural language generation', *Proc. Ninth Int. Joint Conf. Artif. Intell.*, Los Angeles, California, August, pp. 799–805.

McKeown, K. R. (1982), 'Generating natural language in text in response to questions about database structure', Ph.D. thesis, University of Pennsylvania, Philadelphia, Pa.
—— (1983), 'Focus constraints on language generation', *Proc. Eighth Int. Joint Conf. Artif. Intell.*, Karlsruhe, W. Germany, August, pp. 582–7.
—— (1985), 'Text generation: using discourse strategies and focus constraints to generate natural language text', in A. K. Joshi (ed.), *Studies in Natural Language Processing*, Cambridge, Cambridge University Press.
McKeown, K. R. & Paris, C. L. (1987), 'Functional unification grammar revisited', *Proc. 25th Ann. Meet. Assoc. Comput. Ling.*, Stanford, Calif., July.
McKeown, K. R., Wish, M. & Matthews, K. (1985), 'Tailoring explanations for the user', *Proc. Ninth Int. Joint Conf. Artif. Intell.*, Los Angeles, Calif., August, pp. 794–8.
Mann, W. C. (1984), 'Discourse structures for text generation', *Proc. 10th Int. Conf. Comput. Ling.*, Stanford, Calif., July, pp. 367–75.
Mann, W. C. & Thompson, S. (1986), 'Rhetorical structure theory: description and construction of text structures', presented at the Third Int. Lang. Generation Workshop, Nijmegen, The Netherlands, August.
Mann, W. C. & Mathiessen, C. (1983), 'NIGEL: a systemic grammar for text generation', USC/ISI Tech. Rep. ISI/RR-83-105, Marina del Rey.
Mann, W. C. & Moore, J. A. (1981), 'Computer generation of multiparagraph English text', *Am. J. Comput. Ling.*, vol. 7, no. 1, 17–29.
Marcus, M. (1980), *A Theory of Syntactic Recognition for Natural Language.*, Cambridge, Mass., MIT Press.
Martin, W. A. (1981), 'Roles, co-descriptors, and the formal representation of quantified English expressions', *Am. J. Comput. Ling.*, vol. 7, no. 3, 137–47.
Matthiessen, C. M. I. M. (1981), 'A grammar and a lexicon for a text-production system', *Proc. 19th Ann. Meet. Assoc. Comput. Ling.*, Stanford Calif., June, pp. 49–53.
Meehan, J. R. (1977), 'TALE-SPIN: an interactive program that writes stories', *Proc. 5th Int. Joint Conf. Artif. Intell.*, August, pp. 91–8.
Moore, R. C. (1981), 'Problems in logical form', in *Proc. 19th Ann. Meet. Assoc. Comput. Ling.*, June, pp. 117–24.
Morik, K. (1986), 'Modelling the user's wants', presented at the First Int. Workshop on User Modelling, Maria Laach, W. Germany, August.
Neches, R. Swartout, W. R. & Moore, J. (1985), 'Enhanced maintenance and explanation of expert systems through explicit models of their development', *Trans. Software Eng.*, 1337–51.
Paris, C. L. (1985), 'Description strategies for naive and expert users', *Proc. 23rd Ann. Meet. Assoc. Comput. Ling.*, Chicago, Ill., July, pp. 238–45.
—— (1987), 'Tailoring object descriptions', *J. Comp. Ling.*.
Patten, T. & Ritchie, G. (1986), 'A formal model of systemic grammar', presented at Int. Lang. Generation Workshop, Nijmegen, The Netherlands, August.
Pollack, M. E. (1986), 'Inferring domain plans in question-answering', Ph.D. thesis, University of Pennsylvania.
Ritchie, G. (1986), 'The computational complexity of sentence derivation in

functional unification grammar', *Proc. 11th Int. Conf. Comput. Ling.*, Bonn, W. Germany, August, pp. 584–6.

Rubinoff, R. (1986), 'Interfacing MUMBLE with TEXT', *Proc. Am. Assoc. Artif. Intell., AAAI-86*, Philadelphia, Pa., August.

Rumelhart, D. E. (1975), 'Notes on a schema for stories', in D. G. Bobrow & A. Collins (eds), *Representation and Understanding: Studies in Cognitive Science*, New York, Academic.

Sacerdoti, E. (1977), *A Structure for Plans and Behavior*, Amsterdam, Elsevier/ North-Holland.

Schank, R., Goldman, N., Rieger, C. & Riesbeck, O. (1973), 'MARGIE: memory, analysis, response generation and inferences on English', *Proc. Third Int., Joint Conf., Artif. Intell.*

Shapiro, S. (1982), 'Generalized augmented transition network grammars for generation from semantic networks', *Am. J. Comput. Ling.*, vol. 8, no. 1, 12–25.

Shortliffe, E. H. (1976), *Computer-Based Medical Consultations*, New York, Elsevier.

Sidner, C. L. (1979), 'Towards a computational theory of definite anaphora comprehension in English discourse', Ph.D. thesis, Cambridge, Mass., MIT.

Silverman, H. (1975), 'A digitalis therapy advisor', Tech. Rep. Tr-143, MIT Project MAC.

Simmons, R. & Slocum, J. (1972), 'Generating English discourse from semantic networks', *Commun. ACM*, vol. 15, no. 10, 891–905.

Stolfo, S., Vesonder, G. (1982), 'ACE: an expert system supporting analysis and management decision making', Tech. Rep. Dept. Comput. Sci., Columbia University.

Swartout, W. R. (1977), 'A digitalis therapy advisor with explanations', Tech. Rep. TR-176, Lab. Comput. Sci., MIT.

—— (1983a), 'The GIST behavior explainer', *Proc. Natl. Conf. Artif., Intell., AAAI*, Washington, DC.

—— (1983b), 'XPLAIN: a system for creating and explaining expert consulting systems', *Artif. Intell.*, vol. 21, no. 3, 285–325.

Szolovits, P., Hawkinson, L. B. & Martin W. A. (1977), 'An overview of OWL: a language for knowledge representation', Tech. Rep. TM-86, Lab. Comput. Sci. MIT.

Wahlster, W., Marburger, H., Jameson, A. & Busemann, S. (1983), 'Overanswering yes–no questions: extended response to nl questions in a vision system', *Proc. Eighth Int. Joint Conf. Artif. Intell.*, Karlsruhe, W. Germany, August, pp. 643–6.

Wallis, J. W. & Shortliffe, E. H. (1982), 'Explanatory power for medical expert systems: studies in the representation of causal relationships for clinical consultation', Tech. Rep. STAN-CS-82-923, Heurist. Program Proj., Dept. Med. Comput. Sci., Stanford University.

Weiner, J. L. (1980), 'BLAH: a system which explains its reasoning', *Artif. Intell*, vol. 15, 19–48.

Wilensky, R., Arens, Y. & Chin, D. (1984), 'Talking to UNIX in English: an overview of UC', *Commun. ACM*, vol. 27, no. 6, 574–93.

Woolf, B. (1984), 'Context dependent planning in a machine tutor', Ph.D. thesis, University of Massachusetts.

Part II Linguistic approaches: in defence of a particular theory—formalism

2 Can a 'parsing grammar' be used for natural language generation? The negative example of LFG

RUSSELL BLOCK*

2.0 Introduction

Lexical Functional Grammar (LFG) is one of the more promising candidates for a general linguistic theory to emerge from the theoretical upheavals of the 1970s. Heavily influenced by computational linguistics and Artificial Intelligence research, it displays a high degree of formalization and lends itself particularly well to computer implementation, but does not present itself as a mere computer formalism—rather, it aims to fulfil what has been a 'longstanding hope of research in theoretical linguistics ... that linguistic characterizations of formal grammar would shed light on the speaker's mental representation of language' (Bresnan & Kaplan 1982: xvii).

Although the tenor of this chapter is largely theoretical, its intent is largely practical, arising out of the desire to 'marry' an LFG-based parser (cf. H.-U. Block & Haugeneder 1986; H.-U. Block & Hunze 1986) with an LFG-based language generator in a joint project—WISBER (Wissensbasierter Beratungsdialog—'Knowledge-Based Advisory Dialog'; Arz 1984). It goes without saying that the elegance of a system is improved if the same formalism can be used for both analysis and generation. And LFG holds out the promise of offering a unified theoretical foundation for both processes (cf. Bresnan & Kaplan 1982: xix).

It should also go without saying that careful preparatory work on the theoretical level is a necessary prerequisite for investing considerable time and energy in implementation. To this end, the author prepared an

* Universität Hamburg, Fachbereich Informatik, Projektgruppe WISBER, Hamburg, W. Germany

extensive report (R. Block 1986a) in an attempt to answer the following three questions:

1. How plausible are LFG's claims to 'psychological reality'?
2. To what extent is LFG superior or inferior to the Standard Theory of Transformational Grammar from which it is ultimately derived?
3. How realistic is LFG as a theory supporting language generation as opposed to language interpretation?

In this chapter, I will concentrate on the third point—the suitability of LFG for language generation—although the other points will be considered in due course. The critique of LFG is based on Bresnan (1982b,c) Bresnan & Kaplan (1982), and Kaplan & Bresnan (1982). In recent months a revision of the theory has been completed and should shortly become generally available.[1] At the moment it is not clear to what extent the following remarks apply to the revised theory as well.

2.1 Theoretical underpinning of LFG

The psychological basis of LFG is what Bresnan & Kaplan (1982: xvii) have termed 'the competence hypothesis'. As originally formulated by Chomsky, the hypothesis claims '. . . that a reasonable model of language use will incorporate, as a basic component, the generative grammar that expresses the speaker-hearer's knowledge of the language . . .' (Chomsky 1965: 9). This hypothesis immediately raises the question of the formal relationship between competence (the generative grammar) and the other components involved in 'language use'. The simplest hypothesis, and the one that was widely tested in the 1960s (cf. Cairns & Cairns 1976), is that the use components employ procedures that are directly modelled on competence. So, for instance, if the theory of competence uses transformations to generate sentences, one would postulate that the language comprehension system would use similar devices to analyse sentences. By the end of the decade, however, experimental evidence led to the abandoning of the 'simplest hypothesis'. Many researchers came to the conclusion that syntactic analysis made use of 'perceptional strategies' based on, but formally different from, transformations (cf. Bever *et al.* 1976).

LFG has taken a different tack. If the Standard Theory of generative grammar has proved inadequate as a model for language comprehension, perhaps what is needed is not additional devices, but a better theory which can unify the description of competence and the language-use components. LFG purports to be such a theory, one which can establish an 'isomorphic relationship between the different knowledge components' underlying all verbal behaviour (Bresnan & Kaplan 1982: xix). I interpret this to mean that theoretical constructs like transformations, which have no place in the theory, also have no place in language analysis and generation.

2.2 Analysis and generation

A Standard Theory (ST) Transformational Grammar generates surface structures by applying transformations to deep structures, which are the output of a set of context-free production rules. Beginning with the start symbol S, the grammar generates all and only all the well-formed sentences of the language for which it is written in essentially the same way a theorem prover generates the theorems of an axiomatic system. One might attempt to parse sentences with such a grammar by using the analysis by synthesis method, i.e. randomly generating sentences and checking to see whether one or more of the well-formed strings thus generated happen to match the input. But, since the number of sentences in any natural language is infinite, this procedure would be hopelessly inadequate unless guided by powerful heuristics to limit this search by synthesis. In fact, it is quite conceivable that some set of heuristics might completely eliminate analysis by synthesis, recovering deep structures directly without reference to transformations. It follows from this that a non-transformational grammar theory, like LFG, might be perfectly adequate for parsing.

If we turn to sentence generation, we find a very different picture. Here an ST grammar provides an excellent model. Starting from a canonic deep structure specified by a set of production rules, we can generate all and only all the grammatical transforms of that deep structure. If we specify in advance which optional transformations are to apply, any sentence of the language can be generated deterministically.[2] On the other hand, an LFG grammar which does not allow transformations is forced to generate on two different levels—f-structure and c-structure—and then to compare the two, looking for a match. This is the case because the theory specifically forbids carrying out any operations on either f- or c-structures (cf. Kaplan & Bresnan 1982: 180). Thus, there is no way to derive c-structures from f-structures.

2.3 An illustrative example

To demonstrate some of the problems involved, let us briefly consider generating the set of grammatical sentences specified by the following

(Lisp-like) logical form, which (ignoring tense) we can take to be the input to the sentence generator:

(1) (believe Alice (think queen (steal knave tarts)))

Taking the transformational approach first, we begin by projecting the logical form (1) on to the deep structure (2) which is specified by the phrase structure rules in the grammar.

(2) [$_{S1}$ Alice believed [$_{S2}$ that the queen thought [$_{S3}$ that the knave stole the tarts.]]]

By successively applying Passive and Raising from right to left (bottom to top) to the NP *the tarts*, we can derive the following set of surface structures:

(3) Alice believed that the queen thought that THE TARTS were stolen by the knave.

(4) Alice believed that the queen thought THE TARTS to have been stolen by the knave.

(5) Alice believed that THE TARTS were thought by the queen to have been stolen by the knave.

(6) Alice believed THE TARTS to have been thought by the queen to have been stolen by the knave.

(7) THE TARTS were believed by Alice to have been thought by the queen to have been stolen by the knave.

If we apply the transformation to the NP *the knave* instead, we can derive four additional sentences from the single deep structure (2). Similarly we can raise and passivize *the queen*, yielding two additional structures for a total of twelve sentences. But this hardly exhausts the possibilities. Raising and passivizing *the queen* is quite independent of passivizing and raising *the tarts*, so we can add four variants of (3)–(4). In addition, whole clauses can be passivized as in:

(8) That the queen thought that the knave stole the tarts was believed by Alice.

Here again the two-clause subject complement allows various combinations of Passive and Raising. We can further complicate matters by adding Extraposition as in:

(9) It was believed by Alice that the queen thought that the knave stole the tarts.

Needless to say, Passive, Raising, Extraposition can apply in the extraposed subject complement, further increasing the number of variants. It is immediately evident that a large number of phrase structure rules (in addition to those required to generate the canonic deep structure (2)) would be required to generate all of the possible surface structures directly, but this is not the only problem.

Notice that the passive matrix clause in (7) is followed by two passive infinitival clauses (VCOMPs, as they are termed in LFG). In the transformational analysis this follows directly from the application of Passive and Raising. The deep structure object of S_3 in (2) cannot advance to the subject position of S_1 without leaving behind passive infinitivals. The necessary surface structure (c-structure) could, of course, be directly generated. The difficulty with direct non-transformational derivation arises from the fact that a passive matrix clause is not always followed by two passive infinitivals, as (10) demonstrates:

(10) The queen was thought by Alice to have believed that the knave stole the tarts.

The structure of (10) in a transformational grammar follows from the fact that the NP *the queen* has been raised and passivized, rather than the NP *the tarts*. An LFG generation component would have to produce both variants (among many others) although only one is appropriate in each case. It might be thought that this problem could be solved by an appeal to f-structure. After all, the decision between passive and active, SCOMP and VCOMP, is made at this level. Here, however, we are confronted with the problem of overgeneration. The grammar is compelled to produce and filter out any number of 'illegal' structures in order to generate the well-formed variants. Raising verbs like *believe* or *think*—in active and passive versions—have to be subcategorized to accept both SCOMPs and VCOMPs. But the appropriateness of the active/passive, SCOMP/ VCOMP configuration depends crucially on the distribution of long-distance dependencies. In (7), for example, S_2 and S_3 have to be passive VCOMPs because the subject NP of S_1, *the tarts*, is coindexed with the empty object node of *stolen* in S_3.

In order to provide appropriate f-structures, we would first have to calculate the effects of such long-distance dependencies, which, as we have seen, is completely unnecessary for generation since they are merely artefacts of transformational operations.

Even given well-formed f-structures, we are confronted with the problem of matching them to independently generated c-structures since the theory does not permit us to derive c-structures from f-structures by transformation. In an actual experiment aimed at generating German c-structures consistent with well-formed f-structures, Meier & Kindermann (1986) determined that they had to generate c-structures incrementally, using the parser to make the match between the two levels. Since the matching procedure could fail, it was also necessary to introduce backtracking into the generator. This seems like a high price to pay for remaining within the constraints imposed by LFG.

2.4 Deletion

In the Standard Theory empty subject nodes were created by transformation. They were either emptied under identity to nodes higher in a phrase marker by Equi (Deletion of Equivalent NPs) as in (1):

(1) John$_i$ wants $\emptyset_i$ to go

or by Indefinite Agent Deletion as in (2):

(2) It is time $\emptyset$ to go.

Later, it was suggested, for reasons which are no longer theoretically relevant (cf. McCawley 1982: 131) that empty nodes should be base-generated and associated with their antecedents (if any) by 'rules of control'. From the point of view of the grammar alone, the two approaches are thoroughly equivalent. The rules of control could serve just as well as conditions for the deletion transformations. The difference between the two approaches first emerges when we consider generation in a slightly broader context. If we assume that sentences like (1) are generated from an underlying knowledge representation in logical form, we can posit something like (3) as the source of (1):

(3) (want John$_i$ (go John$_i$))

The logical form expresses the speaker's (or machine's) knowledge that it is John who wanted John to go. I don't see how it would be possible to avoid specifying all the arguments to all the predicates at some level of logical representation. But if the argument *John* in the embedded clause is represented in logical form and not represented in surface structure, it must be deleted somewhere along the way. Furthermore, it is clear that it must be deleted in the grammar since not all verbs take subjectless VCOMPs:

(4) *John$_i$ believed [$\emptyset_i$ to go]

A grammar formalism like LFG, which denies in principle the possibility of deletion transformations, could at best beg the question here, claiming that deletion takes place outside the grammar proper but with reference to information about subcategorization which is inside the grammar.

2.5 Another kind of overgeneration

In R. Block (1986a) I noted that one consequence of direct generation of c-structures is that an excessive number of phrase structure rules is necessary in order to generate all the well-formed c-structures corresponding to a given f-structure. Another consequence is that the phrase structure rules have to overgenerate. That is, in order to produce all of the well-formed c-structures the rules have to generate some c-structures that never correspond to an f-structure. This effect can be illustrated with the process of question formation. Consider the declarative-question pair (1)–(2):

(1) John has seen the book.
(2) Has John seen the book?

In a standard transformational account, the question (2) is derived from the structure underlying (1) plus the addition of a question operator Q:

(3) Q John has seen the book.

The question operator Q triggers obligatory subject–verb inversion, yielding (2). Since LFG does not allow operations on c-structures, both (1) and (2) have to be generated directly. This can be done with the following c-structure rules in the spirit of Kaplan & Bresnan (1982: 228):

(4) S → (AUX) NP VP
(5) VP → (AUX) V NP

To generate the declarative (1), we select the optional AUX in rule (5). To generate the question (2), we select the optional AUX in rule (4) instead. But, as the authors themselves are aware, according to the rules we can generate the following strings as well:

(6) *Has John has seen the book?
(7) *John seen the book.

In (6) the optional AUX was selected in both rules and in (7) it was selected in neither rule. In order to generate two well-formed sentences we have to take two ill-formed strings into the bargain. Now to be sure, LFG has procedures for garbage collection that allow us to get rid of structures like (6) and (7). But why generate garbage in the first place when a simple permutation transformation generates the correct form and only the correct form?

Strings like (6) and (7) are clearly artefacts of the theory that requires that they be generated in order to get the correct forms as well. It is difficult to imagine that we could find any independent justification for them. That is, to the best of my knowledge, no language which forms questions by subject–verb inversion also alternatively forms questions by repeating the AUX as in (6). If there were such a language, providing independent motivation for writing rules like (4) and (5) in order to make the AUX proceed and follow the subject NP, LFG would be forced to explain why its general filter mechanisms fail to rule the structure out.

What about the question operator Q we assumed for the transformational theory? Is it also an artefact necessary to make things come out right? Here we can bring both external and internal evidence to bear. First of all, we can note that there are languages which form yes–no questions with an initial question particle. Sentences (8) and (9) are the equivalents of (2) in Yiddish and Latvian, respectively:

(8) (Yid.) ci hot John gesen dos bux?
(9) (Latv.) Vai Jānis ir redzējis to gramatu?

The Yiddish example is quite relevant here since Yiddish displays the same verb–subject inversion for questions as does German (and English with the addition of *do*-support). In Yiddish the abstract question operator is optionally realized as the particle *ci*.

Internal evidence also lends some substance to the abstract question operator. Old English, as a well-behaved Germanic language, followed the same topicalization and verb–subject inversion rules as modern German or Yiddish (among others). Over the course of time the V-II principle (the finite verb must stand in second position in main clauses) has become severely restricted. Leaving aside instances of so-called stylistic inversion, which is optional, we find that there are two instances in which V-II is obligatory in modern English:[3] with fronted negations and fronted questions as the following examples illustrate:

(10) He said the book was where?! (echo question)
(11) Where did he say the book was? (*wh*-question with fronting of *wh*-word)
(12) I have never seen such a mess.
(13) Never have I seen such a mess. (negative statement with fronted neg.-adv.)

If we posit the question operator Q, subject–auxiliary inversion in yes–no questions can be accounted for in precisely the same way as *wh*-questions and negations with fronting:

(14) Q did he say that?

In German, where anything at all in fronted position will trigger verb–subject inversion, we can extend the same explanation to imperatives with the imperative operator IMP:

(15) IMP mach (du) das Fenster auf!

Hence the transformational analysis not only works more efficiently, avoiding overgeneration, but also provides a unified account of several phenomena in several different languages.

2.6 Conclusion

For the reasons presented here, among others (cf. R. Block, 1986a), we have reached the conclusion that an attempt to generate natural language within the theoretical framework of LFG is unrealistic. Similarly the hypothesis that there is an 'isomorphic relationship between the different knowledge components' underlying all verbal behaviour (Bresnan & Kaplan 1982: xix) cannot be maintained. At least, separate formalisms for parsing and text generation are indicated. Initial attempts to implement a transformational generator yielded very positive results. That is, we are able immediately to generate correct German sentences from canonical Phrase Structure Trees derivable from logical structures without recourse to matching procedures or backtracking. Full-scale implementation will have to await completion of work on problems involving ellipsis and pronominalization, generation of unambiguous referential noun phrases, dialog control, and choice of stylistic transforms. These questions occupy our major interest and go beyond the considerations of the 'random sentence generator' discussed here.[4] We are convinced, however, that a theoretically well-founded, efficient sentence generator will be at the heart of every generation system, and that such a generator will not be based on a parsing model.

Notes

1. For a preview, see Wedekind (1986), who also points out the complications caused by generating with two levels of representation.
2. Of course, this and every other generator will have to be constrained so that they do not generate grammatical but otherwise unusable sentences, i.e. sentences that are too long, contain multiple centre embeddings, etc.
3. Verb-subject inversion also occurs in conditionals like *Had he been there, he would have seen it*, where *if* has been left out in the conditional clause. I am not sure how this phenomenon is related to the instances discussed in the text.
4. For an implementation of a transformational generator for a large fragment of German, operating on a 'flat' Verbalized Structure, see Busemann (1984).

Bibliography

Arz, J. (ed.) (1984), *WISBER: Wissensbasierter Beratungsdialog, Vorhabensbeschreibung*, Saarbrücken, Universität des Saarlandes FR 10.2 Informatik IV.
Bever, T., Katz, J. & Langendoen, D. (1976), *An Integrated Theory of Linguistic Ability*, Sussex, The Harvester Press.

Block, R. (1986a), 'Lexical functional grammar and natural language generation', WISBER Bericht Nr. 10, Universität Hamburg.
—— (1986b), *Revolution und Revision in der generativen Theoriebildung*, Tübingen, Gunter Narr Verlag.
Block, H.-U. & Haugeneder, H. (1986), 'The treatment of movement rules in a LFG-parser', *Proceedings of Coling '86*, Bonn, pp. 482–6.
Block, H.-U. & Hunze, R. (1986), 'Incremental construction of C- and F-structure in a LFG-parser,' *Proceedings of Coling '86*, Bonn, pp. 490–3.
Bresnan, J. (ed.) (1982a), *The Mental Representation of Grammatical Relations*, Cambridge, Mass., MIT Press.
—— (1982b), 'Control and complementation', in J. Bresnan (ed.), pp. 282–389.
—— (1982c), 'Passive in lexical theory', in J. Bresnan (ed.), pp. 3–86.
Bresnan, J. & Kaplan, R. (1982), 'Grammars as mental representations of language', in J. Bresnan (ed.), pp. xvii–lii.
Busemann, S. (1984), 'Surface transformations during the generation of written German sentences', Hamburg, Research Unit for Information Science and Artificial Intelligence, Report ANS-27, to appear in L. Bolc (ed.), *Natural Language Generation Systems*, Berlin,
Cairns, C. & Cairns, H. (1976), *Psycholinguistics: A Cognitive Approach*, New York, Holt, Rinehart and Winston.
Chomsky, N. (1957), *Syntactic Structures*, The Hague, Mouton.
—— (1965), *Aspects of the Theory of Syntax*, Cambridge, Mass., MIT Press.
Jackendoff, R. (1972), *Semantic Interpretation in Generative Grammar*, Cambridge, Mass., MIT Press.
Kaplan, R. & Bresnan, J. (1982), 'Lexical-functional grammar: a formal system for grammatical representation', in J. Bresnan (ed.), pp. 173–281.
Kindermann, J. & Meier, J. (1986), 'An efficient parser for lexical functional grammar', *Proceedings of GWAI '86*, Ottenstein, pp. 143–8.
Kleinecke, D. (1986), 'Review of Bresnan (ed.) *The Mental Representation of Grammatical Relations*', in *Computer Linguistics*, vol. 2, no. 2, 127–9.
McCawley, J. (1982), *Thirty Million Theories of Grammar*, Chicago, University of Chicago Press.
Meier, J. & Kindermann, J. (1986), 'Generierung mit Lexical-Functional Grammar', *Proceedings of GWAI '86*, Ottenstein, pp. 113–18.
Netter, K. (1986), 'Getting things out of order', in *Proceedings of Coling '86*, Bonn, pp. 494–6.
Wedekind, J. (1986), 'A concept of derivation for LFG', *Proceedings of Coling '86*, Bonn, pp. 487–9.

3 The application of unification for syntactic generation in German

HELMUT HORACEK*

3.0 Introduction

For various reasons, general methods that have been proved useful in parsing natural language are worth examining in generation, too. Unification grammars have recently done a good job in parsing, but they have rarely been applied in generation up to now. When this is actually done, a large benefit can be expected from the simplicity and power of unification. Moreover, the syntactic coverage is made very explicit. A parser based on a unification grammar can be transformed into the basis of a generator by only a few changes. The expected benefit is a unique source of grammar that is available in a readable format. Once this work has been done for a basic fragment, the coverage can be extended for parsing and generation simultaneously.

3.1 Unification in the generation process

Motivated by the expected benefits we have decided to use LFG, the Lexical Functional Grammar (Kaplan & Bresnan 1982) as a common basis for syntactic parsing and generation in the German version of the natural language interface LOQUI (see, for instance Wachtel (1985). This interface has been developed by the Hamburg group of the ESPRIT project LOKI.

3.1.1 Benefits of unification for the generation process

Why did we decide to use the LFG-mechanism for generation? First, we think that the LFG-formalism is a very convenient tool to describe grammatical relations effectively and in a linguistically adequate manner.

* Research Unit for Information Science and Artificial Intelligence, University of Hamburg, Hamburg, W. Germany.

Second, unification also is a beneficial method for other parts of the generation process. We will demonstrate this by a short example.

When elements of a semantic representation are mapped on to words some of the grammatical functions associated with a particular word might not be filled at the same time this word is created. Only the selection restriction for an eventual filler is included in the mapped structure in order to ensure the grammaticality of the text. This provides the basis for the check if a substitution by a certain paraphrase is feasible or not. Thus the creation of a phrase like

*der Mitarbeiter von Generierung
(the person who works on generation)

will be excluded; its content can be expressed by:

der Mitarbeiter eines Projekts ueber Generierung
(the person who works on a project which is about generation)

There is no literal translation in English; thus the inacceptability of the first phrase is not reflected in the English sentence. On the other hand, when *arbeiten an* is selected instead of *Mitarbeiter* it is possible to substitute the project by its topic because the match based on the respective categories is successful in this case.

3.1.2 *Problems with unification in syntactic generation*

Despite the overall benefits of unification, syntactic problems in generation tend to be treated by some kind of transformations in practical systems, mostly in a rather efficient way. The reason for this preference seems to be caused by the inconveniences involved in the application of unification. It has been argued that LFG is not particularly useful either for generation or for a free word order language like German (Block 1986). In both domains the backtracking mechanism is much overused. This is especially the case when relying on the LFG-formalism alone and on grammars of a style that has been found frequently when confronted with the description of a fragment of English. On the other hand, backtracking is, in principle, avoidable in generation.

Furthermore, a straightforward design of rules is often inexact in the sense that some ungrammatical phrases are not excluded. This is comparatively harmless in parsing or can even be interpreted as robustness, but it is completely unacceptable in generation.

3.1.3 *Some approaches dealing with unification*

Consequently, only very limited work has been done so far on generation by applying a linguistically motivated source grammar based on unification. Just recently, a few approaches have been presented relying on LFG (Meier & Kindermann 1986; Doerre & Momma 1987) and GPSG (Busemann 1987), the Generalized Phrase Structure Grammar (Gazdar *et al*. 1985). The first two approaches were mainly concerned with the correct generation of a sentence which is implicitly specified by a completely instantiated functional structure (f-structure). They did not consider any structural properties of a source grammar which, quite naturally, could be exploited to increase the efficiency significantly.

In order to improve the efficiency, Busemann (1987) uses a criterion which expresses the number of expansion steps necessary to reach a lexical item. Thus the most promising rule is selected out of the set of all applicable ones. The idea is to discover an unsuccessful expansion of a rule as early as possible to keep the extra effort for backtracking low. This overhead is somehow reduced because successfully generated subtrees are stored for later reuse. Nevertheless, Busemann admits that there is a price to pay for the independence of the generator and the grammar.

In our view, the design of a source grammar and its efficient use by the generator are important tasks which have not yet been paid the necessary attention. Consequently, we have tried to develop guidelines for a skilful design of a source grammar balanced by the needs of generation and parsing. In this chapter we will put the emphasis on the efficient use in generation.

3.2 Techniques for a skilful grammar design and its efficient use in syntactic generation

3.2.1 *Handling of the free word order*

When applying a unification grammar a big difficulty is the efficient handling of the free word order. This could be done, in principle, by backtracking but this approach is neither satisfactory for parsing nor for generation. Partial (successful) results of the parser would be lost this way. On the other hand, when the syntactic part of the generation process is started, it should be quite clear which word order is preferable in the actual instance.

In order to get control over the choice of word order we have introduced meta-variables with undetermined grammatical functions for the slots of NPs and PPs in clauses. Such a variable is not fully instantiated until the rule it is part of is actually applied. The idea of using grammatical meta-functions has already been raised in Netter (1986). A flat constituent structure fits very well with this approach, enabling one to obtain a flexible production of various orders of constituents. We will again refer to this point when discussing verb phrases.

The actual preferable order of constituents is selected in advance for each clause. There exists a standard order for German which appropriately is changed if there is a *Wh*-question or when a constituent is to be focused. This is done by a list of grammatical functions indicating the appropriate order in an actual instance. This list is obtained by means of adapting the standard order of constituents according to the dialogue structure. This is done for each (sub)clause separately. In reality, a constituent to be focused on is moved in the first place if a main clause is to be generated. The same procedure is performed if the speech act is a request for a constant (when the constant is a constituent). As the subject takes the first place in the standard order it becomes second after such a move, which is the desired result. Focusing by movement in the last position has not been considered yet but it can be achieved by applying the same method. Moreover, a legal order of constituents cannot be achieved on the basis of the case roles alone, which we have done as a first approach. Additional features, for instance 'FOCUS', 'PRO' and 'SPEC', have to be taken into account in some cases: this has been demonstrated in Emele (1987).

In the following figures we have introduced some conventions that enable us to denote syntax rules in a compact way: 'γ' for the Kleene-star operator and '!' for the denotation that the respective constituent occurs once at most. 'G' is a grammatical meta-function and 'NPP' is either a NP or a PP.

The FIRSTNP feature is used to trigger the presence or absence of a constituent in front of the finite part of the verb. In case this rule is applied to parse a sentence, the FIRSTNP feature is an indicator of whether the utterance is a yes/no question or not. In generation this feature is set in advance and the preferred alternative is produced.

It can be argued that the introduction of a grammatical meta-function does not necessarily run counter to the idea of LFG. It can be seen as a

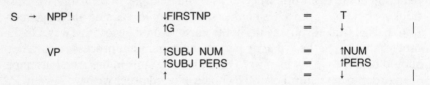

Figure 3.1 Rule to expand a sentence in a noun phrase and a verb phrase (or just a verb phrase)

convenient way of describing a class of rules concisely. The actual rule (selected from this class) is chosen by instantiating all occurrences of the meta-function to grammatical functions rather than by backtracking over closely similar rules. In the case of parsing, the instantiations take place at the end of a parsed sentence clause. In the case of generation, the instantiation is performed before the process starts. Moreover, if there is more than a single clause to be generated, there must be an indication for each clause as to which rule is to be applied when generating the clause.

The introduction of a meta-function and the choice of a flat constituent structure contribute essentially to the avoidance of backtracking in the generation process. Some other skilful decisions in designing the grammar rules are necessary to avoid backtracking almost completely.

3.2.2 *Discontinuous constituents*

Another problem is constituted by the fact that the inapplicability of a certain rule might not be discovered until the last stage of its execution. This defect frequently arises with discontinuous constituents, for instance in complex German verb phrases. Assuming a natural position for the equations, the appropriate auxiliary cannot be determined until the non-finite part of the verb phrase is considered. This is the type of situation where we favour a movement of the critical equations (determining the features of the sentence in this case). Furthermore, the envisioned flatness of the F-structure is achieved by the introduction of non-standard equations in the verb phrase rule.

This technique is, of course, opposite to the usual design of rules which is mainly oriented to the needs of parsing. In fact, the corresponding parsing component is not affected much by this change, because there always exists the possibility that the last word in a sentence (being a verbal part) completely changes the functional description of the whole sentence.

As a consequence we have chosen several rules for verb phrases differing in the number and category of the components of the verb. The tense and the voice of a clause and the syntactic features of the main verb determine unambiguously the appropriate rule. Therefore, these rules are designed such that the critical features are matched at the earliest possible stage. In the syntax rule in Figure 3.2 this applies to the equation with 'STENSE' (for Sentence TENSE). If this match succeeds it is a guaranteed fact that the appropriate rule has been selected. Again, it does no harm when the rule is applied for parsing because there is no complete information present unless the VPART constituent has been analysed completely.

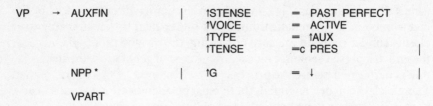

```
VP    →   AUXFIN           |   ↑STENSE      =  PAST PERFECT
                               ↑VOICE       =  ACTIVE
                               ↑TYPE        =  ↑AUX
                               ↑TENSE       =c PRES          |

          NPP *            |   ↑G           =  ↓             |

          VPART
```

Figure 3.2 Rule to expand a verb phrase (with tense past perfect and voice active)
into the finite verb part, any number of constituents, and the finite verb
part (which is a perfect participle in this case)

3.2.3 *Inheritance of features*

This subtask highlights one of the inconveniences that occur when the
pure LFG-formalism is applied to generation. Theoretically, all lexicon
entries are potential candidates to be unified with the actual feature set. As
a search of the entire lexicon is clearly an unacceptable approach in
practice, we have decided to provide the necessary information in advance.

When a particular word is selected in the verbalization process, some of
its features are copied into the respective functional description, namely:
the gender for nouns and a marker for proper names and some syntactic
information for verbs; the particle, if existing, and the auxiliary that is
necessary to build the past perfect tense. This information is always
sufficient to be able to evaluate fully the equations specified in the syntax
rules and to select the canonical form of a word. As our German lexicon
contains stem forms, this is all we need because the eventual access to an
appropriate irregular form is achieved later by the morphological synthesis.

```
NP    →   DET
          ADJP !           |   ↑NUM         =  ↓NUM
                               ↑GEND        =  ↓GEND
                               ↑CASE        =  ↓CASE
                               ↑AMOD        =  ↓             |
          N
```

Figure 3.3 A simplified rule to expand a noun phrase into a determiner, at most
one adjective phrase and a head noun

When forming the German past tense form of a verb the appropriate
auxiliary (*haben* or *sein*) depends on the main verb. This is expressed by the
equation that unifies 'TYPE' (denoting the type of an auxiliary) and 'AUX'
(denoting the auxiliary that a main verb requires for the past tense). When

'AUX' is known at the time when 'AUXFIN' is generated, no backtracking is required.

A simplified noun phrase rule points out the necessity that the gender of the head noun must be known in order to generate the correct form of an eventually existing adjective (phrase) that precedes the head noun.

3.2.4 *Distinction between NP and PP*

We favour the distinction between an NP and a PP to be made by a single feature (named PTYPE—see Figure 3.4). The benefit is mainly manifested in the ease of creating an NP or a PP and of manipulating it in other parts of the generation process in the same way. The syntax rules for noun phrases and prepositional phrases respectively are almost identical to the rule of a relative pronoun which might be preceded by a preposition or not. Note the fact that the redundant equation that checks the existent of 'PTYPE' excludes all unnecessary attempts to generate a preposition at the earliest possible stage.

NPP	→	PREP	|	↑PTYPE	|
		NP	|	↑ = ↓	|
NPP	→	NP	|	↑ = ↓	|
RELP	→	PREP	|	↑PTYPE	|
		RELPRON			
RELP	→	RELPRON			

Figure 3.4 Rules to expand a noun (or prepositional) phrase (or a placeholder for a relative pronoun) into a preposition (if necessary and a noun phrase (a relative pronoun)

Particular accuracy is required in designing the rules expressing the relations between a head of an NP (or PP) and its determiner or the absence of a determiner. Mistakes in this respect can easily result in proper names accompanied by a determiner or in ordinary nouns without a determiner in cases where they should have one.

3.3 An example

We will complete our presentation by the discussion of the generation of a full sentence from a suitable f-structure which is shown in Figure 3.5. The

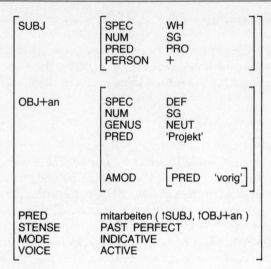

Figure 3.5 Functional Structure for the sentence *Wer hat an dem vorigen Projekt mitgearbeitet? (Who worked on the previous project?)*

structure is associated with information about the required (surface) speech-act. Additionally, a desirable topicalization may be specified, which can be achieved by an appropriate constituent movement, if it is consistent with the surface speech-act. Otherwise the topicalization specification is suppressed. In our example, no topicalization is specified and a request for a constant (namely the filler of the 'SUBJ' slot) is required (see Wachtel (1985) for the terminology and classification of speech-acts). Strictly speaking, this information is redundant in this particular case because it is the only possible choice which is consistent with the value of the 'SPEC' feature ('WH') in the 'SUBJ' slot.

Before the f-structure can be transformed by the grammar rules, the precise order of constituents has to be determined according to linear preference rules, the speech-act and the topicalization specification. The result is the order in which the meta-functions 'G' are instantiated to yield the respective cases present in the f-structure ('SUBJ' and 'OBJ + *an*' in our example). This procedure is an implicit selection of the suitable rule out of a set of virtually existing ones applicable to a sentence (denoted in Figure 3.1). In our example the standard order ('SUBJ' precedes 'OBJ + *an*') is adopted. Moreover, the substructure in the 'SUBJ' slot is augmented by a 'FIRSTNP T' feature value pair because of the speech-act, thus assuring that this NP will be placed in front of the finite verb. After this preliminary preparation the rule in Figure 3.1 can be applied to the f-structure.

The first occurrence of the meta-function 'G' is instantiated to 'SUBJ', and the value of the 'FIRSTNP' feature ('T') in the respective submatrix cares for the attachment of the 'SUBJ' slot to the 'NPP' constituent. As part of this operation, the appropriate surface case, nominative, is inherited. By the application of other rules (not listed here), which refer to the value 'PRO' of the feature 'PRED', the first word of the sentence (*Wer*) is generated. The remainder of the original feature matrix is passed to the next rule, which is concerned with VPs.

A couple of rules similar to the one in Figure 3.2 may be tested eventually, but they are quickly rejected when the 'STENSE' and 'VOICE' features are checked. The right one is selected because these key features match. For the 'AUXFIN' part (this category identifies a lexical item) the suitable auxiliary (*hat*) is created and we can turn our attention to the next (and last) constituent.

As for the 'SUBJ' case the meta-function 'G' is instantiated appropriately (to 'OBJ + *an*' in this case) and the surface case (accusative) is inherited. In addition, a 'PTYPE *an*' feature-value pair (triggered by the '+ *an*' appendix in the 'OBJ' case) is inherited. The existence of this feature is responsible for the right selection between the two alternate branches of the 'NPP' rule in Figure 3.4. A mistake in this case can become quite expensive. Thereby the preposition (*an*) is generated and the next subphrase, an NP, is considered.

According to the rule in Figure 3.3, the determiner (*dem*), the adjective (*vorigen*), and the head noun (*Projekt*) are generated in precisely this order. The rules actually used are significantly more complex covering some of the peculiarities of the syntax of German noun phrases. Nevertheless, the design technique and its effect is based on the same principles as demonstrated for other phrase types: testing the critical equations at the earliest possible stage, thus reducing the overhead caused by an eventually necessary backtracking to the evaluation of a few equations only.

Finally, the 'VPART' in the rule of Figure 3.2 is addressed (yielding the participle *mitgearbeitet*) and the generation of the sentence is finished.

3.4 Summary

The overall goal of this task was the creation of general guidelines for the design of rules and for keeping reasonable control over the order of their execution greatly to reduce the shortcomings mentioned above. As a result, we basically recommend the following principles:

— denoting a whole class of rules by a single one by means of meta-variables;

— evaluating critical equations at the earliest possible stage by moving them to the far left of the body of a rule;
— adopting a non-standard design of rules supporting a representation that is mostly convenient for other parts of the generation process;
— adding additional equations that do no harm in a parsing process in order to exclude ungrammatical phrases (at an early stage) in cases that are easily overlooked.

Consequently, an economic and short grammar that makes the coverage of the system easily readable can be designed following the principles stated above. When the special techniques proposed to control the order of rules are applied appropriately, the preferred text version is generated as the first alternative.

Bibliography

Block, R. (1986), 'Lexical functional grammar and natural language generation', WISBER Bericht Nr. 10, Universitat Hamburg.

Busemann, S. (1987), 'Generierung mit GPSG', GWAI-87, Geseke, Springer Verlag, pp. 355–64.

Doerre, J. & Momma, S. (1987), 'Generierung aus f-Strukturen als struktur-gesteuerte Ableitung', GWAI-87, Geseke, Springer-Verlag, pp. 54–63.

Emele, M. (1987), 'FREGE: Ein objektorientierter FRont-End-GEnerator', GWAI-87, Geseke, Springer-Verlag, pp. 64–73.

Gazdar, Gerald, Klein, Ewan, Pullum, Geoffrey & Sag, Ivan (1985), *Generalized Phrase Structure Grammar*, Oxford, Basil Blackwell, p. 276.

Kaplan, Ronald M. & Bresnan, Joan (1982), 'Lexical-functional grammar; a formal system for grammatical representation', in Joan Bresnan (ed.), *The Mental Representation of Grammatical Relations*, London, MIT Press, pp. 173–281.

Meier, Justus & Kindermann, Joerg (1986), *Generierung mit Lexical-Functional Grammar (LFG)*, Geseke, Springer-Verlag, pp. 113–18.

Netter, K. (1986), *An LFG-Proposal for the Treatment of German Word Order*, Bonn, pp. 494–6.

FKI HH, Wachtel, T. (1985), 'Discourse structure', LOKI-Report NLI-1.1, Hamburg.

4 Concerning the logical component of a natural language generator

SIMON C. DIK*

4.0 Introduction

In this chapter I argue for the following points:

(i) A natural language generator NLG which is to form part of an integrated natural language-using system NLU can only work properly or 'sensibly' if it is connected to a knowledge base KB, and provided with a logical component LC which is capable of modelling aspects of natural reasoning.

(ii) NLG will have to work with structures or representations from which natural language expressions can be generated; KB will have to be formulated in structures in terms of which knowledge can be represented; LC will have to work with structures in terms of which rules for natural inferencing can be defined.

(iii) An optimal solution for NLU requires that the NLG-structures, the KB-structures, and the LC-structures are set up in such a way that they can most easily be converted into each other; preferably, the three components should work in terms of the same structures.

(iv) It is proposed that such an optimal solution could be reached if the structures in question are taken to be 'predications', as defined in the theory of Functional Grammar (FG); the logic based on this idea may be called a Functional Logic (FL).

(v) Some properties of FL are introduced, and some examples are given of how the combined system FG-FL might work within an integrated NLU.

* Institute for General Linguistics, University of Amsterdam, Amsterdam, The Netherlands

4.1 Some requirements on NLG

A minimal, necessary condition on NLG is that it be able to produce linguistic expressions of some natural language. However, if this were the only requirement imposed on NLG, then the highest goal to be achieved by the system would be the random production of arbitrary, well-formed linguistic expressions. If we wish to regard NLG as a module in an integrated NLU, this is obviously not sufficient. We not only want NLG to be able to produce arbitrary linguistic expressions; we want it to be able to produce expressions that fit in with the content and situation, to give sensible and relevant answers to our questions, to ask questions that are appropriate to the communicative situation, etc. In short, we want it to be able to produce linguistic expressions in the way in which natural language users produce such expressions. If this is our aim, we may even want it to produce ill-formed linguistic expressions, as long as these are communicatively adequate. For that is something that natural language users very often do.

A first requirement on such an 'intelligent' NLG is that it be connected to some knowledge base, and be able to exploit the contents of that knowledge base. For example, if we ask the system 'What's the time?', and it is in fact ten past twelve, then we want it to answer 'Ten past twelve'. And in order to be able to do so it must obviously know that it is ten past twelve: it must know the time, and it must be able to connect this knowledge to its NLG in such a way that the appropriate linguistic expression is generated. For this to be possible the knowledge base KB must contain or be able to form some representation of the knowledge 'The time is ten past twelve', the NLG must be able to form some representation from which the appropriate linguistic expression is produced, and there must be a possibility for connecting the knowledge representation and the linguistic representation to each other. One way for a system to know some fact X is for that system to contain some representation R(X) which contains the knowledge of the fact X. However, there is another way in which a system can be said to know something. This is when the system does not CONTAIN X, but is able to infer X from the knowledge that it contains. Consider the following example:

(1) Knowledge: (a) The Abbey of Royaumont is north of Paris.
                     (b) The Abbey of Royaumont is south of Chantilly.
    Question: (c) Is Chantilly north or south of Paris?
    Answer: (d) Chantilly is north of Paris.

In this example the system does not 'know' that Chantilly is north of Paris in the sense of containing some sort of representation of this fact. Nevertheless, if it would answer 'I don't know', we would not accept that answer. We would say, rather, that if a system knows (a) and (b), it also knows (d). But this presupposes that there is a second way of 'knowing' something, in the sense of being able to infer something by virtue of a logical competence. We can thus define:

(2) System S knows fact X =
   (i) S contains a representation of X;
   (ii) S contains knowledge K and a logical component LC such that X
        can be validly inferred from K by virtue of LC.

In order to be able to handle our example (1), our system must possess the following logical facilities:

(3) a. 'A is north of B' and 'B is south of A' are each other's converses.
         Therefore:
            (i) A north of B $\longleftrightarrow$ B south of A
     b. 'A is north of B' and 'A is south of B' are transitive relations.
         Therefore:
           (ii) (A north of B) & (B north of C) $\rightarrow$ (A north of C)
          (iii) (A south of B) & (B south of C) $\rightarrow$ (A south of C)

Using this logical knowledge it must, in the case of (1), be able to construe the following inference:

(4) (a) The Abbey of Royaumont is north of Paris.
     (b) The Abbey of Royaumont is south of Chantilly.
     (c) Therefore, by (3a) (i) from b:
          Chantilly is north of the Abbey of Royaumont.
     (d) Therefore, by (3b) (ii) from (c) and (a):
          Chantilly is north of Paris.

It is evident that if this pattern of reasoning is to work, the logical rules must be able of operating on pieces of knowledge such as (4a) and (4b); and since an intermediary conclusion such as (4c) can play a role in further inferencing towards (4d), the representation type of the conclusions must be the same as that of the premises.

In other words, the logical component LC must be able to work on representations of the knowledge base KB; and these representations must in turn be capable of being connected with the representations underlying linguistic expressions (i.e. from which NLG can produce the relevant linguistic expressions).

4.2 Towards one unified language of representation

It is evident from the example given that an adequate NLG will have to be connected with a KB and an LC. Each of these components requires certain forms of formal representation:

— NLG requires some sort of underlying structure from which linguistic expressions can be produced;
— KB requires some kind of formal structure in which knowledge can be represented;
— LC requires some sort of structure on which logical operations can be performed.

The sets of structures required for these different purposes may be called 'languages' in the wider, more abstract sense of the term. We thus need a language L_{li} for linguistic representation; a language L_k for knowledge representation; and a language L_{lo} for logical representation. Obviously, the expressions of these different languages must be such that they can be most easily converted into each other. It would, in fact, be ideal if these languages were identical, i.e. if the same structures could be used for linguistic representation, knowledge representation and representation of logical form.

We shall assume by hypothesis that this ideal can in fact be implemented. In other words, we act on the strong hypothesis that:

(5) $L_{li} = L_k = L_{lo}$

We shall further assume that this unified representation language (URL) not only defines structures that can be used as input to NLG, but also the structures that can be considered as output of a natural language parser NLP. We can then say that expressions in URL form the output of NLP, the input to NLG, the content of KB, and the input and output to LC. Our next question is: what are the properties of URL? In our answer to this question we make use of the theory of Functional Grammar (FG). FG is a general theory concerning the syntactic, semantic and pragmatic properties of natural languages. FG has been developed so as to reach high levels of typological, pragmatic and psychological adequacy, which can be defined as follows:

TYPOLOGICAL ADEQUACY: applicability to natural languages of any type.

PRAGMATIC ADEQUACY: compatibility with how linguistic expressions are used in communicative interaction.

PSYCHOLOGICAL ADEQUACY: compatibility with what is known about how human natural language users operate in producing and interpreting linguistic expressions.

In order to reach these levels of adequacy, FG assumes that linguistic expressions can be analysed in terms of more abstract underlying structures called predications. These predications are taken to contain all those elements which are essential to determining the form of the linguistic expressions on the one hand, and its content on the other. The structure of the predication is assumed to be highly identical across different languages. Thus, linguistic expressions with widely different syntactic structures will look quite similar at the level of the underlying predication.

Let us illustrate the properties of the FG predication by one example. Consider the following more or less equivalent sentence from English and Japanese:

(6) a. The children are playing in the bath.
    b. Kodomotachi wa ofuro no naka de asonde imasu
       child-plur Top bath of inside in in play-ing be-pol-pres
       'The children are playing in the bath'

Careful inspection of these constructions reveals a great number of differences. For example, Japanese word order is SXV, Japanese has postpositions rather than prepositions, 'in X' is expressed as 'in the inside of X', there is a Topic marker *wa*. Semantically, however, the content of (6a) and (6b) is highly similar. The only real communicative difference is that the Japanese auxiliary *imasu* signals 'politeness', as against the non-polite *iru*. Such a distinction cannot be made in English.

The underlying predications for (6a) and (6b) would be as follows:

(7) a. $\text{DEC(Pres Progr play}_V \text{ (dmx}_i\text{: child}_N(x_i))_{\text{AgSubjTop}}$
          $(\text{d1x}_j\text{: bath}_N(x_j))_{\text{Loc-int}})$
    b. $\text{DEC(Pol Pres Progr asobu}_V \text{ (dmx}_i\text{: kodomo}_N(x_i))_{\text{AgSubjTop}}$
          $(\text{d1x}_j\text{: ofuro}_N(x_j))_{\text{Loc-int}})$

These two predications obviously differ in the lexical predicates that they contain: *play/asobu*, *child/kodomo*, *bath/ofuro*. Apart from this, however, they only differ in the element Pol ('polite'), which is present in the Japanese, but not in the English predication. This corresponds to the fact that English does not have this possibility of grammatically encoding politeness.

All the other differences between (6a–b) are attributed to the expression rules of English and Japanese, i.e. to those rules which serve to map underlying predications on to linguistic expressions. These rules, which determine the form, the order and the intonation pattern of the expression, are obviously quite different in the two languages.

A predication such as (7a) expresses the following information:

(8) Speaker declares (DEC) that at the moment of speaking (Pres) an action of playing is going on (Progr), with a definite (d) set of more than (m) one child as Agent, and located (Loc) inside (int) a definite single (1) entity called a bath; further, the Agent term defines the perspective (Subj), and is the contextually defined entity (Top) about which the expression gives us some further information.

It will be clear that we take predications such as (7a) and (7b) as expressions of our language of linguistic representation L_{li}. This, combined with our hypothesis (5), brings us to the more particular hypothesis that we wish to explore, namely:

(9) Basic Hypothesis:
The language of FG predications = the language URL = L_{li} = L_k = L_{lo}

The hypothesis implies that FG predications form the output of NLP, the input to NLG, the content of KB, and the expressions on which LC operates. The logical component that operates on FG predications is called Functional Logic.

As for knowledge representation it should be added that we assume that knowledge can be divided into perceptual and conceptual knowledge; that perceptual knowledge is represented in 'images' of some kind; and that conceptual knowledge is stored in the form of predications.

In the rest of this chapter I will concentrate on the logical part of this theory, embodied in Functional Logic. It is clear that many aspects of the present theoretical framework must remain out of focus in the present chapter. I therefore give some general references here.

FG has been proposed in Dik (1978) and further developed in Dik (1980) and other publications, such as Bolkestein *et al.* (1985a, 1985b). Computational applications of FG are discussed in Dik (1986b). Kwee (1979, 1987) has developed a program for randomly generating English sentences in terms of FG. The use of an FG—like language for the purposes of knowledge representation is discussed in Dik (1986a) and Weigand (1986). Finally, note that predications such as (7a–b) are so close to each other that this level of analysis would constitute the ideal bridge for translating from English to Japanese and vice versa. This idea has been implemented for translation from English to French in van der Korst (1987).

4.3 Aspects of Functional Logic

By a 'logic' we can in general understand a system which defines valid patterns of reasoning, while excluding invalid patterns. A valid pattern of reasoning is a sequence of expressions $E_1, E_2, \ldots, E_n, \ldots, E_m$, such that, if $E_1 \ldots E_n$ are taken to be correct, then E_m must necessarily also be taken to be correct. By 'correct' we shall often understand 'true', but we may also operate with other correctness values such as 'sincere', 'appropriate', etc. In such a pattern, $E_1 \ldots E_n$ may be called the premises, and E_m the conclusion.

A logical system can be defined in terms of a syntax and a semantics. The syntax tells us what sorts of expressions can occur in patterns of reasoning; the semantics tells us how these expressions can be interpreted. As for Functional Logic, the syntax has been defined as coinciding with the language of underlying predications as determined by FG. Thus, expressions such as (7a) and (7b) are well formed in the logical syntax of English and Japanese, respectively. Note that, to the extent that these expressions have language-dependent properties, the corresponding logics will likewise have such language-dependent properties. However, since the predications of one language largely coincide with those of another language, their logics will show a large degree of overlap. In fact, it is mainly the logical properties of the language-dependent lexical predicates, such as *play*, *child*, *bath*, which will have to be formulated for each language separately.

The semantics of a logic can be divided into two sub-sections. One is concerned with the interpretation of the expressions defined as well-formed by the syntax; the other is concerned with the rules which define which sequences of expressions constitute valid patterns of reasoning. These can be called Rules of Interpretation and Rules of Inference, respectively.

In order to determine the Rules of Interpretation we need an ontology in terms of which the syntactic expressions can be interpreted. By ontology we understand the set of entities that we talk about by means of the expressions; 'entity' is here taken in the widest sense, including not only persons and things, but also events, facts, rules, laws, etc. Standard Logic often takes 'reality' or 'the real world' as its point of departure for determining the ontology. Thus, a statement such as:

(10) The Abbey of Royaumont is north of Paris.

is interpreted in the following way:

(11) a. ABBEY OF ROYAUMONT refers to the Abbey of Royaumont.

b. PARIS refers to Paris.
c. IS NORTH OF refers to the set of ordered pairs ‹x, y› such that x is to the north of y.

So far, all reference can be taken as reference to entities in reality. However, this cannot be the whole story. Consider a text such as the following:

(12) In a faraway country, a long time ago, there were three cities, Abba, Edde and Oppo. Abba was north of Edde, and south of Oppo.

It is clear that we must be able to reason in terms of these expressions (for example, we must be able to conclude that Oppo was north of Edde), even though we have no idea whether or not (12) describes any kind of reality. For such reasons as these, logic has widened its ontology so as to comprise 'the set of all possible worlds'. Example (12) describes a possible world in terms of which the expressions involved can be interpreted. A problem about the notion 'set of all possible worlds', however, is that this notion is not epistemologically restricted. By this we mean that it is taken to be irrelevant whether or not a person knows the relevant section of the set. In actual reasoning, however, we are necessarily restricted by the limitations of our knowledge: we can only talk and reason about entities to the extent that these entities are represented in our knowledge base.

Epistemological restrictions are quite evident if we attempt to simulate intelligent processes by computational means: the computer can only talk and reason about entities to the extent that we have taught it what these entities are. I take it that precisely the same applies to human beings: we can talk and reason about things only to the extent that we know these things. Whether or not these things have counterparts in the real world is a secondary matter. But this implies, in fact, that the things that we talk and reason about exist in our knowledge rather than in reality; for if they do not exist in reality, they can ONLY exist in our knowledge; and if they do exist in reality, we can only talk and reason about them TO THE EXTENT THAT they exist in our knowledge. In this way, we arrive at the conclusion that logical expressions should be interpreted in terms of a mental or epistemological ontology: the worlds that we talk and reason about are mental worlds.

4.4 Picture theory

We may thus conclude that we interpret and evaluate linguistic expressions in terms of mental representations of pieces of knowledge. Such mental representations have been called MENTAL MODELS (Johnson-Laird 1983) or

DISCOURSE MODELS (van Dijk & Kintsch 1983). I use the term (mental) PICTURES, in the sense in which I can say that I picture something, i.e. create a picture of something.

Some important properties of pictures are the following:

(A) Pictures consist of knowledge; knowledge may be perceptual or conceptual; pictures will therefore consist of perceptual and conceptual representations. But for conceptual representations we have assumed that they take the form of predications. Therefore, the language in which pictures are coded is partially identical to the language in terms of which linguistic expressions are analysed.

(B) Pictures are epistemological objects. They are therefore subject-dependent. My picture is not necessarily identical to your picture, and may be different again in some respects from his or her picture.

(C) Pictures are dynamic entities: they may be created, modified and destroyed.

(D) Pictures are necessarily limited and finite: nobody has a complete picture of anything.

(E) Different pictures may at the same time be relevant to interpretation and reasoning.

Let us exemplify some of these properties by some examples. Consider again the example given in (1). This example is taken from the 'Final Announcement' for this workshop, which says:

(13) The Abbey of Royaumont is 30 km north of Paris, 12 km south of Chantilly.

Why are these statements made? In order for me to determine whether they are true or false? No: they are made in order for me to be able to construct a picture concerning the location of the Abbey of Royaumont. Before I got this information, my picture of the situation was more or less as follows:

(14) a. Workshop will be held at Abbey of Royaumont.
    b. Abbey of Royaumont is somewhere near Paris.
    c. Paris is about 500 km south of Amsterdam.

Now obviously I do not doubt the correctness of the information given in the Final Announcement. I assume that the organizers give me this information in order to help me to get to the Workshop. I therefore use this information to update my picture in the following way:

(15)   N
                         Amsterdam
                          458 km

Chantilly
12 km
Abbey of Royaumont
30 km
Paris
S

Although I have never been to Chantilly or to Abbey of Royaumont, this picture will now help me to find these places. Also, I can now reason in terms of the information contained in the picture. For example, I may now conclude that, if the information I have received is correct, Paris must be 42 km south of Chantilly. This example exemplifies some aspects of the properties (A), (B), (C) and (D) above.

As for property (E), consider the following example. Suppose A and B have been to the same movie, and afterwards say:

(16) A: That movie was horrible.
      B: I found it splendid.

It is clear, then, that they have different pictures concerning the movie in question. What is true in A's picture about the movie is false in B's picture, and vice versa. However, not only do they have different pictures, they will also keep track of each other's pictures, as far as these have been revealed in the communication. The situation could be displayed as follows:

(17)

In A's picture AP it is true that the movie was horrible; however, AP contains, as a sub-picture, A's picture of B's picture BP in which it is true that the movie was splendid. Likewise for BP. The configuration in (17) has obvious consequences for the further development of the communication between A and B. For example, A may continue with (18a), but not with (18b):

(18) a. A: I completely disagree with you.
      b. A: I fully agree with you.

In order to explain this, we need to know both A's picture and A's picture of B's picture.

Note that, as a consequence of the idea that statements are evaluated with respect to pictures, it follows that what is true in one picture may be false in another. Therefore, we shall have to interpret Truth in terms of the relation 'Statement S is true/false in picture P'. In other words: 'Vérité au-deçà des Pyrenées, erreur au-delà' (Pascal, *Pensées*: 60).

4.5 Components of a Functional Logic

It is customary to divide logic into different sub-theories, according to that aspect of logical form of which they characterize the logical properties. Thus, we have propositional logic, predicate logic, the logic of classes, etc.

Functional Logic can likewise be divided into different sub-theories in terms of the various 'domains' which can be distinguished in the predication. The global subdivision of the predication and the corresponding components of FL can be displayed as follows:

(19) a. Illocutionary Logic: deals with the logical properties of illocutionary operators such as DECLARATIVE, INTERROGATIVE.
  b. Predicational Logic: deals with the logical relations between whole predications.
  c. Predicate Logic: deals with the logical properties of predicates and predicate operators such as Present, Progressive, etc.
  d. Term Logic: deals with the internal logical properties of terms, including term operators such as Definiteness, Number, Quantification, etc.
  e. Lexical Logic: deals with the logically relevant properties internal to lexical predicates.

4.5.1 *Illocutionary Logic*

Illocutionary Logic will deal with those conclusions which can be validly drawn on the basis of the illocutionary value of the predication. In FG, this illocutionary value is captured by means of predication operators such as DEC (declarative), INT (interrogative), IMP (imperative). We can thus say, briefly, that Illocutionary Logic deals with the logical properties of illocutionary predication operators. What kinds of phenomena are to be accounted for by Illocutionary Logic? Suppose that some speaker or writer X tells me that:

(20) The Abbey of Royaumont is 30 km north of Paris.

This statement may be represented as DEC(ϕ), where ϕ is the predication 'The Abbey of Royaumont is 30 km north of Paris'.

If it is assumed that X is sincere in presenting (20), then I may conclude:

(21) a. X believes that ϕ is true: ϕ is true in X's picture.
   b. X believes that I do not know that ϕ: the truth value of ϕ is undefined in X's picture of my picture.
   c. X wants me to know that ϕ: X wants me to add ϕ as a true predication to my picture.

These conclusions can be drawn on the basis of the declarative character of (20), plus the normal communicative assumption that X is sincere. The conclusions warranted on the basis of DEC can thus be formulated in a rule of interpretation for DEC under normal communicative circumstances. Likewise, interpretation rules for INT, IMP, etc., must be provided which capture those inferences which can be validly drawn on the basis of an occurrence of linguistic expressions with those illocutionary values.

4.5.2 *Predicational logic*

Predicational Logic will deal with those phenomena which are captured in standard propositional logic: conjunction, disjunction, negation, implication and equivalence of predications. This must be done, however, in a way which respects the linguistic properties of those relations. For this reason, Predicational Logic will have some special properties concerning the following phenomena:

(i) *Sequential conjunction*   Predicational Logic will have to account for the fact that certain forms of conjunction cannot be truth-functionally defined. Consider a famous case such as:

(22) a. She drank arsenic and died.
   b. She died and drank arsenic.

These two expressions are clearly not semantically equivalent. The reason is that not only is the truth of the conjuncts a determining factor for the truth value of the whole conjunction: also the temporal sequence between the events described in these conjuncts is essential. We will have to capture this in a special definition for sequential conjunction ⊗ along the following lines:

(23) ϕ ⊗ ψ is true iff ϕ is true and ψ is true and the state of affairs described by ϕ precedes the state of affairs described by ψ in time.

(ii) *Partial predications*   The problem of partial predications can be illustrated with the same example (22a). We have silently assumed that this construction consists of two whole predications ϕ and ψ, and thus equivalent to:

(22)′   She drank arsenic and she died.

Note, however, that in principle (22)′ could be used to describe two events involving different participants, both referred to by *she*. Example (22)′ therefore does not guarantee co-reference in the way that (22a) does. For that reason it would be preferable to be able to interpret (22a) directly as representing two predications involving the same person, than to analyse it via the extended version (22)′. Predicational Logic will have to develop some way of bringing this about.

(iii) *Conditional constructions*   One of the most conspicuous cases of lack of fit between propositional logic and natural language is the analysis of conditional constructions in terms of material implication. Since a material implication $\phi \rightarrow \psi$ is truth-functionally defined as true unless ϕ is true and ψ is false, it allows for a lot of combinations of predications which are not normally expressed by *if . . . then* constructions in natural languages. I believe that a way out of this problem can be found in Picture Theory: natural language conditionals may be interpreted as a means for creating a hypothetical picture, differing at some crucial point from the picture we are (supposed to be) entertaining at the moment of speaking, in such a way that certain conclusions may be drawn by comparison of the hypothetical picture with our actual picture.

Consider the following example:

(24)   If John goes to the party, Mary will go too.

In the normal usage of this construction it is assumed that speaker and addressee do not know whether John is going to the party (nor whether Mary is going to the party). Example (24) is then used to create a hypothetical picture in which these two events are linked to each other. Should it turn out later that John is indeed going to the party, then, if (24) is taken to be true, we may conclude that Mary is going to the party as well. On the other hand, should it turn out that Mary is not going to the party, then, if (24) is taken to be true, we may conclude that John is not going to the party either.

The idea of the conditional as a means for creating an alternative picture is even clearer in the case of counterfactuals:

(25)   If John went to the party, Mary would go there too.

in which it is assumed that speaker and addressee are aware of the fact that John is, in fact, going to the party.

4.5.3 *Predicate Logic*

FL Predicate Logic will be rather different from standard predicate logic because of the fact that the theory of quantification is considered part of term structure rather than predicate structure. Consider the following simple case:

(26) a. All humans are mortal
     b. Standard Logic analysis: $\forall x(H(x) \rightarrow M(x))$
     c. Functional Logic analysis: $M(\forall x: H(x))$

In standard logic the universal quantifier is treated as a propositional operator, which turns a propositional function into a proposition.

In FG and FL, on the other hand, the universal quantifier is treated as a term operator, which turns a propositional function into a quantified term. There is thus a term *all humans*, which refers to the full set of entities that are human, and the predicate *mortal* is applied to that term. Thus, quantification will not be treated at the level of predicate logic.

What is treated at this level is:

(i) *The general theory of relations*   For example, the notion 'converse relation' could be defined at the level of Predicate Logic in the following way:

(27) $F = \text{conv}(G)$ iff $F(x_i)(x_j) \longleftrightarrow G(x_j)(x_i)$

This would thus be the formal rule needed to account for the relation given in (3a) above.

Likewise, other relational properties such as (ir)reflexivity, (a)symmetry, and (in)transitivity will be defined at this level.

(ii) *The theory of Tense, Aspect and Mood*   To the extent that Tense, Aspect and Mood distinctions are expressed by grammatical (rather than lexical) means, they are captured by means of predicate operators such as Pres and Progr in example (7) above. These operators will be semantically interpreted at the level of Predicate Logic. These interpretations will take some such form as the following:

(28) a. Progr   :the state of affairs designated by the predication is unfinished at the relevant reference point t_r:

t_r

b. Pres   :t_r = the moment of speaking and the state of affairs designated by the predication coincides with t_r.

Such definitions as these for the full system of predicate operators of a language can then be used for explicating those patterns of reasoning which crucially involve distinctions of Tense, Aspect and Mood. For example:

(29) The children are playing in the garden.
Therefore: a. The children have not yet finished playing in the garden.
Not: b. The children have not yet started playing in the garden.

(30) a. John has counted the pigeons.
Therefore: John has been counting the pigeons.
b. John has been counting the pigeons.
Not therefore: John has counted the pigeons.

4.5.4 *Term Logic*

For typological and semantic reasons, FG analyses terms according to the following general schema:

(31) $(\omega x: \phi_1(x): \phi_2(x): \ldots : \phi_n(x))$

where x is the term variable symbolizing the entity to be identified by the term, ω stands for one or more operators, and each $\phi(x)$ is an 'open predication in x', i.e. a predicational function containing x as its only free variable. The open predications serve as 'restrictors' which progressively narrow down the set of potential referents of the term, through the repeated relation ':', to be read as 'such that'.

As an example, consider the following term:

(32) a. the red car that John bought
b. $(d1x_i: car_N(x_i): red_A(x_i): Past\text{-}buy_V(d1x_j: John_N(x_j))_{Ag}(x_i)_{Go})$

Here, 'd' and '1' represent the term operators 'definite' and 'singular', respectively. The whole term indicates that we are to identify a definite singular entity x_i such that x_i is a car, such that x_i is red, such that John bought x_i.

Term Logic will be concerned with the semantic interpretation of this kind of term structure. On the one hand, this involves a specification of the semantic effect of the restrictors which are successively stacked on to each other; on the other hand, it involves a definition of the semantic and pragmatic contribution of the various term operators. For the present example, we would need such definitions as the following:

(33) a. d: speaker assumes that addressee can identify the intended
         referent by independent means.
     b. 1: the cardinal number of the set to be identified is 1.

As noted before, the theory of quantification will thus form part of Term Logic in FL.

4.5.5 *Lexical Logic*

A certain class of inferences can be validly drawn on the basis of the lexical meanings of the predicates occurring in the predication. For example:

(34) a. John kissed Mary.
         Therefore: John touched Mary.
     b. John was kept awake by a fly.
         Therefore: John was kept awake by an insect.

Obviously, in order to account for these inferences, we must analyse the meaning of *kiss* and *fly* in such a way that they come out as hyponyms of *touch* and *insect*, respectively: 'kissing is a certain kind of touching' and 'fly is a kind of insect' must thus in some way be retrievable for such inferences as (34a–b) to be warranted by FL. Since there is nothing in the forms of words such as *kiss* and *fly* from which such inferences could be derived, it is clear that what is required is an analysis of lexical meaning and its logical properties. This is the area of Lexical Logic.

In FG-FL, the desired result is achieved in the following way: first, each lexical predicate is by definition part of a predicate frame, a structure which defines its essential formal and semantic properties. The entries in the lexicon are thus predicate frames rather than isolated predicates. Second, each predicate frame in the lexicon is associated with a set of meaning postulates of the following general form:

(35) $F(x_1) \ldots (x_n) \rightarrow G(x_1) \ldots (x_n)$

These meaning postulates stipulate that if one applies a predicate F to a series of term $x_1 \ldots x_n$, then one is committed to accept that also G is assigned to this series of terms.

In the case of the examples given in (34), the relevant entries would take the following form:[1]

(36) a. $kiss_V(x_1: \langle human \rangle (x_1))_{Ag}(x_2: \langle concrete \rangle (x_2))_{Go}$

$\rightarrow$

$touch_V(x_1)_{Ag}(x_2)_{Go}(d2x_i: lip_N(x_i))_{Instr}$

'to kiss something is to touch it with the lips'

b. $fly_N(x_1)_\phi \rightarrow insect_N(x_1)_\phi$

'a fly is an insect'

From these examples it can be seen that not only the left-hand side, but also the right-hand side of a meaning postulate takes the form of a predicate frame. This has the formal advantage that the right-hand side can be substituted for the left-hand side in any predication in which the latter occurs. In this way, predications entailed by other predications through lexical meaning can be derived from these predications by rather simple formal operations.

Note that meaning postulates are one-way implications which do not necessarily add up to a definition of the meaning of the lexical item. Only when a set of meaning postulates is such that the arrow can be reversed can we speak of a meaning *definition*. For example, (36a) does not provide a full definition of *kiss*, since we may touch something with the lips without actually kissing it. In order to arrive at a full definition, we need something extra. We might hypothesize, for example, that the addition of 'in order to express affection' sufficiently differentiates kissing from any other kind of lip-touching. Assuming this to be correct, we can extend (36a) to a full-fledged meaning definition in the following way:[2]

(37) $kiss_v(x_1: \langle human \rangle (x_i))_{Ag}(x_2: \langle concrete \rangle (x_2))_{Go}$

$\longleftrightarrow$

$touch_V(x_1)_{Ag}(x_2)_{Go}(d2x_i: lip_N(x_i))_{Instr}$
$(d1x_j: [express_V(x_1)_{Ag}(ix_k: affection_N(x_k))_{Go}](x_j))_{Purp}$

To the extent that such a definition is correct, it can be used to produce full paraphrases of given predications, and also to account for inference patterns of the following type:

(38) John touched Mary with the lips in order to express affection.
    Therefore: John kissed Mary.

4.6 Conclusion

Let us, by way of conclusion, return to the reasoning pattern given in (1). We can now see how such a pattern would be accounted for in FL:

— We assume a parser which is able to reconstruct the FG underlying predications of the linguistic expressions (a) and (b).

— We need the information that 'A is north of B' and 'B is south of A' are each other's converses. Since this is a lexical property of these words, that information will be stored in their lexical entries. The rule of Predicate Logic given in (27) then tells us what operations are warranted by this fact.

— We need the information that 'A is north of B' is a transitive relation. This, too, will be coded in the lexical entry for *north*, and a general rule of Predicate Logic will tell us what sorts of operations are warranted in the case of transitive relations.

— When a system is provided with this sort of information, it can automatically derive conclusions from given premises through simple substitution operations.

— Obviously, we need some sort of strategy or heuristics to arrive at the desired conclusions (rather than at any random warranted conclusion).

— Finally, we assume a generator which is able to map predications on to the linguistic expressions that can be used to express them.

Along these lines, then, we may hope to arrive at an integrated model of NLU, in which linguistic, epistemological and logical competences co-operate and communicate through one common idiom: the language of underlying predications.

Notes

1. Predicates within ‹ › indicate selection restrictions on the argument positions; Go = Goal or Patient; Instr = Instrument.
2. i = indefinite; Purp = Purpose. The last, rather complex term can be read as: 'for the purpose x_j defined by x_1's expressing affection'.

Bibliography

Bolkestein, A. Machtelt, de Groot, Casper & Mackenzie, J. Lachlan (eds) (1985a), *Syntax and Pragmatics in Functional Grammar*, Dordrecht, Foris.
—— (1985b), *Predicates and Terms in Functional Grammar*, Dordrecht, Foris.
Dik, Simon C. (1978), *Functional Grammar*, Amsterdam, North-Holland (1981, Dordrecht, Foris).
—— (1980), *Studies in Functional Grammar*, London, Academic Press.
—— (1986a), 'Linguistically motivated knowledge representation', Working Papers in Functional Grammar 9, Amsterdam, Institute for General Linguistics.
—— (1986b), 'Functional Grammar and its potential computer applications', in (1986d).

—— (1986c), 'Generating answers from a linguistically coded knowledge base', in (1986d).

—— (1986d), 'Two papers on the computational application of FG' (1986b and 1986c), Working Papers in Functional Grammar 18, Amsterdam, Institute for General Linguistics.

Dijk, Teun A. van & Kintsch, Walter (1983), *Strategies of Discourse Comprehension*, New York, Academic Press.

Johnson-Laird, Philip N. (1983), *Mental Models*, Cambridge, Cambridge University Press.

Korst, Bieke van der (1987), 'Twelve sentences: a translation procedure in terms of Functional Grammar', Working Papers in Functional Grammar 19, Amsterdam, Institute for General Linguistics.

Kwee, Tjoe-Liong (1979), 'A68-FG(3): Simon Dik's funktionele grammatika geschreven in algo168 versie nr. 03', Publications of the Institute of General Linguistics, University of Amsterdam, No. 23.

—— (1987), 'A computer model of Functional Grammar', in *Natural Language Generation: Recent Advances in AI, Psychology and Linguistics*, Dordrecht/Boston, Martinus Nijhoff Publishers.

Weigand, Hans (1986), 'An overview of the conceptual language KOTO', paper, Dept. of Mathematics and Computer Science, Free University, Amsterdam.

Part III Implementational issues

5 Two approaches to natural language generation*

GIOVANNI ADORNI†

5.0 Introduction

In any man–machine interaction, information flows in two directions: input from user to machine, and output from machine to user. When a computer system is given the task of conveying information to the user, it is important that the system be able to output the information in a way and using a language that the user can understand. Computer generation of natural language (NL) is a significant part of the solution to this problem.

The general goal of NL generation in the artificial intelligence paradigm is to take some internal representation of the meaning of a sentence and convert it into a surface-structure form, that is, to produce an NL text. There is a considerable variety of such systems, reflecting differences in the type of internal representation used and in the purpose for which the text is generated. Representation schemes have included largely syntactic dependency trees (Klein 1965), stored generation patterns (Weizenbaum 1966; Winograd 1972), and several versions of semantic nets (Goldman 1975; Herskovits 1973; Shapiro 1979). Applications have included automatic paraphrasing or machine translation of an input text (Habel *et al.* 1977; Wilks 1973; Lytinen 1986), providing NL communication with the user of an interactive program (Grishman 1979; Waltz 1978; Woods *et al.* 1972), or simply testing the adequacy of the internal representation (Simmons & Slocum 1971; Wong 1975).

An NL generation package must be essentially composed of a comprehensive, linguistically justified grammar and a knowledge representation

* This work has been partially supported by the Italian Ministry of Education within the ASSI project on Artificial Intelligence and by EUREKA project PROMETHEUS (subproject Pro-Art).

† *Department of Communication, Computer and System Sciences, University of Genoa, Genoa, Italy*

formalism that can encode different kinds of information. In addition to these components, a general discourse generator must take into account the knowledge of the reader and a model of the discourse structure. In this area, some researchers have looked at the psychological mechanisms underlying discourse production (Clippinger 1975; Kempen 1978; Kempen & Hoenkamp 1987) and have studied explicit discourse models and the planning of speech acts for communication in a given context (Appelt 1981; Cohen 1978; Cohen & Perrault 1979; Hovy 1985; Kempen 1987; McDonald 1980; McKeown 1981). A number of directions for future research have been opened up by the recent successes of unification grammars (Bossie 1981; Hasida & Isizaky 1987; Shieber 1985). Unification grammars, among their other virtues, allow the selection of syntactic structures to be partially based on features of the text which account for textual coherency and appropriateness. One of the previously mentioned directions in research is towards improvement of the practicality of generation technology by developing tools to reduce the amount of 'handcrafting' involved in interfacing a generation system to an application. The automatic generation of portions of a lexicon for a particular application could be a great benefit.

In this chapter two NL generation modules are described. The first module is oriented only to the translation of the internal representation of the NAUSICA system (Adorni *et al.* 1981). NAUSICA is a semantic-based language interpreter which has been developed with the main goal of providing a suitable conceptual-handling background to an integrate vision-manipulation system (Adorni *et al.* 1984a; DiManzo *et al.* 1986). Concept representation in NAUSICA is based on the Conceptual Dependency (CD) formalism (Schank 1975). This formalism has been slightly modified to be able to describe properly a set of about 600 Italian words, which is rather representative of the dictionary used in common conversations. The semantic interpreter is interfaced with a transformational grammar (Chomsky 1957) by means of a 'sentence translator' that performs the following tasks:

(i) it associates a semantic value to each word, that is, a conceptual dependency network (cd-net) or a sub cd-net;
(ii) it looks for interactions between the sub cd-nets associated to each word to build a general framework for whole sentences;
(iii) it looks for a proper filler of each identified semantic case.

The rules used by this sentence translator to perform (ii) and (iii) are usually dependent only on the conceptual primitives contained into the sub cd-nets, even if some particular words can invoke special demons. More details on the adopted formalism, the lexicon and the structure of the sentence translator can be found in Adorni *et al.* (1981, 1983).

The second module describes a generation procedure producing English written sentences from formal representations of their meaning (generated by WEDNESDAY system (Stock *et al*. 1983; Stock 1986)). The following considerations refer to salient aspects of WEDNESDAY:

(i) The words bring all the information necessary to combine one with another the semantic contents present in the sentence;

(ii) the network assembling process is driven by word expectation mechanism. That means that even anomalous or, in some case, unpredicted situations may be analysed;

(iii) the lexicon brings a great part of what is needed by assembling a sentence: syntax and semantic elements.

To each word both a declarative aspect and a procedural one are associated. Expectations and instructions for linking nodes with semantic contents can be brought in by other words. Data are put in precise search spaces. A management of work units and short-term memories is present. It is important to note, though, that the making of the semantic network takes place in a global long-term memory, while syntactic data and operations are in a highly structured short-term memory. WEDNESDAY can be looked at as an interpreter for a dictionary describing language. For a sentence to be analysed the interpreter will execute its words in succession. A characteristic of the meaning representations used in the second module described in the chapter (and derived by WEDNESDAY system) is that they are 'relatively' universal. In fact they bear no trace of the language into which they will be eventually mapped. It is the production procedure that imposes a language-specific form on the final sentence that is produced. In principle, from a given meaning representation, sentences in a number of different languages can be produced, provided that the production procedure for each language is available. Neither of the described systems represents a general discourse generator nor includes a model of the intended reader of the text and a model of the discourse structure and control. In the last section of the chapter some considerations of the two approaches are sketched out.

5.1 NL generation from a conceptual dependency network

Production of NL sentences starting from a cd-net introduces at least three major problems:

(a) the use of conceptual relationships, to obtain a sentence in NL from the words;

(b) the choice of the syntactic relationship, derived from conceptual semantics, which tie words together;

(c) the choice of the words which must be used in the sentence.

With reference to point (c), the words which must be used in the sentence should be the words which 'best' convey the meaning represented by the cd-net. The most meaningful words to be chosen are verbs, nouns and adjectives which indicate conceptual relationships (e.g. conceptual structures, states and changes of state), since they carry a large amount of conceptual information which is spread throughout the underlying structure of the CD system. With reference to points (b) and (a), since the study of syntactical rules is not the focus of this work, and since a great deal of work has already been done in this area, it was decided to design the system to use an existing formulation of Italian syntax (Genot 1973). The structure of the system discussed below is depicted in Figure 5.1 (Adorni & DiManzo 1983).

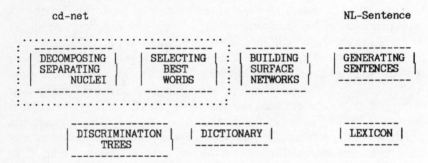

Figure 5.1 Structure of the system

In this figure, the first step performed by the system is the decomposition of a cd-net; in fact, every cd-net can be decomposed into two sub cd-nets linked together by a conceptual relationship (result, causation . . .). This process can be recursively applied until a cd-net is found which can no longer be decomposed. After this decomposition, the system tries to associate a meaning to this sub cd-net which interacts with the next step 'selecting the best words'. For this purpose, tree-like structures are used: discrimination trees (d-trees) (Goldman 1975). The nodes of these trees contain tests about the structure and conceptual cases of a sub cd-net; the leaves represent the Italian words, through pointers to the dictionary which contain the words together with their syntactical characteristics.

Similar structures can also be found in the BABEL system (Goldman 1975), but unlike BABEL, there are some d-trees devoted to testing the possibility of merging two sub cd-nets with the aim of obtaining a single word: merging trees (m-trees). If it is not possible to apply an m-tree to two sub cd-nets, but if it is on the contrary necessary to apply two d-trees to the two sub cd-nets, this means that in the Italian sentence there are two coordinated phrases. Both d-trees and m-trees can be represented by the syntax.

```
TREE          :: = name: STRUCTURE
STRUCTURE :: = NODE | STRUCTURE NODE
NODE          :: = TESTS y NODE n NODE | word | failure
TESTS         :: single__test TEST
TEST          :: = and TESTS | or TESTS |
```

The access to the tree is performed on the basis of the following information contained in the sub-cd nets: type (action, state, state__change . . .) and conceptual primitives (ptrans, move, write . . .) or conceptual states (isa, physical__state, gratification . . .). A list containing d-trees and m-trees is associated with every primitive action, state or state__change. M-trees can also be omitted.

With the aim of generating an Italian sentence it is necessary to have information like subject, object, complements, adverbs, etc.; furthermore, with the aim of generating an Italian paragraph it is necesary to know what coordination and subordination links must be established between the sentences. This information is extracted directly from the conceptual nuclei (looking at the relationships between the sub cd-nets) and it is introduced into an intermediate structure: the surface network (s-net). The s-net is then used to perform the right organization of words in the output sentence. This step is necessary for the Italian sentences because, unlike the English language, it is not possible to establish a priori a generally true fixed order of the elements of a sentence. When an s-net for a verb is built, the system analyses the following verb looking first of all for the links between them. In order to determine which is the main phrase, it is necessary, at this point, to verify the deepness difference in the s-net between the link and the verb previously analysed. When the s-net is completed, the moods and tense are associated with the corresponding verbs, reading in the s-net the information concerning the conceptual nucleus tense and the temporal relationships between the main phrase and ths subordinate. The mood of the main phrase is always indicative, except in the case of the hypothetical period for which the tense is determined on the basis of the temporal features of the action which are provided from the input cd-net. The tenses are chosen on the basis of the graph in Figure 5.2 (★ ☆ refer to a period, ■ □ to the time in which the action occurs, and -- are length indicators).

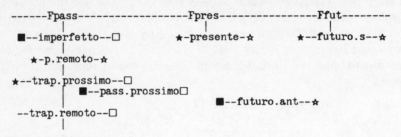

Figure 5.2 Tense table

For the dependent phrases a different analysis has been carried out, depending on the kind of subordinate; for each kind the mood and tense has been decided according to the features of the main phrase and to the temporal relationships between the main phrase and the dependent phrase.

One of the main problems of the production of Italian sentences is the generation of complements. The complements can be grouped in two classes:

— complements typical of a verb, which play a specific conceptual role characteristic of that verb;
— complements independent of the verb, which can be present in any conceptualization (adverbs specified by the Action Aiders . . .).

A set of functions has been associated with every class of verb with the aim of building the first class of complements. The second class is generated by standard functions valid for all verbs.

During the last step, the sentence is generated starting from the s-net and making use of a set of rules derived from an Italian transformational grammar. These rules allow the reconstruction of the final sentence on the basis of the s-net labels concerning the main conceptualization of the input cd-net. At this stage the system interacts with a lexical dictionary of the Italian language (LEXICON) to extract the information about the surface words. For this purpose, a set of functions has been defined, which allow for correct plural generation and correct verb conjugation in all moods and tenses of the three conjugations. During sentence generation some general functions are activated that analyse complements and subjects to avoid subject repetition (this is the case, for example, of co-ordinate phrases, or phrases which use pronouns). Also some functions are defined within the system, which avoid the use of the article before proper nouns, include the proper prepositions (both subordinate and co-ordinate), build combinations of prepositions and articles, and deal with more than one attribute referring to the same name.

Let us suppose that we have the cd-net of Figure 5.3 as input to the system. It is possible to notice in AND with the ATRANS primitive nucleus, a specification of the time (t1) in which the action occurs (two days before the action PTRANS specified by t2) and a specification of the place in which the actor is present at the action time. This cd-net is generated by the NAUSICA system (Adorni *et al*. 1981) according to the structure in Figure 5.4. As a consequence of the decomposition and separation of the conceptual nuclei, the nucleus associated with ATRANS primitive is firstly located in a table (see Table 5.1). Analysing the label 'e10' the system realizes that the ATRANS d-tree has to be applied and, according

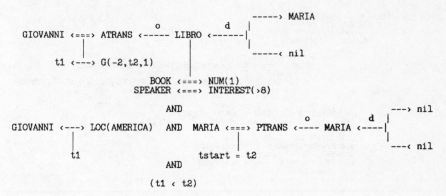

```
                                              -----> MARIA
                              o          d  |
  GIOVANNI  <===>  ATRANS  <----- LIBRO  <-------|
        |                          |            -----< nil
     t1 <---> G(-2,t2,1)           |

                         BOOK    <===> NUM(1)
                         SPEAKER  <===> INTEREST(>8)

              AND                                        ---> nil
                                          o          d  |
GIOVANNI <---> LOC(AMERICA)   AND  MARIA <===> PTRANS <---- MARIA <----|
        |                                |                     ---< nil
        t1                          tstart = t2
              AND

         (t1 < t2)
```

Figure 5.3

```
cd10                 t102                 x10
  type    rel          t_zero  (   t0)      type    spatial
  relat   and          etaq10               rel     in
  link    (a10 y10)     name    ptrans      help    ((GIOVANNI)(AMERICA))
a10                     obj     (MARIA)    q10
  type    rel        y10                    type    action
  relat   and          type    comp         actor   (MARIA)
  link    (b10 d10)     op      .           at      etempq10
b10                     t1      (t102 t101)  action  eteq10
  type    rel          t0      (   t0)    etempq10
  relat   and        etae10                 type    s_a
  link    (d10 x10)    name    atrans       tstart  t102
d10                     obj     (LIBRO pli pl2) pli
  type    rel          rec_to  (MARIA)       type    versus
  relat   and        z10                     status  interest
  link    (e10 z10)    type    timep         value   (> 8)
e10                     gsma    g            da_a    ((SPEAKER) verpli)
  type    action       quant   1          pl2
  actor   (GIOVANNI)   init    t102         type    num
  at      etime10      inrel   -2           value   (1)
  action  etae10     t102                   name    (LIBRO)
etime10                t_zero  (   t0)    verpli
  type    .t                                 type    descriptive
  time    t101                               name    (LIBRO)
t101
```

Figure 5.4 Example of cd-net generated by NAUSICA system

to the nucleus features, the verb *dare* is produced (see Figure 5.5). This verb is stored in a table (see Table 5.2), and the information already used is deleted from Table 5.1. This process is applied recursively until Table 5.1 is empty. In Table 5.2 there is no information about the complements present in the sentence: they can be retrieved anyway on the basis of the labels in column 2.

Table 5.1

a10	y10	and
b10	q10	and
d10	x10	and
e10	z10	and
e10		action

Table 5.2

dare	2	e10	z10
and	2		
essere_3	2	x10	
and	1		y10
partire	1	q10	

```
ATRANS:  OBJ = type POSS
              y ACTOR = DIR_TO
                  y prendere
                  n ACTOR = DIR_FROM
                      y AA_GIUST > 1
                          y meritare
                          n INSTR = type PTRANS and ACTOR(PTRANS) = ACTOR(ATRANS)
                              y portare
                              n DIR_TO(ATRANS) = type POSS and T_START(POSS) < T_START(ATRANS)
                                  y rendere
                                  n dare

                      n ...
         OBJ = type OWNERSHIP and ACTOR = DIR_FROM(ATRANS)
              y DIR_TO = type DO and T_START(ATRANS) < T_START(DO)
                  y pagare
                  n DIR_TO(ATRANS) = ACTOR(ATRANS_1)
                    and DIR_TO(ATRANS_1) = ACTOR(ATRANS)
                    and REL(ATRANS) = type R(ATRANS_1)
                    and REL(ATRANS_1) = type R(ATRANS)
                      y comperare
                      n ...
              n ...
```

Figure 5.5 Partial view of ATRANS d-tree

```
PTRANS:  ACTOR = OBJ
              y INSTR = type MOVE and OBJ(INSTR) = ISA GAMBE
                  y AA_VOLTE(INSTR) "characteristic number"
                      y correre
                      n camminare
                  n DIR_TO = nil
                      y T_START = not nil
                          y partire
                          n ...
                      n DIR_TO = IN or DIR_TO = SU
                          y DIR_FROM = DAVANTI or DIR_FROM = VICINO
                              y entrare
                              n T_START = not nil
                                  y partire_per
                                  n T_END = not nil
                                      y arrivare_a
                                      n andare
              n INSTR = type PTRANS and ACTOR = ACTOR(INSTR) and ACTOR = OBJ(INSTR)
                  y ...
                  n DIR_TO = IN STOMACO
                      y OBJ = ISA FLUIDO
                          y bere
                          n OBJ = ISA CIBO
                              y mangiare
                              n ingerire
                  n ...
```

Figure 5.6 Partial view of PTRANS d-tree

```
via10                        g2                          s6
   regg    part                 gender   male               regg    via10
   verb    (DARE v1)             art      det                verb    (PARTIRE v7)
   subj    (GIOVANNI g2)         numb     sing               subj    (MARIA g8)
   c_obj   (LIBRO g3)        g3                          v7
   c_term  (MARIA g4)            gender   male               neg     nil
   c_time_det (2 GIORNI)         art      indet              rifl    nil
   c_spatial (AMERICA g5 IN)     numb     sing               cond    nil
   subord  ((time_anter s6)      feat     (INTERESSANTE)     form    finite
v1                           g4                              mode    congiuntivo
   neg     nil                  gender   female              tense   imperfetto
   rifl    nil                  art      det             g8
   cond    nil                  numb     sing                gender  female
   form    finite           g5                               art     det
   mode    indicativo                                        numb    sing
   tense   pass
```

Figure 5.7 S-net generated from Figure 5.4

Analysing Table 5.2 starting from the first row, the system finds the verb. To locate the subject of the action and the related complements (if present) a list has been associated with each verb in the dictionary. The list associated with the verb *dare* is:

((mcsubj pact)(mcobj pobj)(mmezzo pinstr)(mcterm prect))

This list says that the complements specific to this verb are the subject, the direct object, the instrument and the indirect object. As a consequence of the application of the functions indicated in the list, the information carried out of the cd-net is introduced in the proper fields of the s-net. Once the specific complements have been analysed, the information not typical of that verb has to be added to the network for further analysis. These operations are replaced for all the verbs present in Table 5.2 which have to appear explicitly in the surface form; the verb *essere__3* (which indicates *to stay in some place*) is not translated in this example as *Giovanni era in America* (*John was in America*), but it is translated only with the locative: *in America*. This is a general PRISE rule: ‹in absence of other conditions introduce the least number of verbs›. In our example, *in America* instead of *John was in America*. The s-net is then built on the way, when the verbs are encountered in Table 5.2, analysing those parts of the conceptual graph referred to by the labels of column 2. At the end of this step the s-net is the one shown in Figure 5.7. As was to be expected, the spatial relationship has become a locative.

The last step, employed in the production of the Italian Sentence, makes use of both the s-net previously built and of the information present in the lexicon. Finally, by analysing a preposition at the time starting from the main phrase (label 'via10' in Figure 5.7) and by exploiting for the complements some ordering criteria previously chosen according to the context (and derived from the Italian grammar), the following output is generated:

(in America Giovanni diede a Maria un libro interessante 2 giorni prima che lei partisse)

(in America John gave Mary an interesting book 2 days before she left)

5.2 NL generation without words meaning analysis

The procedure described in this section produces written sentences in a particular language starting from formal representation of their meaning stated in term of logical predicates (units with one or more arguments) (Adorni & Massone 1987). Every predicate has a label; labels are useful in recursive units, i.e. units that take another unit as their argument. This kind of meaning representation is produced by a sentence comprehension procedure (Stock *et al*. 1983; Stock 1986) which reads NL sentences. In order to translate (lexicalize) a meaning representation (MR) into words, the procedure makes use of a dictionary. The dictionary is a list of lexical entries; each lexical entry is made up of a name and a meaning. The meaning is a list of units identical to units in MR except that literal codes replace number codes. Literal codes are introduced in the dictionary to allow a general representation of entries; these literal codes are then associated with number codes when a specific sentence is considered. The entries of the dictionary do not correspond to whole words but to a set of abstract symbols: the whole words can then be obtained by suitably combining the corresponding symbols.

The list of units of a lexical entry can be divided into semantic units (COGNI), representative of the meaning of a word, and control units (HEADS), which are not representative of the meaning of a word but which take part in the generation of the whole word starting from the MR. Some entries lack semantic units, others control units. The reason for the distinction between semantic and control units is due to the fact that semantic units refer to the meaning of a lexical entry which is independent of the language considered; the control units are, on the contrary, specific of a particular language and allow the generation of the sentences of that language. A lexical entry can contain a lexicalization request (LESS) and some tests (TEST). As an example, consider the following lexical entries in Figure 5.8. To choose the right units of the entry SEE-, all tests have to be solved. If XA is the subject, then the control units (XA (MARK NOM)) and (XB (MARK ACC)) are selected. If, on the contrary, the sentence is in the passive form, then the control unit (XB (MARK NOM)) is chosen, and the procedure of lexicalization is called in order to produce the whole word *by* and the suffix *-ed*.

```
(SEE- ((MAIN CA)                                    (GIRL- ((COGNI (CA (GIRL XA)))
       (COGNI (CA (SEE XA XB)))                              (HEADS (XA (PERS 3)))))
       (TEST (SUBJ XA)
             (HEADS ((XA (MARK NOM))
                     (XB (MARK ACC))))))           (A ((COGNI (CA (UNDEF XA)))))
       (TEST (SUBJ XB)
             (HEADS ((XB (MARK NOM))
                     (LESS (COGNI (PASS CA))       (-S ((COGNI (CA (MANY XA)))
                           (HEADS (XA (MARK BY))))))))))             (HEADS (XA (MARK PLUR)))))
```

Figure 5.8

```
((C1  (GIRL X1))
 (C2  (UNDEF X1))
 (C3  (SEE X1 X2))
 (C4  (MAIN C3))        "a girl saw the flowers"
 (C5  (PAST C3))
 (C6  (FLOWER X2))
 (C7  (MANY X2))
 (C8  (DEF X2))
 (C9  (SUBJ X1)))
```

Figure 5.9 Example of input list

The generation procedure is composed of two subparts: a lexicalization procedure (LP) and an ordering procedure (OP). LP, starting from an MR in the form previously described, produces the unordered set of words composing the final sentence. The ordered sequence of words is then produced by OP on the basis of LP results and of the original MR. The task of the ordering procedure is then to find out a correct sequential order of the words in the final sentence.

The basic operations of LP are identifying a particular unit in the input list and finding a lexical entry in the dictionary that includes that unit as part of its meaning. The choice of the lexical entry is driven by a MAXIMUM OVERLAP PRINCIPLE: 'if the dictionary includes two or more entries having that unit as part of their meaning, LP selects the entry that shares the maximum number of units with the input list'. Basically LP is a procedure specifying which lexicalizations have to be made and in which order; it is made up of ten steps.

STEP 1: lexicalizing sentences declaration.
All input lists contain one and only one unit with a C argument and the predicate MAIN (CMAIN). The first thing LP does is to identify the MAIN argument in the input list (IL) and its declarative, i.e. the unit that declares the content of the MAIN argument. In the list of Figure 5.9 (which will be considered throughout this section) the MAIN argument is C3 and its declaration is the unit (C3 (SEE X1 X2)). The corresponding lexical

entry (the root verb SEE-) is then selected from the dictionary on the basis of the semantic units and stored in a temporary memory (TM), together with the corresponding node C3. The arguments of the sentence's declaration are stored in a list (AL). In this entry a test on the subject is present which is immediately solved to select the right control units, making use of the unit (C9 (SUBJ X1)). LP verifies also if in the control units a LESS request is present (not in our example); if this is the case, another entry is selected on the basis of the LESS arguments. The LESS request can be recursive, that is it can appear also in the new entry; the selection of entries continues until an entry without LESS request is found. At the end of step 1 the situation is as follows:

IL: ((C1 (GIRL X1))   AL: (X1 X2)
    (C2 (UNDEF X1))
    (C5 (PAST C3))   TM: ((C3 SEE-))
    (C6 (FLOWER X2))
    (C7 (MANY X2))
    (C8 (DEF X2)))

STEP 2: lexicalizing the subject.

All units referring to the subject of the sentence are searched in the input list. One or more lexical entries are extracted from the dictionary using the maximum overlap principle: In this case the principle fails, and three different entries are selected, corresponding to unit (a), *GIRL*-, which is a root; unit (b), -*O*, which is a suffix; unit (c), *A*, which is a full voice. (a) and (b) are stored in TM, (c) is stored elsewhere, in a special list called word memory (WM). The suffix -*O* is then associated to the root *GIRL*-; suffix and root are then deleted from TM and a new element (C1 GIRL- -O) is added to WM. Moreover, the argument X1 is deleted from AL and units C1 and C2 are removed from IL. Here is the situation at the end of step 2:

IL: ((C5 (PAST C3))   TM: ((C3 SEE-))
    (C6 (FLOWER X2))   WM: ((C2 A)(C1 GIRL- -O))
    (C7 (MANY X2))   AL: (X2)
    (C8 (DEF X2)))

STEP 3: lexicalizing the progressive predicate, if present.

For some sentences a progressive (PROGR) predicate is present in a unit of IL. In these cases, LP lexicalizes that unit at step 3, producing in TM the suffix -*ing*. The suffix is associated in WM either to the root verb lexicalizing at step 1 (e.g. *the girl was laughing*) or to the root verb *be*- produced by a LESS request (e.g. *the girl is being nice*).

STEP 4: lexicalizing the perfect predicate, if present.
This step is devoted to the lexicalization of the PERF predicate, if IL contains it. In these cases, LP produces in TM the suffix *-ed* which is associated in WM either to the root verb lexicalized at step 1 (e.g. *the girl has laughed*) or to the root verb *be-* produced by a LESS request (e.g. *the girl has been nice*).

STEP 5: lexicalizing a finite tense, if present.
All sentences include necessarily a unit with one of the following predicates: PRES (present), PAST (past), FUT (future). Lexicalization of PRES and PAST predicates produces in TM respectively a suffix *-s* or *-O* and *-ed* which is associated in WM to a root according to the rule already used for steps 3 and 4. In our example a PAST predicate is present, a suffix *-ed* is generated and added to TM; then it is associated to the root verb SEE- and stored in WM. The PAST unit is then removed from IL. A FUT predicate, if present, is lexicalized with the whole word WILL (or SHALL).

STEP 6: lexicalizing a not finite tense, if present.
NFT (not finite tense) unit is a feature unit and it is therefore never originally present in IL: it comes out as a result of lexicalization of WILL (or SHALL). Lexicalizing a NFT unit means generating in TM a suffix *-O* which is added to the root verb lexicalized at step 1 if TM contains a root verb without suffix (e.g. *the girl will laugh*); otherwise it is associated to root verbs *be-* or *have-* generated by a LESS request (e.g. *the girl will be laughing*).

STEP 7: lexicalizing additional arguments, if present.
LP checks the content of AL. If AL is not empty, it means that additional arguments are present in IL. In our example X2 is still in AL: as a consequence step 2 is repeated for X2; all units referring to X2 are now considered, generating the root *FLOWER-*, the suffix *-S* and the whole word *A*. This step is recursive since the declaration unit can contain any number of arguments. At every recursive the analysed argument is removed from AL and the lexicalized units are removed from IL. The recursion stops when AL is empty. At the end of this step we have:

AL: NIL
TM: NIL
IL: NIL
WM: ((C21 GIRL- -O)(C2 A)(C3 SEE- -ED)(C6 FLOWER- -S)(C8 THE))

Since IL is now empty, LP for the sentence of Figure 5.9 is completed.

STEP 8: lexicalizing additional arguments of previous units, if present.
It may happen that one unit containing one argument of the sentence's
declaration includes a further argument. In this case step 8 of LP lexicalizes, in whatever order, all units referring to this argument (i.e. *the child
saw Mary's father*, the linguists referred to the end of the sentence, and so
on). Step 8 is recursive.

STEP 9: lexicalizing adverbials.
An adverbial unit is a unit that has CMAIN as argument and has not
already been lexicalized during the previous steps. The list of Figure 5.10
contains the adverbial unit (C6 (DEEP C2)), which is lexicalized with the
entry DEEPLY. Step 9 is recursive since an IL can contain more adverbial
units.

```
((C1(DOG X1))
 (C2 (SLEEP X1))
 (C3 (MAIN C2))
 (C4 (PRES C2))
 (C5 (PROGR C2))    "the dog is sleeping deeply in the garden"
 (C6 (DEEP C2))
 (C7 (IN C2 X2))
 (C8 (GARDEN X2))
 (C9 (ONE X2))
 (C10 (DEF X2))
 (C11 (DEF X1))
 (C12 (ONE X1)))
```

Figure 5.10 Example of input list with adverbial unit and additional arguments

STEP 10: lexicalizing additional arguments of adverbial units, if present.
An adverbial unit may have additional arguments besides CMAIN.
Consider, for example, unit (C7 (IN C2 X2)) of the list shown in Figure 5.9.
Step 10 is concerned with lexicalization of units in the list having these
additional arguments. These units, in turn, may contain other arguments;
in such cases something similar to step 8 is executed.

The result of LP is the word memory in which every element can be
either a whole word or a pair root-suffix. A special step of LP transforms
every pair root-suffix into a whole word according to a set of rules typical of
the language considered. This step of LP is strongly dependent on the NL
considered. In our example we will have:

((C1 GIRL)(C2 A)(C3 SAW)(C6 FLOWERS)(C8 THE))

The task of the ordering procedure is to order the words generated by
LP; for this purpose, the original meaning representation is needed. OP is
made up of two parts. The first part generates a fixed word order for each

sentence type of the target language. This assumes that all languages have an intrinsic word order, independent of the fact that in some languages (e.g. English) sentences have a rather fixed word order, while in others (e.g. Italian) they have a more variable one. In this work only this first part is considered, but OP has a second part which, starting from the fixed word order, gives as output the actual (in some languages variable) word order of the generated sentence. Whereas LP may be assumed to be 'quasi-universal', OP is language-specific or, at least, language-type-specific. In the following the ordering procedure for a specific language, i.e. English, is described. Basically, the OP examines the units in the MR in a certain order and, for each unit examined, it transfers the word linked to it from WM to a final workspace: actual sentence (AC) (Adorni & Massone 1987; Cumming 1986). Firstly, OP finds the CMAIN declaration in the sentence; OP then identifies the argument of this unit that has a NOM control unit. If IL includes a unit with this argument and DEF or UNDEF as predicate, OP moves the word linked to that unit from WM to AC and it becomes the first word of AC. Then the other words referring to the argument are moved to AC.

WM: ((C3 SAW)(C6 FLOWERS)(C8 THE))
AC: (A GIRL)

Then OP looks in IL for the FT predicate and moves the corresponding word to AC. The same operation is then performed for the predicates PERF and NFT. Then OP produces the CMAIN word if it has not yet been produced. The next step is devoted to the other arguments of the sentence's declaration, starting with the argument having an ACC unit in its lexical entry (X2 in our example). The article is generated first and then the noun:

WM: NIL
AC: (A GIRL SAW THE FLOWERS)

Then the other declaration arguments are considered and, finally, the adverbial units.

A multi-clause sentence is composed of a list of units including two or more CMAINS, each with its own declaration. The LP for multi-clause sentences must first identify the main CMAIN and apply to it the LP for one-clause sentences. During this application, the LP will encounter another CMAIN (a subordinate CMAIN). The procedure for the main CMAIN is then immediately interrupted and the LP for one-clause sentences starts all over again with reference to the subordinate CMAIN; when this task is completed, LP resumes the procedure for the main CMAIN at the point of interruption and brings it to completion. The same 'interrupt–resume' mechanism can be used to extend the ordering procedure to multi-clause sentences.

5.3 Concluding remarks

In this chapter two different approaches to the problem of natural language generation have been presented. The first approach described is strongly dependent on the particular kind of meaning representation (conceptual dependency network). This approach has been introduced anyway because of the facilities it provides for self-generation of the translation rules and the updating of the dictionary, which result in a great degree of flexibility in learning new words and redefining the conceptual representation formalism to cover new applications (Adorni *et al*. 1984b). Each discrimination tree organizes the set of tests required to select one word from among those whose meanings are based on a given primitive; all these words can be distinguished from each other by looking at the restrictions imposed on the connected conceptual cases. Hence, a different discrimination tree must be defined for each primitive. Discrimination tree generation is carried out in two steps. During the first step all the viable subgraphs which are relevant to the same discrimination tree are selected and inserted into a list. Subgraph selection is performed scanning the dictionary and looking at the conceptualization associated with each word. In the second step every subgraph list is processed to build the corresponding discrimination tree. Discrimination trees are binary trees and the building criterion is quite simple. At first, the intersection of all subgraphs is computed in order to obtain the minimal common subset of features (it is never empty, because all the subgraphs within the same list share at least the same primitive). The minimal intersection defines the set of tests associated with the root of the tree. Then the last discarded feature is selected and the set of subgraphs is subdivided into new sets, characterized respectively by the presence and absence of such a feature. This rule is applied again to every new set until all the sets obtained contain no more than one full subgraph.

The PRISE system (Adorni & DiManzo 1983), which is based on this approach, is a language generation module which accepts as input a conceptual dependency network, produced by the NAUSICA system (Adorni *et al*. 1981), describing the concepts to be uttered. The basic design constraint has been the ability of self-defining its own decision rules. Therefore, PRISE 'learns' what conceptual primitives and relationships are used to build the surface network and how Italian words can be associated with them simply by exploring the dictionary; only the knowledge related to the syntactic rules of the Italian language is embedded in the system.

The meaning representations used in the second approach do not involve any analysis of the meaning of the words. However, their format is compatible with lexical decomposition, and the procedure described accepts, without requiring modification, lexically decomposed meaning representations. The generation procedure described is composed of two subparts: a lexicalization procedure and an ordering procedure (Adorni & Massone 1987). The lexicalization procedure, starting from a meaning representation in terms of logical predicates, produces the unordered set of words composing the final sentence. The ordered sequence of words is then produced by the ordering procedure on the basis of lexicalization results and the original meaning representation. The task of the ordering procedure is then to find out the correct sequential order of the words in the final sentence. The ordering procedure is made up of two parts. The first part generates a fixed word order for each sentence type of the target language. This assumes that all languages have an intrinsic word order, independent of the fact that in some languages (e.g. English) sentences have a rather fixed word order, while in others (e.g. Italian) they have a more variable one. Whereas the lexicalization procedure may be assumed to be quasi-universal, ordering procedure is language-specific, or at least, language-type-specific. The meaning representation used in this approach is produced by the WEDNESDAY system (Stock *et al*. 1983; Stock 1986).

Bibliography

Adorni, G., Ansaldi, W., DiManzo, M. & Stringa, L. (1981), 'NAUSICA: Natural language understanding system: the Italian language case analyzed, *Rivista di Informatica*, vol. 11, 39–88.

Adorni, G. & DiManzo, M. (1981), 'PRISE: production of Italian sentences', *Proc. AICA '83*, Naples, September, pp. 389–400.

Adorni, G., DiManzo, M. & Ferrari, G. (1983), 'Natural language input for scene generation', *Proc. 1st Conference of the European Chapter of the ACL*, Pisa, September, pp. 175–82.

Adorni, G., DiManzo, M. & Giunchiglia, F. (1984a). 'From descriptions to images: what reasoning in between?', *Proc. 6th European Conference on Artificial Intelligence*, Pisa, September, pp. 359–68.

—— (1984b), 'Adaptive natural language generation', in I. Plander (ed.), *Artificial Intelligence and Information: Control Systems of Robots*, Amsterdam, Elsevier/North-Holland, pp. 77–80.

Adorni, G. & Massone, L. (1987), 'Toward a language independent generator of sentences', *Applied Artificial Intelligence*, vol. 1, 53–75.

Appelt, D. E. (1981), 'Planning natural language utterance to satisfy multiple goals', Ph.D. dissertation, Stanford University, Stanford.

Bossie, S. L. (1981), 'A tactical component for text generation using a functional grammar', Technical Report MS-CIS-81-5, University of Pennsylvania, Philadelphia.

Chomsky, N. (1957), *Syntactic Structures*, The Hague, Mouton.

Clippinger, J. H. (1975), 'Speaking with many tongues: some problems in modeling speakers of actual discourse', *Proc. TINLAP 1*, MIT, Cambridge, Mass, June, pp. 68–73.

Cohen, P. R. (1978), 'On knowing what to say: planning speech acts', Technical Report 118, University of Toronto, Toronto.

Cohen, P. R. & Perrault, C. R. (1979), 'Elements on plan based theory of speech acts', *Cognitive Science*, vol. 3, 177–212.

Cumming, S. (1986), 'The lexicon in text generation', Workshop 'On Automating the Lexicon', Marina di Grosseto, May.

DiManzo, M., Adorni, G. & Giunchiglia, F. (1986), 'Reasoning about scene descriptions', *Proceedings of the IEEE*, vol. 74, no. 7, 1013–25.

Friedman, J. (1969), Directed Random Generation of Sentences, *Communications of the ACM*, vol. 12, no. 6, 40–6.

Genot, G. (1973), *Grammaire de l'Italien*, Paris, Presses Universitaires de France.

Goldman, N. M. (1975), 'Conceptual generation', in R. C. Schank (ed.), *Conceptual Information Processing*, Amsterdam, North-Holland.

Grishman, R. (1979), 'Response generation in question-answering systems', *Proc. 17th Annual Meeting of the ACL*, La Jolla, pp. 99–101.

Habel, C., Schimt, A. & Schweppe, H. (1977), 'On automatic paraphrasing of natural language expressions', Technical Report 3/17, Semantic Network Project, Technische Universität, Berlin.

Hasida, K. & Isizaky, S. (1987), 'Dependency propagation: a unified theory of sentence comprehension and generation', *Proc. 10th International Joint Conference on Artificial Intelligence*, Milan, August, pp. 664–8.

Herskovits, A. (1973), 'The generation of French from semantic structure', Technical Report 212, Stanford Artificial Intelligence Laboratory, Stanford.

Hovy, E. H. (1985), 'Integrating text planning and production in generation', *Proc. 9th International Joint Conference on Artificial Intelligence*, Los Angeles, August, pp. 848–51.

Kempen, G. (1978), 'Sentence construction by a psychologically plausible formulator', in R. Campbell and P. Smith (eds), *Recent Advances in the Psychology of Language, Vol. 2: Formal and Experimental Approaches*, New York, Plenum Press.

— (1987), 'A framework for incremental syntactic tree formation', *Proc. 10th International Joint Conference on Artificial Intelligence*, Milan, August, pp. 655–60.

Kempen, G. & Hoenkamp, E. (1987), 'An incremental procedural grammar for sentence formulation', *Cognitive Sciences*, vol. 11, no. 2.

Klein, S. (1965), 'Automatic Paraphrasing in Essay Format', *Mechanical Translation*, vol. 8, no. 3, 68–83.

Lytinen, S. (1986), 'Dynamically combining syntax and semantics in natural language processing', *Proc. 5th National Conference on Artificial Intelligence*, Philadelphia, August.

McDonald, D. D. (1980), 'Natural language production as a process of decision making under constraint', Ph.D. dissertation, MIT, Cambridge, Mass.

McKeown, K. R. (1981), 'Generating natural language text in response to questions about data-base structure', Ph.D. dissertation, University of Pennsylvania.

Schank, R. C. (1975), *Conceptual Information Processing*, Amsterdam, North-Holland.

Shapiro, S. C. (1979), 'Generalized augmented transition network grammar for generation from semantic networks', *Proc. 17th Annual Meeting of the ACL*, La Jolla, pp. 25–9.

Shieber, S. M. (1985), 'An introduction to unification approaches to grammar', Tutorial Session, 23rd Annual Meeting of the ACL, Chicago, July.

Simmons, R. & Slocum, J. (1971), 'Generating English discourse from semantic networks', *Communications of the ACM*, vol. 15, 891–905.

Stock, O. (1986), 'Dynamic unification in lexically based parsing', *Proc. 7th European Conference on Artificial Intelligence*, Brighton, July, pp. 212–21.

Stock, O., Castelfranchi, C. & Parisi, D. (1983), 'WEDNESDAY: parsing flexible word order languages', *Proc. 1st Conference of the European Chapter of the ACL*, Pisa, September, pp. 106–10.

Waltz, D. L. (1978), 'An English question-answering system for a large relational data-base', *Communications of the ACM*, vol. 21, no. 7.

Weizenbaum, J. (1966), 'ELIZA: a computer program for the study of natural language communication between man and machine', *Communications of the ACM*, vol. 9, 36–45.

Wilks, J. A. (1973), 'An artificial intelligence approach to machine translation', in K. M. Colby (ed.), *Computer Models of Thought and Language*, San Francisco, Freeman, pp. 114–51.

Winograd, T. (1972), *Understanding Natural Language*, New York, Academic Press.

Wong, H. K. T. (1975), 'Generating English sentences from semantic structures', Technical Report 84, Dept. of Computer Science, University of Toronto, Toronto.

Woods, W. A., Kaplan, R. & Nash-Webber, B. (1972), 'The lunar sciences natural language information system: final report', BBN Report 2378, Bolt Beranek & Newman Inc., Cambridge, Mass.

6 The production of spoken dialogue

GEORGE HOUGHTON AND MARK PEARSON*

6.0 Introduction: motivation and aims

This chapter describes certain aspects of a computational model of the production of spoken language in a simple conversational domain. At the most general level the model attempts to integrate the study of language production into the more general study of purposeful activity. Language is seen as a tool for achieving communicative goals, these goals themselves arising from attempts to achieve higher-level goals. Even the most highly simplified theory of dialogue inevitably involves the interaction of many components and sources of knowledge (knowledge of the world, the addressee, the current discourse, linguistic knowledge and so on) of sufficient complexity that a computer model becomes the only practical way of testing its predictions in any detail. In this work we have attempted to design the relevant components so that they are each of interest in their own right, and so that they will fit together to accomplish the overall task of producing utterances which effectively convey a particular message in a particular context of discourse. As a whole, the model may be taken as a minimum specification of the type of resources required to produce spoken dialogue.

In contrast with this work, most computational models of language generation concentrate on the production of printed monologues (e.g. Davey 1978; McDonald 1983; Mann 1983; McKeown 1985; and many chapters in the current volume). This emphasis on written text, as opposed to spoken dialogue, the usual form of human language production, means that many of what must be considered the central problems of language generation remain barely explored. On the one hand, the production of printed output allows one to ignore the numerous problems inherent in speech generation, in particular the use of intonation, accentuation and rhythm, and the interaction of these factors with the segmental properties

* Experimental Psychology, University of Sussex, Falmer, Brighton, UK

of utterances. On the other hand, the generation of monologues does not require the study of what one might roughly designate 'co-operative dialogue management'. This subsumes a whole variety of issues such as the need to take into account what other speakers say (and how they say it); the representation of past dialogue and its influence on new utterances; the usefulness of notions such as dialogue game and speech acts and the control of 'illocutionary force' and the use of 'indirect speech acts'. For instance, monologue generators characteristically produce sequences of the same kind of sentence, so the problem of choice of dialogue move or speech act type does not arise. (Generally declaratives are produced, though instruction generators produce a series of imperatives.) Dialogue generators, on the other hand, must know when and how to ask questions, make requests, offer suggestions, give orders, etc., and also how to respond to such moves (cf. Cohen 1978; Power 1979; Allen & Perrault 1980; Allen 1983). It is well known that the use of many syntactic, lexical and prosodic devices can only be understood in relation to factors present in spoken dialogue, where the speaker is addressing his or her remarks to a co-present other in a shared situational and conversational context. (See, for instance, Givon (1979). Gazdar (1980) discusses a wide variety of discourse-related pragmatic constraints on production.) Moreover, in English at least, the existence of prosodic options affects syntactic and lexical choices. Consider the following dialogues. (The word in upper case in the second utterance of each pair indicates the location of the nuclear pitch accent. The type of pitch movement used (according to the model described later in the chapter) is given in parentheses):

(1) (a) Does Jack live here?
    (b) He DOES.   (FALL)
(2) (a) Jack lives here.
    (b) He DOES?   (HIGH RISE)
(3) (a) Who lives here?
    (b) HE does.   (FALL)

Utterances (1b) and (2b) are syntactically and lexically identical yet have quite different discourse roles, which are conveyed by the choice of pitch accent on *does*. The point is that the choice of the words *He does* in each case only makes sense if the grammatical system somehow 'knows' that intonational devices are available to convey the speaker's intended meaning. Dialogue (3) illustrates the same point in relation to accent placement. The same words are used again, but to quite different effect, the deictic emphasis being realized by the placement of the nuclear fall (the same accent as is used in dialogue (1)). There is nothing 'natural' about this use of prosody; it is a purely conventional feature of English. (The reader might like to consider how the (b) utterances in each dialogue might be expressed in, say, French.)

The remainder of the chapter outlines some components of a computer model of spoken dialogue which the authors (along with Steve Isard) have been working on at Sussex.[1] Section 6.1 gives a general overview and Section 6.2 provides rather brief descriptions of the syntactic and prosodic components of the model.

6.1 Outline of the model

To make some headway in this area, we have used a type of model first developed by Richard Power (see Power 1974, 1979) in which two 'actors' inhabiting a simple micro-world co-operate to achieve simple, practical goals. The particular world we use in this work (an elaboration of Power's) consists of two spaces, IN and OUT, separated by 4 DOORS of different colours. These doors may be OPEN or CLOSED and in addition each door has a BOLT which may be UP or DOWN. The world also contains a number of BLOCKS of different sizes, shapes and colours which can be picked up and carried around. The goals that the two actors, named Fred and Doris, attempt to achieve involve changing the positions of objects in the world (including themselves). In the course of building and executing plans to achieve these goals the actors may need to help each other, for instance, to obtain information or to get certain tasks performed. It is at these points, where communication between the separate actors is required, that conversation arises.

To illustrate this we provide a dialogue produced by the system described in Houghton (1986). (The linguistic output of this system is tree structures with phonologically specified words on the leaves. In this example the output has been transcribed into written English.) In this dialogue, Doris and Fred are both in. Doris wants a particular block, which Fred is holding, to be out. She thinks Fred can move, but he can't. Doris can't push doors, and believes that you get to be holding something by being handed it.

Doris — Fred.
Fred — Yes.
Doris — I want the small blue block to be out.
Fred — I see.
Doris — Can you push?
Fred — Yes.
Doris — Could you push the green door?
Fred — OK.

Doris   —   Go through it.
Fred   —   No, Because I can't move.

[At this point Doris has to change her plan (for Fred to go through a door while holding the block) so that she is the agent and not Fred. The preconditions of the revised plan are then tested. A door is open but she is not holding the block.]

Doris   —   Hand the small blue block over to me.
Fred   —   OK.

[Doris goes through the door with the block which is now out. Her goal is achieved and the system therefore terminates.]

In this model the production of ordinary discourse is viewed as being organized on three levels. At the highest level, a conversation is generally ABOUT something and appears to be the expression of some kind of purpose understood by the participants. Each 'turn' in the discourse is related somehow to this overall purpose and gains its relevance by virtue of the contribution it makes towards achieving the purpose of the interaction (Grice 1967).

Within this gross structure, a conversation can be seen as a repetitive sequence of 'turn-taking'. Thus there is a level of 'exchange pairs' or 'dialogue games' where one participant opens an exchange and defines its type and the other is expected to respond in an appropriate manner (Power, 1979; Goffman 1981; Stubbs 1983; Levinson 1983; Wunderlich 1980).

Finally at the third level, there is the individual utterance. Here the speaker has a particular intended message (a 'communicative intention') in mind and a goal which the expression of this message is intended to help achieve (for instance, she may wish to get something done, to find something out, or to make known a promise). The speaker's task at this level is to express her intended message in the language which the participants are using.

It will be clear that, as we move from problems concerning the first level down to those at the third, we move from the general domain of purposeful human activity down to the specifically linguistic domain. The program described here reflects this hierarchy in the structure of behaviour. Its overall organization is diagrammed below (Figure 6.1). In the boxes on the left (under the heading 'PROCESSES') are the types of planning activity involved at each level followed by their role in the organization of the participant's actions. In the boxes on the right, there is first the kind of long-term knowledge required at each level (which the associated processes have access to) and then the kind of short-term structures which must be built (by reference to long-term knowledge) in the generation of

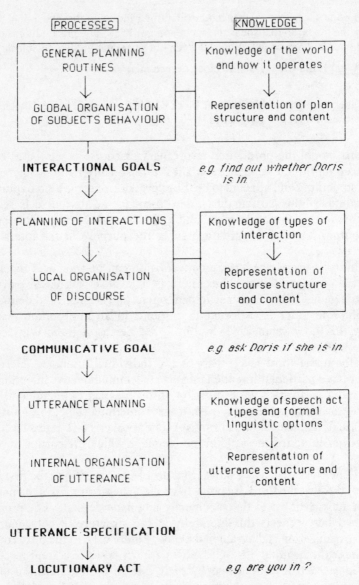

Figure 6.1 The organization of the model

specific acts. Between the process modules there are labels suggesting the kind of information which is passed from one level to the next to activate processes at that level. No more will be said in this chapter concerning levels 1 and 2; the interested reader is referred to Houghton (1986) and Houghton & Isard (1987).

6.2 Producing spoken utterances

6.2.1 *Segmental generation*

The generation of the segmental form of utterances in this system is due to the model described in Houghton (1986), which produces dialogues such as that shown above. In the model, the speaker is seen as using the resources available in his or her language to achieve particular communicative or expressive tasks. Thus, as well as representing the resources themselves, we must also model the act of choice amongst the behavioural options defined by these resources. Apart from the semantic content of a given communicative intention, various other kinds of information influence the course of generation. For instance, many forms in human languages are responsive to dynamic aspects of the discourse context. For the correct use of anaphorical devices and other varieties of referring expression one requires, at the least, knowledge of the state of the discourse, what things have been mentioned and in what connection, and some idea of what one's addressee knows about (cf. Bosch 1983; Clark & Haviland 1977; Clark & Marshall 1981; Rochester & Martin 1977). In addition, information from the language itself often plays a crucial role. A common example is the agreement of, say, determiners and adjectives, with the grammatical 'gender' of a co-occurring noun and the agreement of a pronoun with the gender of the WORD for the class of its referent.[2]

In this work, the making of the required linguistic decisions is modelled as the process of traversing sets of system networks, a network representing a set of interrelated and interdependent options (as described in Systemic Grammar, e.g. Halliday & Martin 1981). (Systemic Grammar was first exploited in automatic language generation by Tony Davey (Davey 1978) in a system which describes the progress of games of noughts and crosses.) Each network is associated with some phrasal category (NP, VP, etc.) of the grammar (see below) and discriminates amongst the range of options defined by the expansions of that category. The set of networks constitutes the interface between the language faculty and the rest of the language user's 'cognitive space'. Which decisions need to be made depends on the language being produced,[3] and the detailed form of networks must be related in some way to the organization of the grammar which affects the realization of the choices made in traversing a network.

Networks generate sets of features, any legal set constituting the record of a path through the network (the features label arcs in the network and a given feature is generated when the arc it labels is crossed). A set of features thus represents a set of linguistically meaningful decisions. The structural realization of these decisions is determined by the substantive linguistic resources available. In this model, these consist of the syntactic component (the 'rules of grammar'), the lexical and morphological component, and the prosodic component. The form of syntactic component is based on work in generalized phrase structure grammar (Gazdar, Klein, Pullum & Sag 1985). In particular, the grammar

(a) is context-free;
(b) makes considerable use of 'complex symbols';
(c) uses 'Linear Precedence' (LP) rules to define word order over sets of rules (individual productions defining only 'immediate dominance' relationships);
(d) associates semantic rules with syntactic rules. (In production we begin with the meaning of some constituent and have to divide up the job of expressing that meaning amongst sub-constituents. We might therefore talk of rules of 'decompositional semantics'—the inverse of the more familiar compositional semantics.)

The expansions in the grammar are themselves fairly complex objects allowing the specification of 'optional' constituents. Along with the use of LP rules and feature variables which are bound from the output of the networks this allows for considerable economy of expression. (More detailed discussion of the form and use of these devices is provided in Houghton 1986).

At first glance, this coupling of systemic networks with a GPSG-like grammar may seem a little odd, but in fact is perfectly natural, on both general and specific grounds. The purpose of systemic networks is to lay out the paradigmatic options available in a language and to illustrate the relations and interdependencies between them. Since any interesting generation model has to make choices amongst the possibilities it defines somehow, the transition-network formalism of SFG might just as well be used, at least in a descriptive capacity, to show what options the model postulates and how they are related (supposing the model does relate them). This can be an aid both to exposition and to comparison between models. More specifically though, GPSG is heavily dependent on feature-based complex symbols. The values of the features which make up a given legal node constrain the set of contexts in which that node can legitimately occur (its 'admissibility conditions'). In terms of production, the feature specification of a node determines the form of its expansion and thus the selection of a given structure is equivalent to the generation of the complex symbol dominating that structure (assuming no free variation within the grammar itself). Since complex symbols are made up of feature specifications, the use of systemic networks to generate the required specification is quite natural. (The compatibility of different linguistic formalisms is often obscured by notational parochialism. Recent work in linguistic metatheory, however, should make it easier to compare and contrast different theories and to make clear underlying similarities. See, for example, Gazdar, Pullum, Carpenter, Klein, Hukari & Levine 1986.)

This scheme is illustrated in Figure 6.2. The box labelled 'Expressive Goal' represents the meaning which the constituent being planned is to convey. The nature of this meaning will of course be different for different constituents. In the derivation of an utterance this sequence of steps will generally occur a number of times. For instance, if the structure chosen the first time through contains a noun phrase, the sequence starts again, at a new level, making noun phrase decisions in order to select a noun phrase structure. Generation is strictly left-to-right with no backtracking, and no transformation or deletion of an already built structure. The box labelled

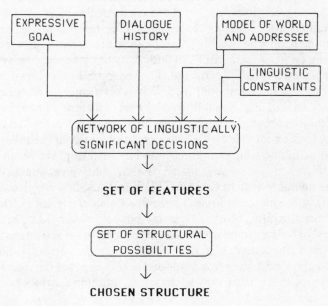

Figure 6.2

'Linguistic Constraints' indicates that generation of syntactic and morphological forms is constrained by lexical information (particularly from content words) and also by decisions already made in earlier parts of the utterance. The need to take lexical constraints (grammatical selection restrictions, lexical gender, etc.) into account before the words determining the constraints are placed in the tree means that generation cannot be achieved in a strictly 'top–down' manner with lexical access occurring only when a lexical node is generated (further discussion of this problem with range of examples is given in Houghton).

As an illustration of this aspect of the model, consider in Figure 6.3 the fragment of network and associated immediate dominance (ID) and linear precedence rules (the ID rule is actually a simplification of one used in the program which also handles relative clauses as a sub-variety of sentence).

In the network diagram the choice points ('OR' nodes) are represented by square cornered brackets, and the labels (features) within the brackets represent the options available at that point. For instance, at node (4) the choice of active or passive voice is made. Oblique cornered nodes (e.g. (1) and (9)) represent 'AND' nodes from which all paths must be taken (since no choice is made, no feature is generated). Arrows indicate further nodes which must be accessed if a particular featural choice is made. So, for instance, the choice of INTERROG at (6) leads to a division between WH and INV at (7), both of which lead to further options. Trailing dots indicate that the network continues or that there are further choices within a node.

The example rule contains three fields. The first labels the rule with subsets of the features derivable from the sentence network. If a set of features produced from the network includes any of these sets (the symbol '|' means 'or'), then this rule is activated. The second field specifies obligatory sub-constituents. Each symbol (in angle brackets) consists of a grammatical category symbol (e.g. NP) followed by a set of features. Those in uppercase are feature constants (values), those in lower-case feature variables (or attributes) looking for values. On some occasion of use of the rule the variables may be bound from the values found in the feature set which caused this rule to be activated. For instance, the variable 'voice' attached to the VP will be bound to whichever of ACTIVE or PASSIVE has been chosen at node (4) in the network. Field 3 specifies a disjunctive set of additional symbols tagged with features. The arrow symbol '→' should be read as 'is realized by' or 'causes to be produced'. If the feature set activating the rule includes the features on the left of the arrow, then the corresponding symbol (right-hand side of the arrow) is added to the output of the rule. In more complex rules more than one such set of additional symbols may be present.

The rule itself specifies no ordering of the constituents producible from

Fragment of Sentence Network

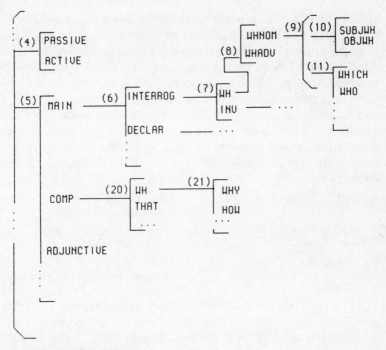

Example grammar rule

SR 1)
  (i)   [DECLAR ACTIVE] | [DECLAR PASSIVE]
        | [COMP] | [ADJUNCTIVE]

  (ii)   <NP (NOM num pers)> < VP (H FIN num pers voice) >

  (iii) { [COMP THAT] → < comp (THAT) >
      | [ADJUNCTIVE] → < advconj (conjtype)>
      | [COMP WH]   → < adv (WH whtype) > }

LP rule

[comp advconj verb (INV) adv] < [NP] < [neg] < [AP PP VP S]

Figure 6.3 Fragment of sentence network

it. This is done by the LP rule which has the form of an ordered sequence of lists of symbols, successive lists separated by the symbol '<' meaning 'comes before'. For an LP rule consisting of n lists, any symbol in a chosen expansion occurring in a list Li, $1 \leq i \leq n$, will be placed before any chosen symbol occurring in a list Lj for i < j. If two chosen symbols occur in the same list, then the order of the two with respect to each other is not stipulated.

The examples provided below illustrate the coordination of network and rule. The single-shaft arrow is used as above (feature realization). The LHS of the arrow gives a (partial) specification of a legal (generable) feature set and the RHS the structure generated (after ordering). The symbol '*⇒' means '(could) eventually generate' and is followed by an example sentence illustrating the structure in question. The feature [MAIN] indicates a matrix (root) clause. [COMP] indicates an embedded (non-root) S, and [ADJUNCTIVE] a sentential adjunct. The realizations of all varieties of these structures are conflated in SR 1. The basic constituents are {NP, VP} and these may be supplemented by any of the additional constituents given in the rule.

(1) [... MAIN DECLAR ACTIVE ...]   → NP(...) VP(ACTIVE ...)
                                     *⇒ 'I want you to be out'

(2) [... COMP THAT ...]   → comp(THAT) NP(...) VP(...)
                                     ⇒ '... that you are out'

(3) [... COMP WH HOW ...]   → adv(WH HOW) NP(...) VP(...)
                                     *⇒ '(Do you know) how you get a bolt
                                        to move'

(4) [... ADJUNCTIVE CAUSAL ...]   → advconj(CAUSAL) NP(...) VP(...)
                                     *⇒ 'because the bolt isn't up'

(5) [... PASSIVE ADJUNCTIVE ...]   → advconj(...) NP(...) VP(PASSIVE ...)
                                     *⇒ 'If a block is picked up'

6.2.2 *Speech generation*

In this section we describe briefly a system for generating intonation contours. This is just one aspect of what has to be done to convert the output of the segmental component into a sayable form, and nothing will be said here about rhythm and duration (but see Isard (1982)). Lack of space constrains us to providing only the barest outline of the system and precludes any detailed theoretical discussion of the function of accent placement and intonation in English. (The reader interested in finding out what some of the problems and approaches are in this area might consult, for instance, Bolinger (1972 a, b); Cooper & Sorensen (1981); Cruttenden (1986); Cutler & Isard (1980); Cutler & Ladd (1983); Gussenhoven (1984); Ladd (1980, 1983); Pierrehumbert (1981); Selkirk (1984).)

The input to the prosodic component is a syntactic tree structure with phonological words on the leaves. The tree is annotated with focus information on noun phrases. (This information is generated during the construction of the tree and used in determining the syntactic form of the

NP. It is left behind as it has implications for accent placement.) The trees produced by the grammar have a fair degree of embedding (particularly right branching), much of it apparently useless as far as planning prosodic form is concerned.[4] The first task undertaken at this stage is to restructure the syntactic tree into an 'accent domain' tree. The two basic processes used are (i) node deletion, whereby the daughters of a node N become daughters of the mother of N, and N disappears; and (ii) node raising, whereby a node (and all sisters to its right) are made right sisters of their mother. As an example of it (i), pre-nominal adjectives are produced by the grammar as part of an AP. At this stage, the AP is deleted, and its daughters are immediately dominated by NP. As an example of (ii), relative clauses (a sub-variety of S) are moved out of NPs, embedded Ss are moved out of VPs. These actions are recursive, and a given node (more precisely, sub-tree) can be gradually passed up the tree. Thus a sentence of the form *This is the cat that ate the rat that swallowed the spider that . . .* , etc., will end up with all the relative clauses as sisters, which provides the appropriate boundaries for the intonation.

These operations typically produce a much flatter structure than the original tree. Its constituents are now 'accept domains', this being a meaningful sub-unit which will contain at least one acceptable word. This flatter structure is then used for assigning prominence levels to the words in the utterance (which ultimately translate into syllabic prominence). There are four levels of relative syllabic prominence which affect both the duration of the syllable and the possibility of pitch excursions involving that syllable.

LEVEL

0 — minimally stressed syllables
e.g. AN apple

1 — unreduced syllables
e.g. bootLACE

2 — stressed syllables
e.g. BOOTlace

3 — accented syllables
e.g. tie your BOOTlace

Type 3 prominence is assigned to words by reference to the informational and syntactic structure of the utterance. It is realized on the main stressed syllable (specified in the lexicon) of the accented word. At this point, certain closed class words (pronouns, determiners, etc.), if they have not been assigned stress above level 0, may be phonomically reduced, for instance the infinitival particle *to* (/tu/) would be reduced to /ta/ (where 'a' = schwa).

In the final sections we briefly describe the part of the model which converts the prosodic description into an actual pitch contour. This involves principally: the selection pitch accent types for accented syllables; the structure of the abstract pitch space; the form of contours within this space; the generation of an abstract contour and finally its translation into Hertz values to be written into the phonemic substance of the utterance.

6.2.2.1 *Abstract specification of contours*   We are currently working on the idea that type of pitch movement can to some extent be determined by reference to the role the utterance plays in the dialogue. For instance, the utterance may be an initiating move, a continuation move (predictable or in some way problematic, say questioning an assumption), a closing utterance or an interruption. It may also be an assertion, a request, a refusal and so on. An assessment of the role of the utterance and its place in the dialogue leads to the selection of a nuclear 'pitch accent' of a particular type, as illustrated in the dialogues at the beginning of the chapter. Utterances often contain notable pitch changes not necessarily associated with the 'nuclear' tone; however, we believe there to be a smaller set of these than there are nuclear accents.

An utterance contour is made up of one or more tone groups and a tone group is a string of pitch accents ending with a nuclear or tonic accent, as is generally assumed within the British intonational tradition (Crystal 1969; Halliday 1967). These pitch accents are associated with particular words, and thereby with particular syllables which are known as accented syllables.

The specification of an accent comes in two parts—accent type and accent level. Levels are explained below. The accent types we have available are the following:

Nuclear:	Fall
	Rise–fall
	Level
	Fall–rise
	Low rise
	High rise
Pre-nuclear:	Fall
	Level
	Low rise

All accents start at the beginning of the vowel in the accented syllable, and end at the beginning of the next accent (if they are pre-nuclear), or at the following tone group or utterance boundary (if they are nuclear). There is one proviso to the above, however, which is that in the case of a rising-tailed nuclear accent the tail itself is not determined relative to the very end of the final syllable in the tone group when that syllable ends in voiceless consonants: if it were the rise might well occur (abstractly) during voiceless consonants and thus be lost. In these cases, then, the effective endpoint of thé contour is aligned with the end of voicing in the final syllable. Falls are allowed merely to fall from a peak towards the baseline (bottom of the pitch range, see below), with no guarantee they will reach the baseline before the end of voicing.

6.2.2.2 *Pitch domain*   The pitch domain is the space in which intonational gestures are planned in response to the information (including accent types) given in the prosodic description. It is a theoretical abstraction, a hypothetical level of representation existing between the prosodic description and the actual spoken utterance. It is thus intended to capture what we believe to be the communicatively and linguistically significant aspects of the form of intonation contours, and abstracts away from a number of speaker-dependent parameters and noise sources which affect the form of the final spoken utterance. We would emphasize that it is not an implementational detail, but a necessary component of any model of speech production.

The pitch domain is a two-dimensional space, with time along the x axis, and 'pitch height' along the y axis. Although we have different options available within the implemented system, we prefer to generate contours on an equal interval log Hertz (Hz) scale rather like a musical stave (i.e. the y axis is non-linear in Hertz). The interval size is specified in semitones and can be varied, thus varying the overall pitch range and allowing the absolute size of pitch excursions to vary in realizing the same kind of pitch movement. Larger excursions (wider intervals) produce a subjective impression of greater 'involvement' in what is being said. The pitch range has a floor, or baseline, which counts as zero pitch height and the contour is scaled above this. A pitch specified as being at a pitch height of level n will be n intervals above the baseline. In principle, an indefinite number of levels above the baseline could be used, within the bounds of articulatory possibility. In practice, the highest level we use is level 3.

The baseline is not level over an utterance, but becomes gradually lower in an attempt to model the effects of the process known as 'declination', an observed overall downdrift in fundamental frequency envelopes during the course of utterances.[5] As the baseline gradually declines, the integer pitch level 'stave' declines in parallel (in log Hz space) above it. A given 'abstract' pitch movement (say a fall from level 3) will be executed in the same way at any point in the utterance. Since the stave is falling this will translate into a lower actual starting and end pitch as the utterance progresses. Furthermore, though the stave is parallel in pitch space, it clearly narrows in frequency (Hz) space as it falls. Consequently a pitch movement executed later in an utterance will produce a smaller absolute change in frequency than the same movement produced earlier, though their abstract specifications in the pitch space will be the same. We have various options available for the shape of the baseline, the one we generally use being a negative exponential curve falling between stipulated start and end pitches. The rate of the fall obviously changes, becoming smaller as the utterance progresses.

The pitch level of an accented syllable will range from high (3), typically the level for a falling pitch accent, to low (0), which will typically be used for a low rise. This will interact with the interval size, so that a level 3 accent will be 9 semitones above the baseline if the interval size is 3, 6 above if the interval size is 2. Since the pitch range is variable, it makes sense to be able correspondingly to vary the rates of the rise and fall in pitch accents. These rates are generated by multiplying the interval size (semitones) by appropriate values for rate of pitch change (intervals per second) to get rates of pitch change expressed in semitones per second.

6.2.2.3 *Contour generation*   The generation of the intonation contour takes place in four stages, as follows. The first two stages constitute the planning stage and relate to the abstract, linguistically conventional level of representation sketched above. The last three constitute the purely phonetic execution phase.

Contour planning

1: The determination from input parameters of the pitch range and the values of the accent targets in semitones above the baseline, and the positions, rates and durations of the pitch movements.

2: The generation of the contour as a succession of straight-line segments in the pitch space.

Contour execution

3: Conversion of the contour to one specified in Hz values.

4: 7-point smoothing—each point in the contour has its value replaced by the mean value of itself and the six surrounding points, producing a more naturally curved contour shape. This COULD be given an empirical interpretation as corresponding to mechanical effects in the vocal tract, which can be expected to apply to discrete and abrupt instructions for pitch change.

5: Micro-intonation and devoicing—this models the effect of particular phonetic segments on the fundamental frequency contour. For instance, the contour drops sharply before voiceless stops and after initial voice-less stops and fricatives. During unvoiced segments the frequency is set to 0.

After the pitch and duration algorithms have completed their tasks, the utterance is converted into a waveform array by means of diphone-based speech synthesizer.

The complete process of utterance production, beginning with the input message and ending with a waveform, is summarized in Figure 6.4.

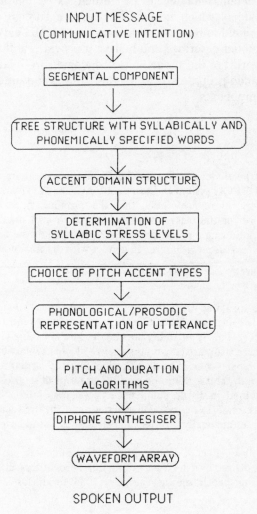

Figure 6.4

6.3 Conclusion

Both as a psychological and practical problem, the production of spoken discourse is central to the study of language generation. The problems involved are immense, encompassing most of theoretical linguistics and phonetics as well as such areas as conversational analysis (Levinson, 1983) knowledge representation and planning. The only feasible strategy, as far as producing detailed models is concerned, is to begin with simple, manageable systems which nevertheless involve enough of the central problems of the field to be of more general interest. We have attempted to do this in the model described and believe it provides both an interesting overall framework for the modelling of dialogue production as well as containing detailed proposals as to the functioning and interactions of the various sub-components.

Notes

1. All aspects of the model described in the chapter have been implemented using the Sussex POPLOG system and run on a DEC Vax 11/780.
2. One might say, more accurately, that the pronoun must agree with the particular word for the class which the speaker has in mind. For instance, compare the following French utterances, which might be said of the same object (the upper-case words agree in gender with the final noun)

(1) Qu'ELLE est BELLE, CETTE maison.
(2) Qu'IL est BEAU, CE batiment.

3. For instance, speaking English properly requires one to manage the use of continuous (*be v-ing*) and perfective (*have v-ed*) aspect (and their interaction with each other). This is an ability not required for speaking German.
4. The original tree structure constitutes a *record* of what syntactic structures were used and in what order. The justification for this structure thus rests on syntactic grounds, and is not to be justified in terms of its prosodic value. It is built and retained in all its detail because (a) it is interesting to see what structure is assigned to a given construction; and (b) the recursive algorithm used builds it automatically and special instructions would have to be built in to prevent it.
5. This is possibly an effect of (among other things) a decrease in the rate of trans-glottal airflow caused by a decrease in subglottal pressure as air gradually leaves the lungs during speech (see e.g. Vaissière (1983) for discussion).

Bibliography

Allen, J. F. (1983), 'Argot: a system overview', in N. J. Cercone (ed.), *Computational Linguistics*, Oxford, Pergamon Press.

Allen, J. F. & Perrault, C. R. (1980), 'Analysing intention in utterances', *Artificial Intelligence*, vol. 15.

Bolinger, D. (1972a), 'Accent is predictable (if you're a mind reader)', *Language*, vol. 48, 633–44.

— (ed.) (1972b), *Intonation: Selected Readings*, London, Penguin.

Bosch, P. (1983), *Agreement and Anaphora: A Study of the Role of Pronouns in Syntax and Discourse*, London, Academic Press.

Clark, H. H. & Haviland, S. E. (1977), 'Comprehension and the given—new contract', in Freedle, R. O. (ed.), *Discourse Processes, Vol. 1: Advances in Research and Theory*, New Jersey, Ablex.

Clark, H. H. & Marshall, C. R. (1981), 'Definite reference and mutual knowledge', in A. K. Joshi, B. L. Webber & I. A. Sag (eds), *Elements of Discourse Understanding*.

Cohen, P. R. (1978), 'On knowing what to say: planning speech acts', unpublished Ph.D. thesis, Dept. of Computer Science, University of Toronto.

Cruttenden, A. (1986), *Intonation*, Cambridge, Cambridge University Press.

Crystal, D. (1969), *Prosodic Systems and Intonation in English*, Cambridge, Cambridge University Press.

Cutler, A. & Isard, S. D. (1980), 'The production of prosody, in B. Butterworth (ed.), *Language Production, Vol. 1.: Speech and Talk*, New York, Academic Press.

Cutler, A. & Ladd, D. (eds) (1983), *Prosody: Models and Measurements*, Heidelberg, Springer-Verlag.

Davey, A. (1978), *Discourse Production: A Computer Model of Some Aspects of a Speaker*, Edinburgh, Edinburgh University Press.

Gazdar, G. (1980), 'Pragmatic constraints on linguistic production', in B. Butterworth (ed.), *Language Production, Vol. 1: Speech and Talk*, New York, Academic Press.

Gazdar, G., Klein, E., Pullum, G. K. & Sag, I. (1985), *Generalized Phrase Structure Grammar*, Oxford, Basil Blackwell.

Gazdar, G., Pullum, G. K., Carpenter, R., Klein, E., Hukari, T. & Levine, R. (1986), 'Category structures', CSRP 71, Cognitive studies program, University of Sussex (revised version in *Computational Linguistics*, vol. 14, no. 1, 1988).

Givon, T. (1979), *Discourse and Syntax: Syntax and Semantics 12*, London, Academic Press.

Goffman, E. (1981), 'Replies and responses', in E. Goffman (ed.), *Forms of Talk*, Oxford, Basil Blackwell.

Grice, P. (1967), 'Logic and conversation', unpublished MS of the William James Lecture, Harvard University.

Gussenhoven, C. (1984), *On the Grammar and Semantics of Sentence Accents*, Dordrecht, Foris.

Halliday, M. A. K. (1967), *Intonation and Grammar in British English*, The Hague, Mouton.

Halliday, M. A. K. & Martin, J. R. (eds) (1981), *Readings in Systemic Linguistics*, London, Batsford.

Houghton, G. (1986), 'The production of language in dialogue: a computational model', D.Phil. thesis, University of Sussex.

—— (forthcoming), *A Computational Model of Discourse Production*, New Jersey, Ablex.

Houghton, G. & Isard, S. D. (1987), 'Why to speak, what to say and how to say it: modelling language production in discourse', in P. Morris (ed.), *Modelling Cognition*, Chichester, Wiley.

Isard, S. D. (1982), 'The synthesis of rhythmic structure', Proceedings of the Institute of Acoustics 1982.

Ladd, D. R. (1980), *The Structure of Intonational Meaning: Evidence from English*. Bloomington, Indiana, Indiana University Press.

—— (1983) 'Even focus and normal stress', *Journal of Semantics*, vol. 2.

Levinson, S. C. (1983), *Pragmatics*, Cambridge, Cambridge University Press.

McDonald, D. D. (1983), 'Natural language generation as a computational problem: an introduction', in M. Brady & R. C. Berwick (eds), *Computational Models of Discourse*, Cambridge, Mass., MIT Press.

McKeown, K. R. (1985), *Text Generation*, Cambridge, Cambridge University Press.

Mann, W. C. (1983), 'A linguistic overview of the Nigel Text Generation Grammar', USC ISI Technical Report RS-83-9.

Pierrehumbert, J. (1981), 'Synthesizing intonation', *Journal of the Accoustical Society of America*, vol. 70, 985–95.

Power, R. (1974), 'A computer model of conversation', unpublished Ph.D. thesis, University of Edinburgh.

—— (1979), 'The organization of purposeful dialogues', *Linguistics*, vol. 17.

Rochester, S. R. & Martin, J. R. (1977), 'The art of referring: the speaker's use of noun phrases to instruct the listener', in R. Freedle (ed.), *Discourse Processes: Advances in Research and Theory*, New Jersey, Ablex.

Selkirk, E. O. (1984), *Phonology and Syntax: The Relation between Sound and Structure*, Cambridge, Mass., MIT Press.

Stubbs, M. (1983), *Discourse Analysis: The Sociolinguistic Nature of Natural Language*, Oxford, Basil Blackwell.

Vaissière, J. (1983), 'Language independent prosodic features', in A. Cutler & D. R. Ladd (eds), *Prosody: Models and Measurements*, Berlin, Springer Verlag.

Wunderlich, D. (1980), 'Methodological remarks on speech act theory', in J. R. Searle, F. Kiefer & M. Bierwisch (eds), *Speech Act Theory and Pragmatics*, Dordrecht, D. Reidel.

7 Natural language generation from plans*

CHRIS MELLISH†

7.0 Introduction

In this chapter we discuss the structure of a system that generates natural language instructions from the sorts of plans generated by AI planning programs (such as NONLIN (Tate 1976)). Our aim is to tackle the problem of organizing relatively large amounts of material (which does not have inherently appropriate structure) and to generate smooth readable text. Since the amount of material we wish to deal with could be large, we have avoided considering expensive global optimization techniques in favour of emphasizing local simplification techniques (analogous to 'peephole' optimizing techniques in compiling). Thus our basic strategy is to

(1) translate the original plan into an expression in a formal MESSAGE LANGUAGE, which can then be transformed by various algebraic 'simplification rules';
(2) translate the resulting message language expression compositionally into an unordered syntactic representation of the text by ordered skeletal rules, using a simple GRAMMATICAL CONSTRAINT SATISFACTION system to enforce grammaticality; and finally
(3) produce an ordered sequence of words by invoking a further set of ordered rules (which may themselves cause local rearrangement of structure).

The resulting system is similar to McDonald's model (McDonald 1983), in that it is basically a direct production system that utilizes an intermediate syntactic representation. The system is also similar to McDonald's in its emphasis on local processing, although there is no attempt to produce a psychological model in our work. Our constraint satisfaction system is implemented by unification, however, so that the effects of local decisions

* The work reported here was made possible by SERC grant GR/D/08876. I am currently supported by an SERC Advanced Fellowship.
† Cognitive Studies Programme, University of Sussex, Falmer, Brighton, UK

can propagate globally without the need for explicit global variables. This is used, for instance, to enforce a simple model of pronominalization (based on that of Dale 1986).

The results of our system are promising, but the texts still lack much of the smoothness of human-generated text. Partly this is because, although the domain of plans seems a priori to provide rich structure that a natural language generator can use, in practice a plan that is generated without the production of explanations in mind seems rarely to contain the depth of information that would yield an interesting natural language account. This is, of course, similar to the problem that Swartout (1983) encountered with expert systems.

7.1 Generating natural language from plans

Planning is a powerful concept in Artificial Intelligence and the state of the art in planning systems allows quite complex plans to be produced with very little human guidance. If these plans are to be for human consumption, they must be explained in a way that is comprehensible to a human being. There is thus a practical reason for considering ways of generating natural language from plans. There are also theoretical reasons why plans are a good domain for studying natural language generation. Although there may be a great deal of material in a given plan, there is a kind of consensus among planning researchers on what sort of information a plan is likely to provide. Thus it is possible that interesting general principles about producing explanations of plans can be formulated, independently of the domains in which the plans are produced.

The input to our natural language generator is the set of data structures created by Tate's NONLIN planner (Tate 1976) working on a planning task (translated into Prolog). Here is an extract of the information taken from a house-building plan, which concerns pouring the basement floor.

```
node(26,action,pour__basement__floor,26).
before(26,[16,24]).
after(26,[23]).
parent(26,34).
tome(basement__floor__laid,26,true).
gost(unsupervised,basement__floor__laid,true,23,[26]).
```

The plan contains a numbered node for each primitive action that must be performed. Node 26 is for the *pour basement floor* action. Nodes 16 and 24 come directly before it in the plan, and node 23 comes directly after it. Node 26 arises from the expansion of a more abstract action *decorate* (node 34). In addition, we have information (TOME facts) about what effects pouring the basement floor has and (GOST facts) which other nodes require these effects to be true.

We have set ourselves the goal of generating from such a plan a single natural language text that explains the actions to be performed and why things have to be done this way. An example of part of such an output is at the end of this chapter. As we shall see, to a large extent the explanatory power of such an account depends on what information is represented in the plan in the first place. In many ways, a system which produces a single monologue from a plan is artificial and unlikely to be very useful compared to an interactive system that can be asked to explain parts of the plan selectively. On the other hand, it provides us with an excellent way of studying the problems of automatically generating large texts.

7.2 Basic framework

Our natural language generation system can be thought of as consisting of four processing stages, as follows:

Message planning
Message optimization
Compositional structure building
Linearization and output

MESSAGE PLANNING can be thought of as the interface between the generator and the outside world. At this stage, the generator must decide 'what to say', i.e. which objects and relationships in the world are to be expressed in language and in roughly what order. We will not discuss message planning further in this chapter, but will instead concentrate on its output and what can be done with it.

The output of message planning is a datastructure called the MESSAGE. The message is expressed in a special message language, which is discussed below. The idea is that message planning may be a relatively simple process and that the resulting message is then 'cleaned up' and simplified by algebraic operations on the expression.

The message is a non-linguistic object, and the task of STRUCTURE BUILD-ING is to build a first description (a functional description much as in Functional Grammar (Kay 1979)) of a linguistic object. We assume here that a 'linguistically motivated' intermediate representation of the text is of value (this is argued for, for instance, by McDonald (1983)). Our structure builder is purely compositional, and so the amount of information that it can take into account is limited. We treat structure building as a recursive descent traversal of the message, using rules about how to build linguistic structures which correspond to local patterns in the message. The recursive descent terminates when it reaches primitive elements of the message. At such points, the system's dictionary is consulted. The system described in Chester (1976) is similar to ours in the local nature of its structure-building component, but Chester builds sentences directly, rather than via structural representations. Mann *et al*. (1982) would call this a 'direct translation' system. A system built in this fashion has the advantage of a very simple control structure and has the potential of having its principles expressed in modular, independent rules. If, on the other hand, the kind of structure built for part of the message could depend in arbitrary ways on structures previously built or on quite separate elements of the message, then such advantages would not obtain.

Once a structural description of a text has been produced, it is necessary to produce a linear sequence of words. This involves deciding on the order in which words are to be produced and carrying out the necessary morphological operations on individual words. Our structural descriptions contain only dominance information and no ordering information, and so a separate set of rules is used to produce a linearization. This is akin to the ID/LP distinction used in GPSG (Gazdar *et al*. 1985). We will not discuss linearization and output further in this chapter.

7.3 The message language

The messages produced by our message planner are expressions in an algebraic message language. This is a language specifically devised for expressing the objects that arise in plans and the kinds of things one might wish to say about them. This language is gradually evolving as we enrich the repertoire of the system. At present, there are six main types of statements ('utterances') that can be made as part of our generated text:

UTTERANCE::=
  do(ACTION)
    — an instruction to perform an action
  result(ACTION,STATE)
    — as 'do', but also mentioning an effect of the action
  expansion(ACTION,ACTION)
    — describing the expansion of an action into subactions
  prereqs(AGENT,ACTION,STATE)
    — describing the prerequisites of an action, with the
    — assumption that a given agent will perform it
  now(STATE)
    — indicating that some state now holds

neccbefore(AGENT,ACTION,ACTION)
  — statement that one action must be performed before another

These 'utterances' mention actions and states, which could be primitive actions and states (as appearing in the plan) or complex actions and states, according to the following rules:

ACTION::=
  then(ACTION,ACTION)
    — two actions in sequence
  achieve(STATE)
    — the action to achieve a state
  wait(STATE)
    — waiting until a state holds
  complete(ACTION)
    — finishing doing a prolonged action
  repeat(ACTION,STATE)
    — doing the action until the state holds
  parallel(ACTION,ACTION)
    — doing two actions in parallel
  PRIMITIVE__ACTION

STATE::=
  and(STATE,STATE)
    — both states hold
  enabled(AGENT,ACTION)
    — an agent is able to perform an action
  done(AGENT,ACTION)
    — an agent has done an action
  doing(AGENT,ACTION)
    — an agent is doing an action
  PRIMITIVE__STATE

The message language provides for the description of actions being carried out by different agents, although in our language generation we currently only allow for a single agent, the reader ('user'):

AGENT::= user

A message consists of a number of 'utterances' linked together by various organizational devices. These indicate various kinds of sequencing and embedding:

MESSAGE :=
  title(ACTION,MESSAGE)
    — labels a piece of text with a title (based on an action)

embed(MESSAGE,MESSAGE,MESSAGE)
 — introduction-body-conclusion type structure
neutral__seq(MESSAGE,MESSAGE)
 — two subtexts produced in sequence, but with no implied relationship
time__then(MESSAGE,MESSAGE)
 — two subtexts produced in sequence, this indicating time order
linked(MESSAGE,MESSAGE)
 — two subtexts produced in sequence, with some unspecified relationship
time__parallel(MESSAGE,MESSAGE)
 — two subtexts produced in sequence, indicating parallelism in time
contra__seq(MESSAGE,MESSAGE)
 — two subtexts produced in sequence, where the second contradicts an
 — expectation created by the first
UTTERANCE

The message language is probably best illustrated by some example expressions, together with the English rendering that our system provides:

```
result(paint,
    and(
      done(user,complete(decorate)),
      enabled(user,lay__finished__flooring)
    )
)
```

(where *paint*, *decorate* and *lay_finished_flooring* are primitive actions) produces the text:

paint the house and you will have finished decorating and be able to lay the finished flooring

The more complex expression:

```
embed(expansion(
          make(pss).
          then(cook(s1),add(saus,s1,s2))
        ),
    time__then(
          do(repeat(stir(s2),boiling(s2))),
          do(add(saus,s1,s2))
        ),
    now(done(user,make(pss)))
)
```

with *make*, *cook*, *add*, *stir*, *boiling* primitive states and actions that take primitive arguments like 'pss' and 's1') yields:

making paprika potatoes and spiced sausages involves cooking the sauce then adding the sausages to the sauce. stir the sauce until it boils and then add the sausages to the sauce. you have now made paprika potatoes and spiced sausages

7.4 Message optimization

There are four main types of simplification rules used in our message optimization system. The first kind tidy up special cases that could be as easily be detected when the expression is constructed. Here is an example of such a rule ([] denotes the empty utterance):

(1) neutral__seq(X,[]) +++>X.

This is to be read as a rewrite rule, with the expression on the left of the +++> being rewritten to the expression on the right. Variables are denoted by names beginning with capital letters. Thus any utterance expression of type 'neutral__seq' will be rewritten by this rule if its second component is empty. Such an expression is rewritten simply to its first component. Incorporating such simplifications into the optimisation stage means that the message planning component can be simpler and more perspicuous.

The second kind of rule expresses knowledge about planning and plan execution. Here are two such rules:

(2) achieve(done(user,Act)) +++>Act.
(3) parallel(X,wait(Y)) +++>then(X,wait(Y)).

Rule (2) expresses the fact that the only way to create a state where you have done an action is to do the action. Rule (3) expresses the fact that waiting is an action that is always postponed until there is nothing else to do. Both of these principles are useful in finding the best way to express a given action.

A third kind of rule really reflects the linguistic coverage of the system in an indirect manner. If there is a special way available for saying a particular kind of thing, then that should be preferred to using a more general technique. Here is such a rule:

(4) prereqs(user,Act,done(user,Act1)) +++>neccbefore(user,Act,1,Act).

It is arguable that such rules should really exist as special-case structure building rules (described in the next section). Such an approach would, however, preclude the use of optimization rules that made further use of the output of such rules.

Finally there are rules that are motivated by notions of simplicity of structure. For instance, the rule:

(5) time__parallel(do(X),do(Y)) +++>do(parallel(X,Y)).

results in an expression with one fewer 'connectives'. Such rules should really be backed up by a (perhaps psychological) theory of the complexity of messages.

Here is an example of how a message language expression can be simplified using these rules.

```
neutral__seq(prereqs(user,
              parallel(achieve(done(user,a1)),wait(s)),
              done(user,a2)),
     [])
```

is simplified by rule (1) to:

```
prereqs(user,
    parallel(achieve(done(user,a1)),wait(s)).
    done(user,a2)
  )
```

which is simplified by rule (2) to:

```
prereqs(user,
    parallel(a1,wait(s)),
    done(user,a2)
  )
```

which is simplified by rule (3) to:

```
prereqs(user,
    then(a1,wait(s)),
    done(user,a2)
```

which is simplified by rule (4) to:

```
neccbefore(user,
    a2,
    then(a1,wait(s))
    )
```

7.5 Compositional structure building

Our structure-building component uses a set of rules for mapping from local message patterns to functional descriptions. These are similar to the functional descriptions used in Functional Grammar (Kay 1979). Here are two mapping rules:

```
linked(X,linked(Y,Z) ==>
        [samesentence,
         conjn = [root =','],
         first = [$X],
         rest = [$linked(Y,Z)]
        ].
prereqs(user,Act,States) ==>
        [samesentence,
         conjn = [root = 'in order'],
         first =
                 [s,
                  pred = [subj = [elided=yes, $user],
                                  aux = [root = to].
                                  pred = [morph = inf, $Act]
                                 ]
                 ],
         rest =
                 [s,
                  pred = [aux = [root = must], pred = [morph = inf,
$States]]
                 ].
```

In each of the rules, the left-hand side is a Prolog pattern to be unified with part of the message. The right-hand side is a functional description, describing the English phrase that is to render that part. In these functional descriptions, expressions preceded by dollar signs represent the places where further information will be contributed by the expansion of subparts of the message. So, for instance, the second rule specifies that further information about the 'pred' of the 'pred' of the 'first' sentence is to come from looking at 'Act' the second component of the part of the message we are concerned with. This part of the message will itself be matched against structure-building rules to result eventually in a complete specification of that phrase. This is what one would expect from a compositional structure builder.

In our system, functional descriptions can contain both the usual specifications of features and values (for instance, the features 'conjn' and 'first' used above) and also the specification of properties (such as 's' and 'samesentence') that the relevant construction has. Some of the properties used are essentially 'macros' for bundles of simpler feature-value and property specifications. 'samesentence', for instance, is defined as being short-hand for:

```
[s,
 pfl=P,
 pfl2=P2,
 first = [focus=F,pfl2=IP],
 rest = [focus=F,pfl=[list,first=IP,rest=P],pfl1=IP,pfl2=P2]
]
```

Values in functional descriptions which begin with capital letters (e.g. 'F' and 'IP') are variables (using a standard Prolog notation). Thus any phrase that has the description 'samesentence' has the 'focus' of its 'first' the same as the 'focus' of its 'rest'. This description will hold of a clause which consists of two conjoined subclauses; the restriction forces the 'focus' of the two subclauses to be the same. This and the restrictions on the features 'pfl', 'pfl1' and 'pfl2' are part of a simple focus maintenance and the pronominalization system based on Dale (1986). The feature 'focus' holds the symbol representing the single world object (or set of objects) that is 'in focus' throughout a sentence, this value being shared by all constituents of the sentence. Only references to this object may be pronominalized within the sentence, and, if any pronominalization occurs, this object is also constrained to be a member of the list which is the value of the feature 'pfl' ('potential focus list').[1] The features 'pfl' and 'pfl2', which have values for most constituents, are used to build a list of the objects mentioned in a sentence. This list of objects is then in general a component of the 'pfl' of the next sentence, and 'pfl2' holds the list, augmented with any objects that are mentioned within the constituent itself.

As the message is traversed by the structure-building rules, more and more information accumulates about the output functional description and its component. The structure-building rules only provide the framework of the final functional description, however, the rest being filled in by a simple GRAMMATICAL CONSTRAINT SATISFACTION SYSTEM. This enforces grammaticality and handles the propagation of feature values that are shared between different phrases (for instance, for number agreement). A declarative specification of the types of legal descriptions and the constraints they must satisfy is pre-compiled into procedures that enforce legality by performing extra unifications when functional descriptions are actually constructed. This, together with the fact that functional unification is implemented by standard logical unification means that the system can be quite efficient. This contrasts with other approaches to using unification and Functional Grammar (e.g. McKeown 1982). McKeown's system does not use its grammar (specification of legal descriptions) until a complete (framework) functional description has been built. Enforcing grammaticality then involves a laborious (partly non-deterministic) traversal of the grammar and functional description. Systems that use Functional Grammar in this way have led to it being wrongly dismissed as too inefficient for use in natural language generation systems. The advantage in using unification from our point of view is that structure building can be compositional but feature values can propagate in a non-local manner without the necessity for the unstructured use of global variables.

7.6 Optimization techniques in language generation

In many ways, a natural language generation system is like an optimizing compiler. Producing some sort of natural language from a symbolic input is not a task of great difficulty, but producing text that is smooth and readable is a challenge. The difference between the two lies in the kinds of optimizations that are made in the process. As with an optimizing compiler, we can seek to produce an optimal solution by a search among all possibilities or through a succession of local transformations (as in peephole optimization). Unfortunately, since the amount of material we have to generate from can be large, a search through all possible natural language realizations (even if we had an evaluation function that allowed a 'best first' strategy) would be infeasible. Mann & Moore address the same problem in their KDS system (Mann & Moore 1981). Their solution is to consider the whole search space but have an incomplete search strategy ('hill climbing'). Whether this produces an optimal solution then depends on whether such a solution arises from the sequence of globally 'best possible' local transformations and this will be hard to establish in most cases. By casting the optimization problem as an algebraic simplification task using a set of simplifying rewrite rules we can make use of established algebraic manipulation techniques. We also hope to be able to use some of the formal results about rewrite rule sets to say sensible things about in what sense our methods will produce 'optimal' results.

   In our current system, there are really only two places where optimizations affecting the quality of the text can be made. The main place, as we have seen, is in the message optimization stage. Certain optimizations can also be made in the structure-building stage, because the rules can direct that a piece of message matching a more specific pattern be realized in a way different to a message matching a less specific pattern. Both of these places involve detecting patterns in the message and thus work from non-linguistic data. We believe, however, that an effective natural language generation system should also be able to perform purely linguistic optimizations in a way that ours cannot. In our system, the compositionality requirement anchors the structure builder firmly to the shape of the message, and yet the message optimizer can only optimize on the basis of reasoning about its own (non-linguistic) domain. Unfortunately, there are certain (language-dependent) 'linguistic tricks' that are not reflected clearly in non-linguistic domains. For instance, whether it makes sense to perform a 'heavy NP shift' depends on the 'size' of the phrase in question, and this in turn depends on the lexical items that the language makes available. There seem to be a number of situations of this kind where information is required about the complexity of linguistic constituents, and these include even segmentation into sentences, which may be problematic when information can be expressed in relative clauses. It is not clear that we can expect a message optimizer to produce uniformly good solutions to these problems, and so a linguistic optimizer has an important role to play. Other places where a linguistic optimizer might be essential is in the introduction of conjunction and ellipsis, which again cannot be planned completely non-linguistically. It would be possible to introduce linguistic optimizations at structure-building time, relaxing the requirement of compositionality (indeed, this is how McDonald (1983) operates). We believe, however, that it could be achieved by a subsequent stage and that it would be conceptually clearer to see it in this way.

7.7 Results and conclusions

Although the small examples above and the general approach we are taking look promising, nevertheless our results with real plans have been somewhat disappointing. For instance, consider in Figure 7.1 the extract from a plan to build a house (this is a standard demonstration plan for NONLIN). It concerns installing the services. In this diagram, time is understood to work from left to right, and a line rightwards from one action to another indicates that the first must precede the second. Only actions are shown in this diagram (no preconditions or effects are shown), and they are abbreviated for reasons of space. Those actions in parentheses are not actually part of installing the services (but are actions that are nevertheless crucial to this part of the plan); they will be described elsewhere in the text. Here is the English produced for this plan fragment (we have added

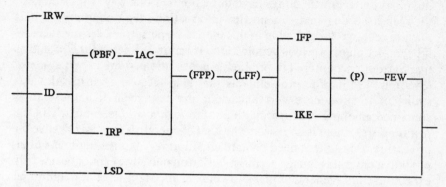

Figure 7.1

capitalization and formatting by hand, and also annotated some of the actions with the abbreviations used above):

Installing the services:
Installing the services involves finishing the electrical work[FEW] and laying the storm drains[LSD]. You must paint the house[P] before finishing the electrical work.
In order to paint the house you must have installed the finished plumbing[IFP] and installed the kitchen equipment[IKE]. You must lay the finished flooring[LFF] before installing the finished plumbing[IFP] and installing the kitchen equipment[IKE].
You must fasten the plaster and plaster board[FPP] before laying the finished flooring[LFF]. In order to fasten the plaster and plaster board[FPP] you must have installed the air conditioning[IAC] and installed the rough plumbing[IRP] and installed the rough wiring[IRW].
Install the drains[ID] and then install the air conditioning[IAC], installing the rough plumbing[IRP]. Meanwhile install the rough wiring[IRW].
You can now fasten the plaster and the plaster board[FPP].
You can now lay the finished flooring[LFF].
You can now install the finished plumbing[IFP] and install the kitchen equipment[IKE].
You can now paint the house[P].
You can now finish the electrical work[FEW].
Meanwhile lay the storm drains[LSD].
You have now finished installing the services.

This account is fairly comprehensible, but is repetitive and quite hard to follow. One reason for the repetition is that the subject matter is really very boring and uninformative. The reader is told WHAT to do but is given no illumination as to WHY things have to be done in this way. Unfortunately, the plan itself does not contain this information—the only preconditions that are required for an action in this plan to be performed are the successful completion of previous actions. One is reminded here of the problems that Sartout encountered in producing explanations from 'expert systems' (Swartout 1983). The problem was that just because a set of rules was sufficient to produce expert behaviour did not mean that those rules contained anything illuminating to put into explanations. Similarly in the planning area, there is no reason why a set of operators that are effective for producing useful plans need contain anything very interesting that can be put into a natural language account. Unfortunately, one cannot necessarily expect machine-generated plans to come at the right level of detail to be really useful to a human being. For instance, a house-building plan which enabled one to see why the rough plumbing must be installed after the drains[2] would be very large, and it would be well beyond the state of the art for such a plan to be produced automatically. Moreover, such a plan would undoubtedly contain a lot of information that was blindingly obvious to a human reader and hence of no interest whatsoever.

The problems with our natural language accounts are, of course, not entirely due to deficiencies in the plans we are working on. One way to reduce the repetitiveness of the about account would be to introduce more variation in the range of devices used to realize the same kinds of message. Another important area we are looking at is ways of extending our message language so that we can represent more kinds of actions and states (for instance, incomplete actions, partial expansions of actions) and hence decompose plan fragments in more interesting ways.

Notes

1. In fact, the situation is slightly more complicated, as 'pfl' is a list of lists. When pronominalization occurs, the focus is constrained to be an element of one of the elements of 'pfl'. Lists are encoded using the features 'first' and 'rest', as is conventional in feature systems.
2. Presumably because otherwise it is hard to make the pipes line up.

Bibliography

Chester, D. (1976), 'The translation of formal proofs into English', *Artificial Intelligence*, vol. 7, p. 261.
Dale, R. (1986), 'The pronominalisation decision in language generation'. DAI Report 276, University of Edinburgh.

Gazdar, G., Klein, E., Pullum, G. & Sag, I. (1985), *Generalized Phrase Structure Grammar*, Oxford, Basil Blackwell.

Kay, M. (1979), 'Functional grammar', *Proceedings of the 5th Annual Meeting of the Berkeley Linguistics Society*, Berkeley.

McDonald, D. D. (1983), 'Natural language generation as a computational problem: an introduction', in M. Brady (ed.), *Computational Theories of Discourse*, Cambridge, Mass., MIT Press.

McKeown, K. R. (1982), 'Generating natural language text in response to questions about database structure', Ph.D. thesis, Computer and Information Science, University of Pennsylvania.

Mann, W. C. & Moore, J. A. (1981), 'Computer generation of multiparagraph English text', *AJCL*, vol. 7, no. 1.

Mann, W., Bates, M., Grosz., McDonald, D., McKeown, K. & Swartout, W. (1982), 'Text generation', *AJCL*, vol. 8, no. 2.

Swartout, W. R. (1983), 'XPLAIN: a system for creating and explaining expert consulting programs', *Artificial Intelligence*, vol. 21.

Tate, A. (1976), 'Project planning using a hierarchical non-linear planner', DAI Report 25, University of Edinburgh.

8 An approach for creating structured text

NATHALIE SIMONIN*

8.1 Introduction

Generation, of either written or spoken text, is a complex task whose components and processes are still poorly understood. While there may be disagreements on the subtleties of the overall architecture, there is no doubt that the task must be divided into a conceptual and a linguistic component. The former deals with content, i.e. what to say and how to organize its parts into a coherent whole, while the latter deals with form, i.e. the determination of the words, morphological adjustments and sentence structure.

Most work on natural language generation has focused on the mapping of given conceptual structures on to linguistic forms. In contrast, relatively little work has been devoted to the determination and organization of the content itself. This is what I will be concerned with here. Specifically, I will focus on the problem of how to generate coherent and well-structured text.

My approach to text generation is motivated by the following two questions: (i) what kind of knowledge is needed to draft a document? and (ii) how do humans go about writing text? It should be noted, however, that my background is in computer science and not in cognitive psychology or linguistics.

Text generation is rooted in the need to communicate complex knowledge structures. In fact, ideas are often too complex to be expressed by a single sentence. Hence, complex structures have to be decomposed into more elementary ones, which may correspond to sentences. In order to enable readers to build a global meaning representation that is equivalent to the writer's original model, they have to be given cues on what the components are, and how to put them together. If the text lacks such instructions, or if the cues are unclear or misleading, then the text is likely

* *Cap Sogeti Innovation, Paris*

to be perceived either as an incoherent set of elements or, worse, as a message having a different goal.

This chapter is organized as follows: in the next section I discuss some general problems of text production. In Section 8.3 I will review related work, and in Section 8.4 I will describe my own approach. In the last section I will offer some conclusions and discuss possible improvements of the system.

8.2 Problem presentation

8.2.1 *The communicative setting*

The kind of text people produce depends on a number of factors: the writer's goals (intentions), the reader's knowledge (expertise), pragmatic factors (setting), and so forth. Communication is a mediated problem-solving activity where rational agents use language in order to satisfy multiple goals (Appelt 1985). In consequence, in order to be efficient, content, shape and text structure have to be sensitive to these goals. Put differently, the conceptual and linguistic choices are pragmatically constrained.

Depending on the situation, and depending on the purpose, one tells a story, tells a joke, gives a description or offers an explanation. The writer structures text so as to catch the readers' attention, to convince them of the validity of an argument, and so forth. If the writer wants to achieve his goals, that is to say, if he wants the text to be read, understood, remembered and followed, he should be brief, clear, convincing and to the point. In other words, he must ease the readers' burden of building a mental model equivalent to his own. In order to do so, the readers must be given cues that allow them to perceive what the building blocks are and what their functional relationship (overall architecture) is.

8.2.2 *The product*

The same content can be expressed by different types of text. Depending on whether one wants to teach, convince or amuse, one produces a specific kind of text. Meaning and text form thus have to be separated, for they fulfil different functions. Different forms (types of text) are used precisely to signal different goals. De Beaugrande (1980) suggests the following typology: descriptive, narrative, argumentative, literary, poetic, scientific, didactic and conversational texts.

It should be noted, however, that different text types may constrain conceptual, textual and linguistic choices in specific ways.

A text is the product of goal-directed activity. As such, it has a beginning (e.g. a setting) and an end (e.g. a resolution). The text itself is an idealized trace of the reasoning process, in the sense that it does not show the mental operations performed on a representation, i.e. transformation, addition or deletion of elements. Texts may also be thought of as a window to the mind, that is to say, they reflect to some extent the way people see or organize the world (mental models).

As the Prague school has convincingly argued (Danes 1974), texts are dynamic entities, which have a unity and a progression. Discourse objects (topics) have to be introduced and gradually developed according to some point of view (temporal, causal, taxonomic). The components have to be linked in such a way that the reader can recognize the structure of the discourse objects as a coherent whole.

8.2.2.1 *The text representation*   Texts are composed of a set of functionally related objects: words, sentences, paragraphs. I distinguish among the following classes of objects: visible objects, abstract syntactic structures, discourse objects, predicates and links.

Texts convey information by various means (e.g. sentence order or syntactic structure). The text representation I shall use includes all information relevant to text structure.

Visible objects: Visible objects are words or word sequences, sentences, paragraphs, chapters and so forth. My system uses these objects as primitives to build a surface representation of the underlying text structure. In doing so it makes explicit the serial and hierarchical position of the discourse entities, as shown in Figure 8.1.

Syntactic components: Sentences are represented in terms of syntactic categories: noun-phrase, verb-phrase, determiner, noun, verb and so forth, as shown in Figure 8.2.

Discourse objects: Every text consists of saying something about some other thing (the referent or discourse topic). In order to predicate something

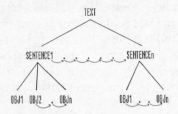

Figure 8.1

"the big mouse" ->

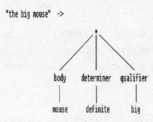

Figure 8.2

about an object, the referent first has to be introduced. Discourse objects can be words, sentences, paragraphs or even more complex entities. In other words, one can predicate something on objects of various complexities.

An important aspect of the underlying meaning of texts can be captured through referential nets, graphs showing what objects have been introduced when, and what has been predicated about each one of them. Take for example:

The main crop is wheat, WHOSE PRODUCTION HAS GREATLY DECREASED. THIS DECLINE has heavily affected the trade balance.

It should be noted that these two predications concern one single object:

the decrease of wheat production.

From my point of view, entire texts can be seen as single discourse objects. In consequence, texts can be represented by an object which mentions the topic, the time and the nature of the links between sentences and paragraphs. This object will be progressively refined during the structuring phase: information may be added, deleted or modified.

Predicates and speech acts: Objects like car, sea, justice and the like are incomplete thoughts. In order to be completed, something has to be said, i.e. predicated about them:

The car is old,
The sea is beautiful

and so forth.

As mentioned above, entire propositions may, in turn, become reference objects, i.e. function as arguments. This is one way of elaborating more complex information structures. For example, the following sentence is composed of three hierarchically related predicates.

The president's decision to lay off 3% of his employees has been criticized by the union.

It should also be noted that the act of predication implies a comment. While predicating something, one cannot but take a stance and communicate one's position with respect to the plausibility of the truth of the message. The speaker may also express his wishes, doubts and so forth. While uttering

'The production of the wheat will increase next year.'

The speaker introduces not only the object wheat production, but he also predicates the fact that there will be an increase and that he is sure about his prediction (metacomment).

Links: The links are the means to make explicit the kind of relationship that holds between two or more entities (e.g. propositions). By unifying the objects with a link, one also creates a new object of greater complexity. Links thus are important in at least two respects: they allow for building objects of various complexity, and they help the reader to perceive unity where there would otherwise only be a set of isolated elements.

A because of B   instead of (A, B)
A and B, but not C   instead of (A, B, C)

Links or discourse markers thus are crucial in any text, as they signal the internal structure of the discourse plan (outline, macro-structure).

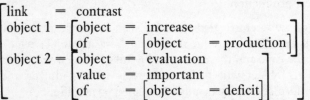

'The production is increasing BUT the deficit remains important.'

Our system determines these links (i) on the basis of conceptual characteristics of the propositions, and (ii) on the basis of pragmatic features of the situation (discourse goals). The choice of these connectives is important for the above-mentioned reasons, but this choice remains delicate as it has to correspond to the readers' point of view. Mismatches in the permissibility of adjacency pairs will result in the impression of incoherence.

8.2.3 *The process*

Text generation involves different kinds of expertise: domain-specific knowledge, rhetorical skill (i.e. in discourse structure), linguistic knowledge and so forth. The whole process may be decomposed into a set of subprocesses:

— determine the content (level of abstraction, what shall be made explicit?);
— determine the relative importance (focusing, subordination);
— integrate (group, form a hierarchy, and order) the information into some overall plan (text-structure or outline);
— chunk the whole into smaller units (paragraphs and sentences);
— generate links between the elements at the various levels;
— introduce, maintain and refer back to discourse referents (determine an adequate level of description, the anaphoric reference, elipsis, and signal topic shifts);
— determine the right words and sentence structure;
— continually revise by considering local as well as global constraints.

and so forth.

Obviously, the order in which the whole process is carried out varies to a great extent among humans as well as for a single person. One often jumps ahead, goes back to his notes, changes the plan, integrates a new thought while deleting another because it does not fit into the plan, or completely modifies the initial goal.

Writing, as compared to speaking, seems to be much more of a controlled or conscious activity, in which the author deliberately cycles through the different stages: determine, organize, revise and express content. At every cycle, information may be fed back, perhaps modifying the structure built so far. The whole process will stop when some defined threshold level, that is, a satisfactory match between intended and obtained result, has been reached.

8.3 Related work

According to de Beaugrande (1980) discourse production consists of the following phases: (i) planning, (ii) ideation (iii) development and (iv) expression. These phases are not necessarily strictly sequential. Each one of them may be more or less dominant, i.e. given more or fewer resources, at a given point in time.

The planning phase consists of goal setting and determining an adequate text type according to the speaker's goals and the listener's profile. The ideation phase deals with the selection of content (What information is relevant? What is the most adequate level of abstraction? and so forth). These two phases are largely language-independent. The next, development, deals with discourse organization, and finally, expression deals with the mapping of conceptual structures on to linguistic forms, words and sentences.

While most work on natural language generation has been devoted to this last phase, there has been some work on the determination and organization of content.

Meehan (1977) was interested in the planning aspect of problem solving. Given a set of characters, beliefs and goals, he generated stories that related the strategies invented by his heroes to achieve their respective goals. As these goals could be in conflict, this planning could become quite complex.

Davey's (1979) system generated commentaries on tic-tac-toe games. His system could determine not only how to say something, but also what to say. In order to do so, it had domain-specific knowledge (i.e. knowledge about tic-tac-toe games), and a user-model. While the former took care of the relevancy of the information to be conveyed (what comments were relevant in a given situation), the latter allowed it to omit those details that could be inferred.

Mann & Moore (1981) were among the first to address the issue of generating multi-sentence strings. Their system produced texts providing instructions about what to do in case of a fire alarm. KDS, which stands for knowledge delivery system, was divided into four components: acquisition, planning, generation and improvement. The first component determined the content, the second planned an outline, the third generated the linguistic form, while the last component revised the whole, suggesting improvements.

This text-evaluation component is original. Actually it is a desirable feature in any text generation system. Unfortunately, the heuristics used by KDS are not linguistically motivated. Furthermore, the system organizes text only at the utterance level. The system has no notion of text or discourse structure. Finally, the system is entirely domain-dependent.

McKeown (1982) was concerned with the production of paragraph-length text in response to questions about the structure and the terminology of a military data base. Starting from the assumption that people answer a given kind of question by a given kind of text, she designed a system in which different text types are associated with different discourse goals. TEXT is the first system to use a real data base and to integrate three major components of generation: the determination, organization and expression of content.

Danlos (1985) has designed a script-driven system that generates wire-service-style news reports. The script controls the input, i.e. what to say, while the discourse grammar and the linguistic component determine the form.

Another promising approach is Mann & Thompson's Rhetorical Structure Theory (1983). These authors studied the possible relationships that hold among the elements at different levels (propositions, paragraphs) of discourse. They list a set of about twenty relations: thesis–antithesis, evidence, justification, reason, motivation, cause, condition, circumstance, background, concession, sequence, enablement, solutionhood, elaboration, restatement, and so forth.

These relationships are very important to any theory of discourse generation. Since they are not always explicit, they often have to be inferred. The problem with this descriptive approach is that it is not clear how to establish the kind of relationship that holds between two discourse units.

8.4 Our approach

I will now turn to my system and describe the different steps it goes through in order to generate text. It should be noted that this work is part of a larger system, developed by Cap Sogeti Innovation. We have a parser and a generator. I will deal here only with the latter.

The process is started by analysing a text taken from a French review called *ATLASECO*. These texts contain information concerning the industrial, economic and agricultural situation of various countries (gross national product, economic balance and so forth). While analysing these texts the system builds a knowledge base. This knowledge base is the starting point for our generator. The system queries this knowledge base and its goal is to build a coherent, well-structured text from the extracted data.

8.4.1 *What information will the system communicate?*

The starting point of the system is thus an unordered list of information, i.e. a set of data extracted from a knowledge base. What information will be extracted depends on the question the system is being asked. Obviously, the following two questions will result in different texts:

(a) what do you know about Algeria?
(b) what do you know about Algeria's agriculture?

The order in which the knowledge base is queried is immaterial to the final text. Put differently, the primitives extracted from the knowledge base have no intended order. Each piece of information can be expressed by a short sentence, for example:

$$\begin{bmatrix} \text{object} = & \text{increase} \\ \text{of} & = \begin{bmatrix} \text{object} & = & \text{production} \\ \text{of} & = \begin{bmatrix} \text{object} & = \text{food crop} \end{bmatrix} \end{bmatrix} \end{bmatrix}$$

$\rightarrow$ 'the food crop production is increasing.'

8.4.2 *How to present it?*

Once we have decided what to say, we are faced with the problem of how to present it. In what order will the information be displayed in the final text? The structuring process can be decomposed into several sub-components. These processes are not strictly sequential, neither are they independent. Actually we use a spy-mechanism in order to know the current state of the system. This allows us to co-ordinate the different processes. The task of the structuring component is to build a text structure. In order to do so, we work on both the CONTENT LEVEL (what to say) and the TEXT-STRUCTURE LEVEL. There is continuous interaction between these two components, one modulating as a function of the other.

Thus, we are not working on the sentence level, but rather on the discourse level. That is, we process the text as a whole and not as a set of isolated elements.

Coherence can be achieved in multiple ways, in particular: (i) through the text's external structure, (ii) by the links that unify the elements to the whole. The former signals what these units are, while the latter specifies the kind of relationships that hold between them. The construction of the text plan is done in subsequent steps:

— searching for all information pertaining to a given topic;
— eliminating redundancy;
— ordering the information according to some point of view (chrono-logically, order of importance);
— generating links between the elements;
— revising the plan.

All of these processes are rule-driven.

8.4.2.1 *Organization of the messages*
Integration into a text plan: Once we know what information we want to communicate, we have to organize the messages into a coherent whole. In

order to do this, the system tries to integrate the data in the right place in the given text model. Intractable residues will be placed in a special paragraph. In other words, the system creates a special paragraph for those items which could not be integrated in any of the available slots of the text structure.

The rules that drive this process are of the following kind:

IF the message deals with agriculture (wheat, oranges and the like), and
IF the message deals with export,
THEN insert the items in the paragraph on 'commercial agriculture'.

As one can see from the example, semantic knowledge is used in order to determine to which category a given item belongs. Recognizing that *oranges* and *wheat* are agricultural products, and knowing that *export* is a commercial activity, the system groups these items under the heading of *commercial agriculture*. Similarly, knowing that wool is a product derived from sheep, and that sheep breed, the message *the production of wool is important* can be integrated in the paragraph on breeding. The efficient integration of data into a given structure clearly implies some form of reasoning.

Elimination of redundancy: Since the same information can be integrated at various places in the plan, redundancies could occur. In order to prevent them, we have decided that information should occur only once, at the most appropriate place in the plan. In order to determine the right place, we have devised a set of rules like the following:

IF the primitive contains some sort of judgement, and
IF it appears in the introduction,
THEN the introduction is the most appropriate place.

Other possibilities are to place the information either in the most specific paragraph, or wherever it first appears. This strategy of order-of-mention will only be used if no other rules apply.

We start by processing the redundancies between the paragraphs in order to reduce or entirely eliminate the redundancies within each paragraph.

The processes of data integration and redundancy elimination can run in parallel, as they are controlled by two different sets of rules. Whenever information appears in more than one place, all but one instance is immediately deleted.

8.4.2.2 *Revision of the text plan*   If our choices with regard to the relative position of the data turn out to be inadequate, then the resulting text will be incoherent. In that case the text structure has to be modified, at least locally. That is to say, information may have to be added, deleted or reordered.

If for a given domain a text plan can be defined in principle, the actual text will nevertheless depend on the nature, the variety and the complexity of the information that it contains.

Modification of the text plan: So far we have worked on the content level; we shall now work on the text-structure level. The system connects, separates, balances or reorders paragraphs, highlights some information as may be needed, and so forth. All these operations concern modifications within or between paragraphs. For example:

IF breeding is more important for the economy of a given country than agriculture,
THEN mention the breeding before mentioning agriculture.
IF a country has a monoculture,
THEN group the introduction, the information concerning the agricultural consumption and the commercial agriculture into the same chapter.

Ordering information: At this point, we consider the information to be in the right place. The final structure starts to take shape. However, we still have to improve its deepest structure. The paragraphs so far are only a set of unordered elements. Hence some order has to be imposed. This kind of linearizing can be done according to various points of view. Objects may be grouped by class membership—units belonging to the same topic are grouped together—by order of importance, by degree of generality (from general to specific), or by chronological or spatial order.

8.4.2.3 *Link creation*   Although the text's external structure has been completed, we still have to work on the internal structure. In other words, we have to make explicit the kind of relationships that hold between the different units (discourse marker, i.e. logical connectives; anaphoric reference, i.e. pronouns, elipsis and so forth). We also have to find ways of avoiding repetition and to factor redundant information.

Combining sentences may entail syntactic transformations within or between clauses. Elements can be combined at various levels. Domain-specific knowledge may be necessary to determine what items can be grouped together in a single sentence. For instance, it is possible to:

— talk about growth and a number:
  'The wheat production is increasing.'
  'The wheat production is 1,300,000 tons.'
  → 'The wheat production is increasing TO 1,300,000 tons.'

— develop a number in terms of percentage:

'The deficit amounts to $100,000,000.'
'This deficit represents 5% of the gross national product.'
→ 'The deficit amounts to $100,000,000, THAT IS TO SAY, 5% of the gross national product.'

— introduce a figure, a percentage or a place:

'This country is the third largest producer of wheat in the world'
'The wheat production is 850 million tons.'
→ 'This country is the third largest producer of wheat in the world WITH 850 million tons.'

— juxtapose similar information.

At this point, the system does not yet lexicalize the concept. It chooses only the adequate conceptual class. For example, the following is used to introduce a restriction:

$$\begin{bmatrix} \text{name} & = \text{restriction} \\ \text{is a} & = \text{link} \\ \text{examples} & = (\text{on the other hand, nevertheless, but}) \end{bmatrix}$$

The actual choice of these links is important in that it may influence the final form of the text. It constrains the place of the connective and the arguments, the kind of ellipsis and so forth.

Obviously, there are many other kinds of links, for example, 'pronouns'.

'The food crop is wheat'
'The food crop production is increasing'
→ 'The food crop is wheat. Its production is increasing.'

The text's internal and external structure being completed, all that remains to be done is to translate this message into French.

8.4.3 *How to say it*

Sentence generation is divided into determining syntactic structure, lexicalization and making the necessary morphological adjustments.

8.4.3.1 *Sentence generation* Starting from functional descriptions representing the text's final structure, the system generates the corresponding linguistic forms.

In order to do so, the system activates the syntactic patterns that are associated with the concepts. Action rules combine these patterns to produce the description of the sentence. For example, the concept *figure* is associated with the syntactic pattern shown in Figure 8.3. These patterns associated with concepts (growth, comparison, alternative and so forth) are somewhat similar to McKeown's rhetorical predicates (1982).

$$
\begin{bmatrix}
\text{cat} & = & \text{sentence} \\
\text{is\_a} & = & \text{figure} \\
\text{object} & = & \text{X} \\
\text{value} & = & \text{Y} \\
\text{unity} & = & \text{Z} \\
\text{qualifier} & = & \text{I} \\
\text{pattern} & = & (\quad
\begin{bmatrix}
\text{X} \\
\text{cat} = \text{gn} \\
\text{qualifier} = \text{I}
\end{bmatrix} \\
& & \begin{bmatrix}
\text{lex} = \text{amount} \\
\text{cat} = \text{verb}
\end{bmatrix} \\
& & \begin{bmatrix}
\text{lex} = \text{Y} \\
\text{cat} = \text{adj\_cardinal}
\end{bmatrix} \\
& & \begin{bmatrix}
\text{lex} = \text{Z} \\
\text{cat} = \text{substantif}
\end{bmatrix})
\end{bmatrix}
$$

Figure 8.3

8.4.3.2 *Morphological adjustments* Words still have to be inflected. For example, in English, regular verbs that end in the past tense with a *y* take *-ied* at the end instead of *yed*. The lexical entries are independent. Each one of them represents a different lexical item. The entries contain semantic, syntactic and morphological information. It is on this basis that the system builds the final form. For example:

$$
\begin{bmatrix}
\text{word} & = & \text{burn} \\
\text{cat} & = & \text{verb} \\
\text{tense} & = & \text{present} \\
\text{person} & = & \text{3d} \\
\text{number} & = & \text{singular} \\
\text{inflection} & = & \text{s}
\end{bmatrix}
\rightarrow \text{burns}
$$

8.5 Conclusion

The present chapter has focused on the necessary expert knowledge to create coherent, well-structured text. The emphasis of our work lay on text structure rather than on expressing a given content. In order to structure the data, the system relies on three kinds of knowledge sources: general knowledge, domain-specific knowledge, and knowledge about the reader. The text is processed as a whole and not as a set of isolated units. The result of the structuring process is a detailed outline, containing syntactic information that might be useful for the final generation.

The structuring process has been modelled as a 'conscious activity' in the sense that the system could evaluate and improve its choices.

The texts generated by the system describe the main features of the agriculture and economy of various countries. The texts contain approximately twenty sentences, each composed of ten to forty-five words. The different kinds of knowledge needed for the various processes are represented by a single formalism, functional descriptions (Kay 1981).

The system uses

— 400 lexical items (which represent 2400 words);
— a semantic network containing 220 concepts, out of which 80 are domain-independent;
— 1 text model, containing 50 paragraphs and subheadings;
— 100 rules for text structuring, and
— 30 rules and syntactic patterns for sentence generation.

The language used is French.

Our current work concerns a component that sits between a natural language front end and a dialogue system specialized in giving advice. This component can assist a user with one of several 'specialist' plans:

— a specialist for presenting a concept;
— a specialist for explaining a solution;
— a specialist for asking for information;
— a specialist for suggesting modifications in order to remove ambiguities or inconsistencies.

Finally, we are also investigating how to achieve a better integration between the text-structuring and the sentence-generation component. Choices at the sentence level may feed back to the text-structuring component, thus requiring changes on the local or global level. I am convinced that in an efficient system these two components have to co-operate.

Bibliography

Appelt, D. (1982), 'Planning natural language utterances to satisfy multiple goals', Technical Note 259, Stanford Research Institute, Menlo Park, Calif.

ATLASECO (1982), *Atlas économique mondial, Le Nouvel Observateur*.

Beaugrande, de (1980), *Text, Discourse and Process*, Norwood, NJ, Ablex.

Danes, F. (1974), *Papers on Functional Sentence Perspective*, The Hague, Mouton.

Danlos, Laurence (1985), *Generation automatique de textes en langues naturelles*, Paris, Masson.

Davey, Anthony (1979), *Discourse Production*, Edinburgh, University of Edinburgh Press.

Dik, Simon (1978), *Functional Grammar, Publications in Language Science*, Dordrecht, Holland, Foris.

Fillmore, Charles (1968), 'The case for case', in E. Bach & R. Harms (eds), *Universals in Linguistics Theory*, pp. 1–90.

Grize, Jean-Blaise (1982), 'Introduction à la logique naturelle et approche logique du dialogue', *Approches formelles de la semantique naturelle*, Publication CNRS-UPS-UTM-ADI.

Gross, Maurice (1975), *Methodes en syntaxe*, Hermann.

Herskovits, A. (1973), 'The generation of French from a semantic representation', Artificial Intelligence, Memo 212, Computer Science Dept. Stanford University, August.

Kay, Martin (1981), 'Unification grammars', internal publication,

McDonald, David D. & Pustejovsky, James D. (1985), 'Description-directed natural language generation', *Proceedings of the Ninth International Joint Conference on Artificial Intelligence*, 18–23 August 1985, Los Angeles, Calif.

McKeown, Kathleen R. (1982), 'Generating natural language text in response to questions about database structure', Ph.D., University of Pennsylvania.

Mann, William C. & Moore, James A. (1981), 'Computer generation of multi-paragraph English text', *AJCL*, vol. 7, no. 1, January–March.

Mann, William C. & Thompson, Sandra A. (1983), 'Relational propositions in discourse', ISI/RR-83-115, November 1983, University of Southern California.

Meehan, James R. (1977), 'TALE-SPIN, an interactive program that writes stories', *Proceedings of the Fifth IJCAI*.

Scardamalia, M., Bereiter, C. & Steinbach, R. (1984), 'Teachability of reflective processes in written composition', *Cognitive Science*, vol. 8, no. 2, pp. 173–90, April.

Searle, J. (1972), *Les Actes de Langage*, Paris, Hermann.

Simonin, Nathalie (1985), 'Utilisation d'une expertise pour engendrer des textes structurés en français', thèse, Université de Paris VI.

Part IV Psychological issues

9 Automatic and executive processing in semantic and syntactic planning: a dual process model of speech production*

TREVOR A. HARLEY†

9.0 Introduction

It is perhaps a truism that while we speak, we also think. Experimental confirmation of this claim is provided by Ford & Holmes (1978), who showed that decisions about syntactic planning must be made on-line during speech production, and Harley (1984), who showed that certain speech errors are best explained by the intrusion of thought into speech. The interaction of the processes of thought and language generation can be manifested in a number of ways. First, we can think about what we say as we say it. Second, we can plan what we say in some detail before we commence articulation. Third, we can consider alternatives to what we are saying before and during speech. Finally, we can think about something totally unrelated to what we are saying. Speech errors discussed in Harley (1984) exemplify these interactions. The speech production processes appear to be extremely flexible, and it is the purpose of this chapter to account for this flexibility.

Possibly the earliest suggestion that the order of the speech production processes is not fixed was due to Pick (1931). Pick produced a modern-looking model of speech production, which comprised six levels of processing. In his model, thought formulation was followed by the realization of the accentuation pattern, sentence pattern, word-finding, grammatization and motor execution. This model is similar to that of Fromkin (1971). However, in Pick's model the sequence was not fixed, but varied depending upon what was to be expressed. In particular, he suggested that speech production would be facilitated if there were a

---

* George Houghton did a very thorough job of reviewing this chapter, and he has improved it immeasurably. Thanks for comments are also due to Siobhan MacAndrew. I am, of course, responsible for any remaining infelicities of style, vagueness and mistakes.

† Department of Psychology, University of Warwick, Coventry, UK

ready-made phrase or sentence available. (Butterworth (1980a) discusses this suggestion in further detail.) Hughlings-Jackson's (1932) work on aphasia is also relevant. Normal speakers usually have language production under 'volitional control', whereas aphasics are often unable to generate novel strings which capture the appropriate underlying proposition.

Butterworth (1980b) also proposed that the order of the speech production processes is not rigidly determined. He suggests that on some occasions the speaker first selects one or two words of the construction, and then constructs a syntactic pattern and intonation contour appropriate to these 'leading decisions'. A similar approach was described as the 'keyword' or 'Variable Priority Hypothesis' by Harley (1982). The central idea was again that there is more than one possible order of processing.

There remains a remarkable convergence of much of the speech error data towards an order of processing as described in Fromkin (1971) and Garrett (1975). This follows the general sequence: 'message' formulation; construction of a syntactic frame; retrieval of the phonological form of open-class items from the lexicon and their insertion into the appropriate slot in the syntactic frame; the specification of closed-class lexical items and functional morphemes; and transduction from phonemes into phonetic features.[1]

It is an obvious weakness of the variable order hypotheses discussed above that they are not process-orientated. It is not clear how the flexibility of speech production processes should be incorporated into a working model. It is suggested that this can be achieved if speech production uses two attentional processes instead of one as in the traditional models. The basis for the distinction between the two processes is founded upon evidence to be discussed below, but also upon an emerging consensus among cognitive psychologists that there is a division between 'automatic' and 'attentional' or 'controlled' processing (Posner & Snyder 1975; Shiffrin & Schneider 1977). Generally, it is agreed that automatic processing is fast, can occur in parallel, is not directly accessible to consciousness, does not use working memory space, is not limited by capacity, and does not show interference effects with other automatic processes. In contrast, controlled processing is slow, serial, capacity limited, uses working memory space, and interferes in dual-task performance with other controlled processing mechanisms. Controlled processing is available by introspection to consciousness, except in the case of what Shiffrin & Schneider label 'veiled' controlled processing, which is inaccessible. There are some problems with this conceptualization (see, for example, Allport 1980; Neumann 1984), but nevertheless it provides a suitable framework with which to begin. However, to avoid too rigid an identification with the Shiffrin & Schneider (1977) approach, the terms 'automatic' and 'executive' processing will be used. At one level of description, automatic processing (AP) can be seen to consist of highly predictable activation pathways; executive processing (EP) consists of a set of strategies which can be used to modify these pathways. The model therefore bears some resemblance to that of Anderson (1983), who proposed that the general cognitive system consists of a spreading activation network, plus a superimposed production system.

According to this hypothesis, there are two types of attentional processes operating in normal speech production. The standard or default (AP) type is fast, fixed in the order of its component processes, and occurs automatically. The EP type is slow and enables variation in the order of processing. Only EP processes can be monitored directly by introspection during production (Levelt 1983). AP processes can only be monitored via their phonological output.

AP processes are probably responsible for the majority of our productions. This component of the model is similar to that of Harley (1984), Stemberger (1985) and Dell (1986). The main process used by this route is SPREADING ACTIVATION. The speech production system is conceptualized as network distributed across a neural substrate. The network contains nodes each of which at any time possesses a level of activation and a threshold at which the node 'fires' and passes on activation to the other nodes to which it is connected. The purpose of the threshold is to speed up processing. Nodes are connected to each other by links which can either be excitatory or inhibitory.

Nodes are organized in LEVELS OF PROCESSING. In the current model, PHONEME NODES are connected to appropriate LEXICAL NODES. The lexical nodes for content words are then connected to a level of concept nodes which encode semantic information about lexical items. They are eventually connected to nodes which represent perceptual information, though probably by many intervening levels. They are also connected to a SYNTACTIC LEVEL which encodes the grammatical roles in which an item can participate. The situation for function words is different, as their conceptual structure is far from clear. It is possible that they are represented at a higher level primarily by connections to the syntactic level and again by the specification of their possible grammatical roles. Nodes within levels are mutually inhibitory (McClelland & Rumelhart 1981). Processing between levels occurs in cascade (McClelland 1979). An example is shown in Figure 9.1.

Lexical access occurs when the activation at a particular node rises above that node's threshold level. Nodes at the same level are in competition with one another because of the inhibitory intra-level connections.

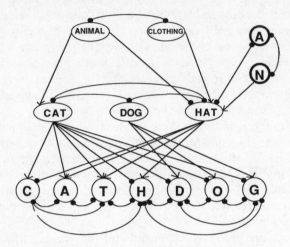

Figure 9.1 Portion of a sample network. This diagram shows connections within and between the conceptual (grossly simplified), lexical, syntactic (again grossly simplified) and phonological levels. Arrows show excitatory connections, dots inhibitory connections. For clarity many connections are omitted. Similarly serial position effects are ignored.

Syntax is embodied within the network by ensuring that the appropriate node reaches its peak activation at the correct time. This view of syntactic processing is compatible with that of Small (1981). This type of model of syntactic processing also sees each lexical entry associated with a syntactic node in a (distributed) network, with either activating (for example, DETERMINER calls NOUN) or inhibitory (for example, ADJECTIVE rules out VERB as an immediately subsequent node) links between them. So with the sentence *The cat loves the dog* the lexical and phoneme nodes for *cat* are inhibited until the DETERMINER node has been fired and the /t/ /ɵ/ /ə/ phonemes output. Needless to say, syntax is extremely problematical, and there is only sufficient space here to indicate that there may be solutions within this framework.

The automatic process is sufficient for converting the source conceptual code into the object phonological code most of the time. Often, there will be additional demands upon processing. It might be necessary to produce a particularly difficult string, or output it very carefully, or otherwise necessitate more planning than the default system can provide. For this executive processing (EP) process is available. The characteristics of these processes include the access and use of working memory during speech production and its proneness to interference. It has the benefit of altering the course and outcome of the default AP processes while enabling the monitoring of intermediate levels of processing. Its cost is that it is slower and draws upon additional resources. EP gates activation by focusing it at particular nodes and hence through particular pathways (see Schneider 1985). The mechanisms responsible for doing this are perhaps best conceptualized as being part of an EXECUTIVE STRUCTURE. The architecture of this model is summarized in Figure 9.2.

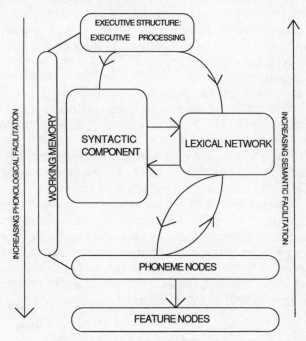

Figure 9.2 The architecture of the speech production system. This diagram shows the general arrangement of levels of processing and their connections. Phoneme nodes are assumed to be transduced into phonetic features. The prosodic level, dealing with stress assignment and the generation of the intonation contour, is omitted. (See Butterworth (1980c) for the relationship between this and the other systems.)

This model has the advantage of being able to reconcile the variable priority idea with the more traditional models, and, as will be shown, can account for a number of other apparently independent phenomena in speech production. It remains to examine these phenomena.

9.1 Evidence for a dual-process model

9.1.1 *Evidence from hesitations*

The analysis of the distribution of pauses in natural speech has revealed much about the time course of natural speech production. (See Butterworth (1980b) for a review.) We can distinguish between MICRO-PAUSES, which tend to be found before less frequent or probable words, and MACRO-PAUSES, which tend to be found at clausal junctures. Micro-pauses reflect transient difficulties in outputting a phonological code of a lexical item given its conceptual code, and macro-pauses indicates of major planning. Henderson, Goldman-Eisler & Skarbek (1966) noted that such pauses show a cyclic pattern. Generally, periods of much pausing alternate with periods of little pausing. The hypothesis is that this is due to periods containing much planning alternating with periods predominately of execution. Butterworth (1975) found that each cycle is approximately five to eight clauses long, and primarily corresponds to an 'idea' in the discourse. These planning cycles therefore appear to represent the planning and subsequent execution of semantic chunks in discourse.[2]

In the current model, the planning phase of each cycle involves much executive processing, whereas the execution phase involves a preponderance of automatic processing. In particular, high-level semantic and syntactic planning can be produced by executive processing. The message plan enters working memory and is prone to interference with other items that have access to it. This is further corroborated with the speech error data. Lexical access and syntactic assembly normally occur in parallel and interactively (Bock 1987) as automatic processes.

9.1.2 *Evidence from monitoring and feedback*

It is well known that we can monitor our own speech, and correct mistakes. However, we can do more than just correct a mistake we have already made. In some instances we are able to stop ourselves making the mistake before it is actually output. Hence we obviously have access to some (unspecified) internal representational level. Levelt (1983) examined spontaneous self-repairs in speech, and favoured a perceptual theory of monitoring. This hypothesis states that subjects parse their 'internal speech' as they do normal 'heard' speech, and hence detect deviations from their communicative intentions. These data impose the minimum requirement upon speech production that speakers can have access to a pre-articulatory code, and that they can modify this without necessarily committing themselves to its articulation. A wide range of material can enter working memory during the course of production (Hitch 1980). EP may have access to working memory; EP processes will often be directly accessible to conscious introspection. Speakers should also be faster and more accurate at detecting errors involving EP processes.

9.1.3 *Evidence from work upon memory and conversational analysis*

Schenkein (1980) has shown that speakers tend to re-use material from earlier in the conversation at various junctures. Speakers utilize pre-existing words, phrases, syntactic structures and even speech-act types. In this case generation does not occur commencing from the initial conceptual input only. Instead, highly activated structures are taken direct and manipulated at the appropriate level in interaction with the conceptual representation and with pragmatic constraints. EP operates on these template structures to override the AP route. Also, the form of previous statements has been shown to affect the way in which new questions are formulated (Levelt & Kelter 1982). Any theory of speech production must account for how this is done. According to the current model, the output of a certain syntactic structure primes that unit and makes it more accessible in the future. Commonly used structures may be stored in a pre-generated form. These will tend to be used rather more frequently than more complex syntactic structures which necessitate executive processing in their construction. Particular lexical items can also be primed in a similar way. The recent access of a particular item will lower that item's threshold, making it easier to access in the future (Morton 1969).

Ellis (1979) argued that a short-term memory buffer is routinely involved in normal speech production. On the other hand, Shallice & Butterworth (1977) described a patient who had a severely reduced digit span, yet who had unimpaired speech. Hence they concluded that working memory is not usually involved in speech production. The dual-process model provides a resolution of this paradox. A reduced digit span suggests an impairment of the EP system, but assuming that AP processes are intact, any such patient should still be able to produce fairly normal speech. However, the theory predicts that they should be incapable of the flexibility discussed here. Their ability to modify their production processes contingent upon circumstances and resources should be greatly reduced.

Lexical access normally occurs by AP mechanisms. Activation is automatically summed and facilitation effects (Harley 1984) are found. An alternative route to lexical access in production is by executive processing. This involves an active, serial search component for a particular phonological code. It is perhaps best exemplified in search in 'tip-of-the-tongue' states (Brown & McNeill 1966). Semantic intentions are matched against the phonological output. EP enables activation to be focused upon a set of particular conceptual nodes. These states possibly originate due to weakly associated inter-level connections between conceptual and phonological nodes. Phonologically related words are incorrectly activated and inhibit the target item. Evidence for intra-level inhibition is provided by work on phonological blocking in tip-of-the-tongue states (Jones & Langord 1987).

9.1.4 *Evidence from aphasia*

Butterworth & Howard (1987) describe the breakdown of speech production which gives rise to paragrammatisms in certain aphasics in terms of a deficit in control structures. In terms of the model described here this would be a failure of the EP system. The analysis of aphasia is complex, and it is probable that there is no simple mapping between components of the model and aphasia types. AP is almost certainly disrupted in all aphasics. For example, Ellis (1985) interprets the neologisms of jargon aphasics within an interactive activation framework similar to the AP processes described here.

9.1.5 *Evidence from speech errors*

These are discussed in detail in Harley (1984, forthcoming). Plan-internal errors are due to AP mechanisms. Non-plan-internal errors show elements of both automatic and controlled processing. Some examples are given.

(1) Target: What do you want to watch?
      Utterance: What do you want to READ?
      Context: The speaker was reading, and thinking 'He can watch TV while I finish this'.
(2) Target: We can discuss in detail what we're going to do.
      Utterance: We can discuss in detail WHERE WE'RE GOING TO LIVE.
      Context: The speaker planned to say next turn: 'I'm a homeless vagrant'.
(3) Target: It's not a danger at the moment.
      Utterance: It's not a DASTRY at the moment.
      Context: The speaker was writing a shopping list. As she spoke she wrote and thought the word 'pastry'. This was unrelated to what she was saying.

Lack of space permits only a cursory analysis of these errors. Each of them shows how working memory contents can interact with the normal speech production processes. Example (1) indicates that we can think about what we say as we say it, example (2) that we can plan in detail before articulation, and (3) that completely irrelevant material can interfere (see also Harley (forthcoming) for further discussion of this point, and for examples of environmental contamination errors). Note also a tendency to maintain syntactic coherence, and the automatic activation of associations by working memory contents. Other errors show that we can consider alternatives to the phonologically specified result of AP processing before and during articulation. In summary, there are both AP and EP sources of error.

9.2 Conclusions

This chapter attempts to set language generation within the wider context of cognitive psychology by showing how a major theoretical distinction between two types of attentional processing has explanatory value within model of speech production. More specifically, it is clear that considerable work remains to be done on integrating attentional processes and interactive activation or connectionist models.

Notes

1. In the Fromkin (1971) and Garrett (1975) models there is no interaction between levels. This has been disputed (see Dell & Reich 1981; Harley 1984; Stemberger 1985).
2. It should be pointed out that this cyclic analysis of pauses is disputed. So, in fact, is the analysis of pauses (see Good & Butterworth 1980).

Bibliography

Allport, D. A. (1980), 'Attention and performance', in G. Claxton (ed.), *Cognitive Psychology: New Directions*, London, Routledge & Kegan Paul.

Anderson, J. R. (1983), *The Architecture of Cognition*, Cambridge, Mass., Harvard University Press.

Bock, J. K. (1987), 'Coordinating words and syntax in speech plans', in A. W. Ellis (ed.), *Progress in the Psychology of Language*, Vol. 3, London, Erlbaum.

Brown, R. & McNeill, D. (1966), 'The "tip-of-the-tongue" phenomenon', *Journal of Verbal Learning and Verbal Behavior*, vol. 5, 325–37.

Butterworth, B. L. (1975), 'Hesitation and semantic planning in speech', *Journal of Psycholinguistic Research*, vol. 4, 75–87.

—— (1980a), 'Introduction: a brief review of methods of studying language production', in B. L. Butterworth (ed.), *Language Production, Vol. 1: Speech and Talk*, New York, Academic Press.

—— (1980b), 'Evidence from pauses in speech', in B. L. Butterworth (ed.), *Language Production, Vol. 1: Speech and Talk*, New York, Academic Press.

—— (1980c), 'Some constraints on models of language production', in B. L. Butterworth (ed.), *Language Production, Vol. 1: Speech and Talk*, New York, Academic Press.

Butterworth, B. L. & Howard, D. (1987), 'Paragrammatisms', *Cognition*, vol. 26, 1–37.

Dell, G. S. (1986), 'A spreading activation theory of retrieval in sentence production', *Psychological Review*, vol. 93, 283–321.

Dell, G. S. & Reich, P. A. (1981), 'Stages in sentence production: an analysis of speech errors', *Journal of Verbal Learning and Verbal Behavior*, vol. 20, 611–29.

Ellis, A. W. (1979), 'Speech production and short-term memory', in J. Morton & J. C. Marshall (eds), *Psycholinguistics, Vol. 2: Structure and Process*, London, Elek.

—— (1985), 'The production of spoken words: a cognitive neuropsychological perspective', in A. W. Ellis (ed.), *Progress in the Psychology of Language*, vol. 2, London, Erlbaum.

Ford, M. & Holmes, V. M. (1978), 'Planning units and syntax in sentence production', *Cognition*, vol. 6, 35–53.

Fromkin, V. A. (1971), 'The non-anomalous nature of anomalous utterances', *Language*, vol. 47, 27–52.

Garrett, M. (1975), 'The analysis of sentence production', in G. Bower (ed.), *The Psychology of Learning and Motivation*, vol. 9, New York, Academic Press.

Good, D. A. & Butterworth, B. L. (1980), 'Hesitancy as a conversational resource: some methodological considerations', in H. Dechert & M. Raupach (eds), *Temporal Variables in Speech*, The Hague, Mouton.

Harley, T. A. (1982), 'There's more than one way . . .', *Proceedings of the European Conference on Artificial Intelligence*, Paris.

—— (1984), 'A critique of top–down independent levels models of speech production: evidence from non-plan-internal speech errors', *Cognitive Science*, vol. 8, 191–219.

—— (forthcoming), 'The intrusion of environmental material into normal speech'.

Henderson, A., Goldman-Eisler, F. & Skarbek, A. (1966), 'Sequential temporal patterns in spontaneous speech', *Language and Speech*, vol. 9, 207–16.

Hitch, G. J. (1980), 'Developing the concept of working memory', in G. Claxton (ed.), *Cognitive Psychology: New Directions*, London, Routledge & Kegan Paul.

Hughlings-Jackson, J. (1932), *Selected Writings of John Hughlings-Jackson* (edited J. Taylor), London, Hodder & Stoughton.

Jones, G. V. & Langford, S. (1987), 'Phonological blocking in tip of the tongue states', *Cognition*, vol. 26, 115–22.

Levelt, W. J. M. (1983), 'Monitoring and self-repair in speech', *Cognition*, vol. 14, 41–104.

Levelt, W. J. M. & Kelter, S. (1982), 'Surface form and memory in question answering', *Cognitive Psychology*, vol. 14, 78–106.

McClelland, J. L. (1979), 'On the time relations of mental processes: an examination of systems of processes in cascade', *Psychological Review*, vol. 86, 287–330.

McClelland, J. L. & Rumelhart, D. E. (1981), 'An interactive activation model of context effects in letter perception—Part 1: An account of the basic findings', *Psychological Review*, vol. 88, 375–407.

Morton, J. (1969), 'Interaction of information in word recognition', *Psychological Review*, vol. 76, 165–78.

Neumann, O. (1984), 'Automatic processing: a review of recent findings and a plea for an old theory', in W. Prinz & A. F. Sanders (eds), *Cognition and Motor Processes*, Berlin, Springer-Verlag.

Norman, D. A. & Shallice, T. (1980), 'Attention to action: willed and automatic control of behavior', unpublished MS.

Pick, A. (1931), *Aphasia* (translated J. W. Brown, Springfield, Ill., Thomas, 1973).

Posner, M. I. & Snyder, C. R. R. (1975), 'Attention and cognitive control', in R. L. Solso (ed.), *Information Processing and Cognition: The Loyola Symposium*, Hillsdale, NJ, Erlbaum.

Schenkein, J. (1980), 'A taxonomy for repeating action sequences in natural conversation', in B. L. Butterworth (ed.), *Language Production, Vol. 1: Speech and Talk*, New York, Academic Press.

Schneider, W. (1985), 'Toward a model of attention and the development of automatic processing', in M. I. Posner & O. M. Marin (eds), *Attention and Performance*, XI, Hillsdale, NJ, Erlbaum.

Shallice, T. & Butterworth, B. (1977), 'Short-term memory impairment and spontaneous speech', *Neuropsychologia*, vol. 15, 729–35.

Shiffrin, R. M. & Schneider, W. (1977), 'Controlled and automatic human information processing—II: Perceptual learning, automatic attending, and a general theory', *Psychological Review*, vol. 84, 127–90.

Small, S. (1981), 'Viewing word expert parsing as linguistic theory', *Proceedings 6th International Joint Conference on Artificial Intelligence (IJCAI)*, pp. 70–6.

Stemberger, J. P. (1985), 'An interactive activation model of language production', in A. W. Ellis (ed.), *Progress in the Psychology of Language*, vol. 1, London, Erlbaum.

10 Incremental production of referential noun-phrases by human speakers

H. SCHRIEFERS* AND THOMAS PECHMANN†

10.0 Introduction

Language production by human speakers has a number of properties which distinguish it from most language generation systems in AI. In particular human language production is very fast and fluent, and speakers have to pay a price for this speed and fluency in terms of occasional speech errors, hesitations, false starts and changes of plans during speaking. One of the most remarkable properties of human language production seems to be that—at least sometimes—we start speaking before we know precisely what we are going to say. That is, planning on the pre-verbal message level, on the one hand, and formulating and articulating, on the other, are carried out partially in parallel. Borrowing a term from Kempen and Hoenkamp (1987) we will refer to this partial parallelism of message planning and formulation activities as INCREMENTAL PRODUCTION. Incremental production seems to be a necessary prerequisite for the fluency and speed of language production. Incremental production guarantees that linguistic formulation processes do not have to wait for the complete conceptual pre-planning of an utterance or even clause. This partial parallelism of message planning and formulation activities seems to be reflected in a class of speech errors which appear to be due to the intrusion of a preverbal message fragment or concept in the formulation process (see, for example, Harley 1984). Although there can be no doubt that natural language is often produced incrementally, there hardly exist any empirical studies concerned with this phenomenon. In the present chapter we will discuss some findings from experiments which give further support to the notion of incremental production together with some data indicating factors which make incremental production strategies more or less likely.

* *Max-Planck-Institut für Psycholinguistik, Nijmegen, The Netherlands*
† *Universität des Saarlandes, Saarbrücken, W. Germany*

10.1 The referential communication task as a tool to study human language production: the paradigm and some results

One method for the empirical study of human language production is to collect corpora of spontaneous speech, and to analyse phenomena like hesitations, pauses and speech errors. Although this method has the advantage that language production is spontaneous and not influenced by experimental laboratory settings, the method also has clear disadvantages. In particular, one has no control over the message which serves as input to the formulation processes. Since, in the present chapter, we focus on the relation between message planning activities and formulation activities, we used an experimental paradigm that is usually called the 'referential communication task'. With this task it is possible to elicit utterances from speakers under conditions which allow quite direct control over the message level input to be fed into the formulator.

In a referential communication task, the subject is asked to give a verbal description of a given target object permitting a potential listener to distinguish this target object from a number of simultaneously displayed context objects. Figure 10.1 gives an example of such a configuration of a

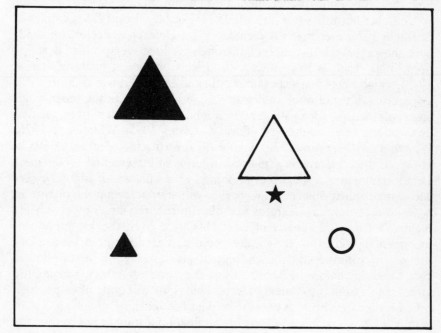

Figure 10.1 A simple example of a referential domain

target object (white triangle) with three context objects. As in the experiments to be reported below, the target object is indicated by a star. In this example, naming the colour and object class of the target object (WHITE TRIANGLE) would be sufficient to distinguish the target object from the context objects. This description would be MINIMALLY SPECIFIED. If the speaker were only to name the class of the target object (TRIANGLE), then a listener could not unambiguously identify the target object. Such a description would be UNDERSPECIFIED. The speaker could, however, also give an OVERSPECIFIED description, i.e. a description mentioning more features than those which discriminate the target object from the context objects. In the example given in Figure 10.1, the speaker could mention the target object's (relative) size in addition to its colour and object class. In this particular case, the overspecified description could either take the format BIG WHITE TRIANGLE or WHITE BIG TRIANGLE.

Below we will first discuss some of the results reported in the literature on referential communication. Then we will make a proposal about how these results can be explained in the framework of incremental language production. Finally we will present some further data which, on the one hand, give additional support to the idea of incremental production, and which, on the other hand, give some first indication about influences which limit the applicability of incremental production strategies.

A number of studies (e.g. Freedle 1972; Ford & Olson 1975; Garmiza & Anisfield 1976; Herrmann & Deutsch 1976; Deutsch & Pechmann 1982) have shown that adult speakers quite often produce overspecified descriptions. This result is in conflict with Grice's 'maxim of quantity' (Grice 1975), which states that a speaker should make his utterance as informative as required, but not more informative than required. On the other hand, and somewhat paradoxically, children tend to produce less overspecified descriptions than adults (e.g. Ford & Olson 1975; Whitehurst 1976; Whitehurst & Merkur 1977; Higgins 1977; Deutsch & Pechmann 1982). How can these results be explained in terms of incremental production? Let us assume that a speaker is presented with a picture of a target object and some context objects. The speaker will start scanning the picture in order to determine the features that discriminate the target object unambiguously from the context objects. However, given the assumption of incremental production, the speaker could start his description even before the visual scanning and the conceptual planning for his description is completed, i.e. before he has identified the features that discriminate the target object from the context objects. That is, he will quite often produce overspecified descriptions because he does not yet know whether a certain feature, like colour, is a necessary discrimination feature or not by the time he starts his description. The time overlap between conceptual planning and formulating would be responsible for the high proportion of over-specified utterances.

Pechmann (cf. Pechmann 1984a,b, 1987) has provided strong evidence for this interpretation. He recorded the eye-movements of subjects during a referential description experiment. These data show that adult speakers tend to start the articulation of the description before they have scanned all objects of a given picture, and that the visual scanning processes are still going on while overt speech has already begun. That is, adult speakers start their description before they know what the discriminating features of the target object are. In contrast, children tended to scan the whole array of objects on a given picture first, and then started with the description of the target object.

Although this interpretation nicely explains referential overspecification in terms of incremental production, it seems to be in conflict with other speaker requirements. Remember the example of an overspecified description given above. This description could either take the format WHITE BIG TRIANGLE or BIG WHITE TRIANGLE. When one asks for speakers' intuitive preferences for one of these two utterances, then the latter will almost always turn out to be by far the preferred one (cf. Martin 1969; Danks & Glucksberg 1971). This has been explained by assuming general rules governing the order of prenominal adjectives (e.g. Martin 1969; Danks & Glucksberg 1971; Ertel 1971).

If this were the case, then one could seriously question the applicability of incremental production in these tasks, since then subjects would always have to wait until they have determined the feature that has to be named first in the description according to this rule before they could start their description. That is, they could not start their utterance with that feature of the target object that becomes available first. And (within the domain of the features colour and size) this feature can be expected to be colour since it is an 'absolute' feature of the target object that can be determined without comparing the target object with the context objects, and it is particularly quickly processed by peripheral vision. However, one might doubt whether the preference for the prenominal adjective ordering SIZE BEFORE COLOR in forced-choice tasks really reflects what speakers actually do when speaking. If they are following an incremental production strategy, then one should find a substantial number of descriptions which do not conform to this rule of prenominal adjective ordering. And indeed, this hypothesis has been repeatedly supported by empirical data (Pechmann in press).

Before turning to some experimental evidence concerning the sketched consequences of incremental production for overspecification and pre-nominal adjective ordering, one additional point has to be made. The idea of incremental production does not mean that a speaker just enumerates the properties of the target object in the order in which they become conceptually available. If this were the case one would expect subjects to produce descriptions which, for example, start with the object class of the target object, followed by additional features (like BALL GREEN BIG). Instead, subjects spontaneously give their descriptions in the form of a well-formed NP which for languages like Dutch, English and German means that the noun has to be preceded by the adjectives. So even when the object class would be the first feature of the target object that becomes available, there would be a strong pressure from the syntactic rules determining the form of an NP to prevent subjects from starting their description by mentioning the object class of the target object. And for the same reason one would not expect subjects to leave out the noun even when the noun is not a discriminating feature since the syntactic rules for a complete NP require the presence of a noun except for elliptic cases. For example, speakers will not refer to a white triangle in the context of black objects by giving the minimally specified description WHITE, but by means of a complete NP (i.e. WHITE TRIANGLE). So mentioning the noun when it is not a discriminating feature cannot be counted as a real case of over-specification. Rather, this is motivated by syntactic rules. And it appears to be quite likely that the pressure to follow such a rule is stronger than the one to follow a rule of prenominal adjective ordering.

Along the same line of argument it could also occur that bigger conceptual units than the object class of the target object become the basic building block of the description. For example, if one presented subjects over and over again with pictures of target objects and context objects from only a few different object classes in a few different colours, then it might happen that the subject would conceptualize the combination of a given colour and object class as one fixed higher order entity which can be modified further by a size adjective.

An NP like BIG BLACK TRIANGLE would then express the notion that there is a basic conceptual unit ‹black triangle› which is BIG, and it would not express the notion that there is a basic conceptual unit ‹triangle› which is BIG AND BLACK. Just as with the noun of an NP, subjects should always name the complete conceptual basic unit (e.g. BLACK TRIANGLE) in their description, regardless of whether colour is a discriminating feature or not, and they should almost never produce descriptions like BLACK BIG TRIANGLE since then they would ‘destroy’ the basic conceptual unit (the speaker would then express the concept of either a ‹triangle› which is BIG and BLACK, or of a ‹big triangle› which is BLACK, but not of a ‹black triangle› which is BIG).

10.2 Some empirical results

We put some of the above ideas to test in two experiments. Both experiments used the referential description task. In Experiment I, subjects saw 101 pictures, each depicting a target object and three to four context objects. In Experiment II, subjects saw thirty-six pictures of a target object and four to six context objects, and thirty-six pictures of a target object with ten to twelve context objects. The experiments mainly differed from each other with respect to the construction of the stimulus materials. In Experiment I, each object was realized in three different levels of size and four colours, with the target object always being selected from the medium level of size. In Experiment II, only two levels of size were realized. In Experiment I, three different classes of objects were used in the construction of the pictures (namely the geometric figures circle, triangle and square) whereas in Experiment II forty-eight different classes of objects were used (namely everyday objects like chair, table, basket, etc.). All these differences between the experiments should lead subjects in Experiment I to conceive of colour and object class together as the basic conceptual unit for their descriptions. In contrast, in Experiment II such a tendency should not be induced.

The most important results for the present discussion can be summarized as follows: in both experiments subjects almost always produced a complete and correct NP, i.e. they always named the object class regardless of whether object class was a necessary discriminating feature or not. This conforms with the idea that there is a strong pressure from syntactic rules to produce a correct NP, and, as a consequence, subjects in this task did not treat object class as a feature which could be omitted when it did not discriminate the target object from the context objects. However, the data also indicate that in Experiment I it was presumably a conceptual unit of object class and colour which formed the basic building block around which subjects constructed their descriptions. This is reflected in two results. First, in Experiment I subjects almost always named the colour of the target object. That is, besides descriptions in which colour is a necessary discriminating feature of the target object, they also named colour in 92 per cent of all experimental trials in which colour was not a necessary discriminating feature. And second, in only 11 per cent of the descriptions consisting of a colour adjective, a size adjective and a noun, subjects produced an NP in which the colour adjective preceded the size adjective.

In contrast, in Experiment II the corresponding percentage of over-specifications regarding colour was clearly lower (as should be expected when colour is not named automatically as part of the basic building block of their descriptions), but with 52 per cent (as compared to 92 per cent in Experiment I) it was still quite high, as should be expected under the assumption of an incremental production strategy. And finally, this went together with a massive increase in the number of NPs of the type ‹colour, size, noun›. Whereas in Experiment I only 11 per cent of the NPs consisting of a colour adjective, a size adjective and a noun showed the ordering ‹colour, size, noun›, the corresponding percentage for Experiment II was 35 per cent. This shows that prenominal adjective ordering does not conform to a fixed, situation-independent rule. Rather, given a situation favouring incremental production strategies, as in Experiment II, there is a high percentage of utterances not conforming to this rule. In contrast, given the situation of Experiment I, there is a strong tendency to form a higher-order conceptual entity of colour and object class, and to treat this entity in much the same way as object class alone in Experiment I.

10.3 Conclusion

There are good reasons to assume that at least a certain amount of simultaneity between conceptual message planning and formulating is a necessary prerequisite for the speed and fluency of human language production. On the other hand, however, there are a number of potential factors that constrain the applicability of incremental production in such a way that human language production does not just become the enumeration of properties or ideas in the order in which they become available. In the present chapter we have presented some empirical evidence that human language production is, at least to some extent, incremental. On the other hand, we have tried to point to some of the factors constraining the amount of admissible and/or tolerable ‘incrementality’. One of these factors was a clear and obvious one, namely the syntactic rules for NPs in languages like Dutch, German and English. We also discussed a second factor which was not so obvious, namely the way in which speakers break down a given visual input into smaller or larger conceptual units or chunks.

Bibliography

Danks, J. H. & Glucksberg, S. (1971), ‘Psychological scaling of adjective order’, *Journal of Verbal Learning and Verbal Behavior*, vol. 10, 63–7.

Deutsch, W. & Pechmann, T. (1982), ‘Social interaction and the development of definite descriptions’, *Cognition*, vol. 11, 159–84.

Ertel, S. (1971), ‘Pränominale Adjektivfolgen und semantische Tiefenstruktur’, *Studia Psychologica*, vol. 13, 127–35.

Ford, W. & Olson, D. (1975), 'The elaboration of the noun phrase in children's descriptions of objects', *Journal of Experimental Child Psychology*, vol. 19, 371–82.

Freedle, R. (1972), 'Language users as fallible information processors: implications for measuring and modeling comprehension', in R. O. Freedle & J. B. Carroll (eds), *Language Comprehension and the Acquisition of Knowledge*, New York, Wiley.

Garmiza, C. & Anisfield, M. (1976), 'Factors reducing the efficiency of referent-communication in children', *Merrill-Palmer Quarterly*, vol., 22, 125–36.

Grice, H. P. (1975), 'Logic and conversation', in P. Cole & J. L. Morgan (eds), *Syntax and Semantics, Volume 3: Speech Acts*, New York, Academic Press.

Harley, T. A. (1984), 'A critique of top–down independent level models of speech production: evidence from non-plan-internal speech errors', *Cognitive Science*, vol. 8, 191–219.

Herrmann, T. & Deutsch, W. (1976), *Psychologie der Objektbenennung*, Bern, Huber.

Higgins, E. T. (1977), 'Communication development as related to channel, incentive and social class', *Genetic Psychology Monographs*, vol. 66, 75–141.

Kempen, G. & Hoenkamp, E. (1987), 'An incremental procedural grammar for sentence formulation', *Cognitive Science*, vol. 11, 201–258.

Martin, J. E. (1969), 'Semantic determinants of preferred adjective ordering', *Journal of Verbal Learning and Verbal Behavior*', vol. 8, 697–704.

Pechmann, T. (1984a), 'Accentuation and redundancy in children's and adults' referential communication', in H. Bouma & D. Bouwhuis (eds), *Attention and Performance 10*, Hillsdale, NJ, Erlbaum.

—— (1984b), 'Überspezifizierung und Betonung in referentieller Kommunikation', unpublished doctoral dissertation, Universität Mannheim.

—— (1987), 'Effects of incremental speech production on the syntax and content of noun phrases', Fachrichtungsarbeit No. 120 der Fachrichtung Psychologie der Universität des Saarlandes.

—— (in press), 'Incremental speech production and referential overspecification', *Linguistics*, vol. 27.

Whitehurst, G. J. (1976), 'The development of communication: changes with age and modeling', *Child Development*, vol. 47, 473–82.

Whitehurst, G. J. & Merkur, A. (1977), 'The development of communication: modeling and contrast failure', *Child Development*, vol. 48, 993–1001.

Part V Educational applications

11 Natural languages are flexible tools: that's what makes them hard to explain, to learn and to use

MICHAEL ZOCK*

11.1 Problem

The psychologist or language teacher interested in text generation may be startled by the following two facts:

(1) Despite our enormous amount of experience in speaking and writing, every so often we fail. Performance errors in natural language are numerous compared to other domains (for example, mathematics).
(2) A great many natural language generators have come to light during the last decade.[1] These systems are truly impressive as far as output is concerned. However, they are of little help to a human trying to express a given content.

One may thus wonder why natural languages are so hard to learn, to use or to explain, and why current computerized systems have so little to say. The answer to those questions may be found in:

(a) the cognitive constraints of the information process;
(b) the structure of the data; and
(c) the underlying assumptions or goals of the application designers.

Points (a) and (b) are clearly related. Humans are resource-limited. Hence the symbols and the mechanisms they can put to use are constrained in specific ways.[2] What those constraints are and how they interrelate is the core of the student's learning task, or the scientist's research task.

* *LIMSI, Orsay, France*

11.1.1 *Cognitive, linguistic and pragmatic constraints*

Natural, as opposed to artificial, languages are flexible. They ought to be because of cognitive, linguistic and pragmatic constraints. The former are universal. Their physical manifestations are the space, time, and channel constraints:

(i) humans, unlike computers, have a very limited short-term memory;
(ii) unless rehearsed, information vanishes after a short time;
(iii) output is sequential; one can utter but one word at a time.

The second constraint, although related to the former, is relative to a given language (for example, word order), linguistic universals being the exception. Finally, the pragmatic constraint consists in limiting the quantity of output—speakers are allotted some definite amount of space and time.

Obviously these constraints have a number of consequences on the organization of the process as well as on the structure of the data. As we can feed only a limited amount of information into the short-term memory (SPACE CONSTRAINT), and as information decays rapidly over time (TIME CONSTRAINT), we have to express our thoughts as fast as possible, keeping the buffer free from overload.

However, buffer clearance cannot be done in just any way. Thoughtless clearance of the working memory, i.e. outputting words in the order of the arrival of their conceptual correlates (FIFO), or processing the concepts one by one (word-to-word processing), may result in poor syntactic planning. As a result one may get stuck in a dead end, choose the wrong word, syntactic category or sentence frame. Planning is thus necessary. On the other hand, if one plans too far ahead, part of the message may be lost by the time one initiates expressing the planned content.

What can one do in a situation where no new material can be fed into the buffer, unless part of it is released, and where too early clearance may result in poor syntactic planning, while late clearance may imply loss of information? We clearly face a resource management problem with regard to the size in coordination of input and output. How far shall we plan ahead, or, corollarily, when shall we start to verbalize? Typically people do not plan sentences entirely in advance; neither do they proceed word by word. The planning and execution units are thus smaller than a sentence, but longer than a word.

As the speaker is confronted with two conflicting demands—(i) clear the buffer as soon as possible in order to avoid overload, and (ii) feed into it enough information to perform optimal linguistic processing—some compromise has to be found. In human processing the conflict is solved by incremental processing (see below).

The channel limitations are a further constraint. The fact that one can utter but one word at a time (CHANNEL CONSTRAINT) may imply transformations. As the order of conceptual fragments does not necessarily correlate with the order of their corresponding linguistic expressions (words), mismatches between input–output order may yield movement of constituents (at least for languages with restrictions on word order). While transformations have the advantage to allow for inclusion of a given conceptual fragment in the sentence under study, thus avoiding global changes (restarting from scratch), they are, computationally speaking, not very elegant, as they imply storage of the element to be transferred.

Finally, the PRAGMATIC CONSTRAINT results in some compromise between ideal delivery and acceptable performance, because if one stops too long between two sentences, the listener may take this as a signal to take his turn.[3]

11.1.1.1 *Flexibility of data and process answer in part of the problem of resource management*

Humans have found ways, psychological and linguistic resources, to deal with the above-mentioned constraints. They have developed strategies, forging the tool in such a way that they can control the whole process despite its complexity (number and complexity of constraints).

For example, incremental processing allows one to overcome the BUFFER CONSTRAINTS: one starts to output before having fully encoded content.[4] While speaking we think. The problem of incremental processing is the negotiation of a good compromise between encoding and expressing content (opportunistic planning).

Incremental processing has the advantage of solving, at least in part, the problem of short-term memory. However, there is a price to be paid. Parallel or time-sharing processes put heavy constraints on the input-output mechanisms. Operating on incomplete conceptual structures, one is never sure of having made the best linguistic choice, as new data (concepts) may turn out to be incompatible with the structure built so far.

As this situation is the rule rather than the exception, it is easy to understand why languages need to be flexible. If they were not, every time we had a mapping problem, we would have to destroy the whole structure and build from scratch. As we all know, this is rarely the case. We usually make only local corrections.

Actually, it is quite remarkable to see to what extent the human system is capable of dealing with poorly planned solutions. Of course, speakers do make a lot of errors, but despite their imperfect performance, the human system hardly ever breaks down completely. A skillful speaker/writer usually finds a way out, even if he is short of words.[5] This robustness is all the more noteworthy as the speaker has to JUGGLE several, sometimes contradictory, DEMANDS. For example, he has to find a good COMPROMISE between

(i) ECONOMY and PRECISION: despite conciseness he wants to be precise (this implies adequate lexical choices);

(ii) PLANNING and EXECUTION, i.e. encoding and expressing content: before saying something one has to think carefully about what one wants to say and how to say it. As we noted already, strict separation of planning and execution (serial processing) may result in loss of information (memory constraint), or in the fact that someone else will take his turn (pragmatic constraint).

What resources do we have to deal with the CHANNEL CONSTRAINT? As was stated earlier, linguistic structures are NOT necessarily ISOMORPHIC with conceptual structures, and that is why we may need to perform transformations. Natural languages are generally fairly flexible with respect to linearization. If this were not so, we would have to start from scratch every time we started verbalizing from the wrong node of a conceptual graph. In order to gain some freedom on linearizing graph-like structures, languages have special devices of which transformations are probably the best known. However, many languages have another device, much more powerful and without the former's shortcoming—Tesnière (1959) called it 'translation'. According to him, translation is a mechanism by which a lexical item can be transferred from one syntactic category to another. For example, a verb may be nominalized, an adjective may become a verb and so forth.[6] I strongly believe that this mechanism is much more commonly used than has generally been recognized.

We have now enough information to answer the first set of questions: (i) why is linguistic performance so imperfect, and (ii) why are languages so hard to learn or to explain?

The MEMORY CONSTRAINTS which force us to operate on incomplete conceptual structures explain, at least in part, the relatively high error rate. The FLEXIBILITY of the system, on the other hand, explains why languages are so hard to learn or to explain. The whole process is organized into modules which communicate to some extent. This is clearly the case for lexical and syntactic choices, one modulating as a function of the other:

IN CASE OF snow . . .	(SNOW = noun)
IF it snows . . .	(SNOW = verb)
He has the NECESSARY tools.	(NECESSITY = adjective)
He has the tools he NEEDS.	(NECESSITY = verb)

11.1.1.2 *Flexibility enhances the efficiency of processing, but this skill is not easily learned*   The advantage of flexibility is the relative freedom of processing: different orders of processing are possible. Priority may be given to lexical or syntactic planning.[7]

The disadvantage of flexibility is that the causal relationships between the choices on the different levels are no longer straightforward. There are several reasons for this:

(i) The choice on one level may affect the range of choices or the outcome of a choice on an entirely different level. For example, an early, pragmatically motivated choice like topic may affect the final syntactic structure (voice). The former belongs to the discourse level, whereas the latter pertains to the sentence level.

(ii) A choice may have several consequences. For example, topicalization may affect lexicalization as well as syntactic structure:

John had inherited some bonds. Just before the crash of the stock market

    he SOLD them to a friend

    *his friend BOUGHT them from him

    *the bonds WERE SOLD to his friend

(iii) The result of a choice may be indirect; it appears only at an intermediate level (for example, it may affect the part of speech). The problem is that the only outcome which is really objective (i.e. accessible to our senses) is the final result (text). Hence we are much less aware of the outcomes on the intermediate levels.

Which choice determines which outcome, or what determines what, is thus far from evident; the decision at one level (at an early stage) may affect the available choices and thus the final outcome (the only one visible) in very subtle ways.

To summarize, the architecture of natural languages seems to be systemic and heterarchical rather than hierarchical. There are dependencies across hierarchical levels, affecting the final form in unpredictable ways. As a result it is hard, even for a native speaker, to tell what choices have what effect, or, put differently, what determines what.

11.1.2 *Why have computer systems at present so little to say?*

Let us now turn to the second question: why have present systems so little to say? The answer is to be found in the goals as well as in the underlying assumptions of the system designers. Obviously these systems were not built with the intent to assist man or to model human performance.[8]

More importantly, current systems are generally rigid. Their lack of flexibility is due to the unidirectional information flow.[9] There is hardly any interaction between CONCEPTUAL (meaning), TEXTUAL (chunking and linearization) and LINGUISTIC decisions (lexicalization and syntactic structures). More precisely, it is generally assumed that:

(i) meaning is something stable which is not altered during the process of mapping conceptual structures on to linguistic structures; and that
(ii) the processor knows in advance in what syntactical terms (part of speech) to express a conceptual fragment.[10]

Such a view entails the mistaken idea that at the onset of articulation the processor knows:

— how to break down a given conceptual structure, i.e. graph, so that each chunk matches any of the available sentence frames; and, in corollary,
— how to express a given conceptual fragment; for example, should a given concept surface as a noun, verb, adjective, etc.

While these assumptions may be true for highly skilled speakers (politicians, reporters) and for stereotyped situations (weather forecasts, sport reports), they are somehow counter-intuitive and inconsistent with natural data. I believe that they have to be relativized with respect to on-line processing, be it speaking or writing. The ordinary speaker/writer frequently fails in his attempts to produce well-formed and coherent sentences. Trying to put too much information into a sentence frame, he becomes unclear (embedding), loses track, or gets stuck in dead ends. Chunking a graph into too small pieces, his utterances lack variety (poor style) or are incomplete.

Translating given conceptual structures into well-formed linguistic strings (sentences) draws on various knowledge sources: textual, lexical and morpho-syntactical. One has to:

— find a adequate discourse structure (overall organization);
— de. rmine paragraph, sentence or clause boundaries, i.e. chunk the whole into smaller, more manageable parts (for example, subgraphs);
— map the concepts on to words, or, more precisely, word-stems; and
— integrate these lexical formatives into an adequate sentence frame, i.e. shape the words (for example, nominalize a given formative), determine their order (linearization), insert function words, and make the necessary morphological adjustments (agreement: subject–verb, noun–adjective, etc.).

In trying to map efficiently a conceptual structure on to a linguistic structure one has to learn three things: (i) what these choices are (forms);

(ii) what they depend on (meaning); and (iii) how the choices interact (implications of each choice).

What I am striving for is to visualize this process, in particular the interaction of the choices. The decomposition of the process should ease the cognitive burden (reduce mental load) while visualization of the inter-actions should make transparent the causal links between meaning (choices) and form (outcomes).

11.2 Goal

In this part of my chapter I will present the outline of a system, which, once implemented, should show how the mapping of conceptual structures on to linguistic forms can be done in a dynamic fashion. The purpose of this system is to show on-line the interdependence of the above-mentioned components. In doing so, it might assist a student learning French, or a writer engaged in the formulation process. Both of them might use it not only to express content, but also to determine empirically how decisions like (i) chunk-size, (ii) topicalization, (iii) lexicalization, or (iv) syntactic structure affect each other, contributing in particular ways to the final form of the content to be expressed.

The system could also be useful for computational linguistics trying to determine the function or motivation of these choices. As a given con-ceptual structure can be phrased in many ways, each version producing a different rhetorical effect, it is important to determine why, when and how these choices are made.[11] For example, under what conditions should one use a subordinate clause? What are the linguistic and pragmatic constraints on topicalization, and so on.

Finally, the system should also allow us to model psychologically relevant behaviour. Thus it should account not only for correct sentences, but also for certain performance errors (false starts, dead ends). For example, what happens if one makes an inadequate choice, e.g. chooses a chunk too big for the available sentence frames? Does one have to start from scratch? What should we do in case of inadequate topicalization?

One of the system's tasks is precisely to model and to elucidate these failures by showing how inadequate choices, or choices made at a very late date (afterthoughts, last minute changes of lexical choice, etc.), may impair performance.

11.3 Outline of a possible solution

The system I have in mind is an interactive syntactic paraphrase-generator.[12] The user provides the data (WHAT TO SAY) and the system helps him to determine the final form (HOW TO SAY IT). Input is given in the form of propositions which are transformed into a conceptual graph. This graph can be translated into several equivalent texts.

These different forms depend (i) on the expressive possibilities of the language, and (ii) on a number of choices to be made by the speaker. As the learner may not know what those choices are, the system will make them explicit, inviting him to watch their outcome. In doing so, the system will not only help to determine the final form, but, more importantly, it will show the implication of each choice. The user can thus empirically find out what determines what, i.e. what controls what. For example, how does topicalization, or a particular lexical choice, affect syntax?

At the moment there are three types of choices the user can make:

—SIZE of CHUNK: by drawing a window one tells the system what parts of the conceptual structure should be integrated into the sentence-frame. For example, one can try to build one large sentence (one huge window), or several smaller ones (series of small windows). The system will try each time to generate a sentence, including all the elements (concepts) contained in the window. As we will see, chunk-size affects not only sentence complexity (embedding) but also the syntactic status of the different elements.

— Focus or TOPICALIZATION: any graph can be linearized in different ways. It is thus important to decide where to start.

— CHOICE of particular WORDS, expressions or SENTENCE STRUCTURE: all of these may be given in a communicative setting by the prior context.

Let us use an example to illustrate this dialogue (see Figure 11.1). Suppose that we want to express the following content:

publish (press
        (decide (Mitterrand
                (nationalize (Mitterrand, banks)))

The system transforms this input into a conceptual graph, showing all the words it knows of in order to express the given concepts. The user chooses among these words,[13] determines the size of the window and the concept with which he wants to start linearization. By drawing a window, he signals what kind of information he wants the system to build a sentence with. Obviously, different choices result in different surface expressions.

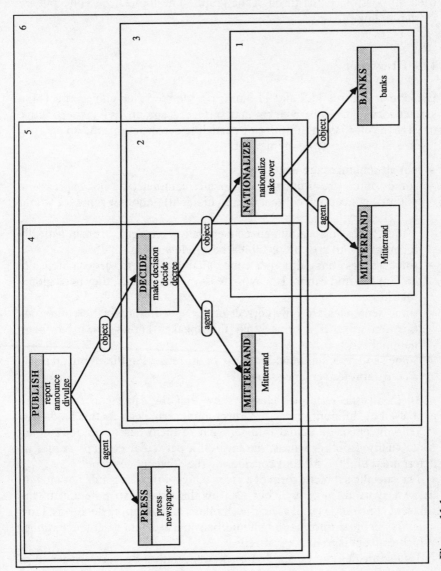

Figure 11.1

In Figure 11.2 the numbers refer to the windows. As we had six windows (see Figure 11.1) we have six numbers. For each window we have tried all possible paths through the graph. The topicalized concepts are written in upper case.

11.4 Discussion

Looking at Figures 11.2 and 11.3 one can see how each choice affects the surface form. The same concept may surface as a noun, as a verb, as active or passive voice, as an infinitive or participle construction, and so on.

Several points may be of interest:

— not all sentences are complete;
— some sentences, although syntactically complete, do not express the planned conceptual content (see 5f, 6i, 6j, 6l)—another sentence would be necessary;
— some expressions, although conceptually complete, are syntactically incomplete but are completable (the window is too small);
— some expressions, although conceptually complete, are syntactically incomplete and cannot be completed—in other words, they need global revision;
— some sentences are only correct under specific pragmatic conditions (for example, 2f assumes that the speaker knows WHAT has been nationalized);
— some sentences sound odd because of the tense. Put differently, tense is a constraint for sentence structure

All in all, the examples clearly show that the same concept may be expressed by different syntactic forms (noun, verb, etc.). As this holds true for all concepts, the actual form of each of them has to be determined contextually. In other words, the form of a particular concept cannot be determined blindly, without considering the adjacent concepts.

The specific syntactic form of a given concept thus depends not only on its own syntactic potential, but also on the expressive potential of the adjacent concepts, as well as on the chunking and scanning decisions. How much conceptual information should be squeezed into a sentence frame? Which concept is to be topicalized?

Two strategies can be applied by the user: either he starts with a given sentence-frame and looks to see if a given conceptual item can be realized, e.g. as a noun, as a verb, etc. (syntax-driven generation), or he starts with a concept, checking whether any of the associated expressions (words) can be integrated into a known sentence-frame (lexical-driven generation). In

1 a) **Mitterrand** nationalizes the banks.
  b) The **nationalization** of the banks by Mitterrand   (...)
  c) The **banks** are nationalized by Mitterrand.
  d) The **banks**, nationalized by Mitterrand   (...)

2 a) **Mitterrand** decides to nationalize.   (?)
  b) **Mitterrand** decides on the nationalization   (...)
  c) **Mitterrand's** decision to nationalize   (...)
  d) The **decision** of Mitterrand to nationalize   (...)
  e) The **decision** made by Mitterrand to nationalize   (...)
  f) The **nationalization** decided by Mitterrand   (...)
  g) The **nationalization** is decided by Mitterrand.

3 a) **Mitterrand** decides to nationalize the banks.
  b) **Mitterrand** decides on the nationalization of the banks.
  c) The **decision** of Mitterrand to nationalize the banks   (...)
  d) The **nationalization** of the banks decided by Mitterrand   (...)
  e) The **nationalization** of the banks is decided by Mitterrand.
  f) The **banks**, nationalized by Mitterrand,   (.../-)

4 a) The **press** publishes the decision of Mitterrand.
  b) The **press** publishes Mitterrand's decision.
  c) The **press** publishes that Mitterrand decides   (...)
  d) The **press**' publication of Mitterrand's decision   (...)
  e) The **publication** by the press of Mitterrand's decision   (...)
  f) The **publication** by the press that Mitterrand decides   (...)
  g) The **decision** of Mitterrand, published by the press   (...)
  h) The **decision** of Mitterrand is published by the press.

5 a) The **press** publishes Mitterrand's decision to nationalize.   (?)
  b) The **press** publishes that Mitterrand decides to nationalize.   (?)
  c) The **publication** by the press of Mitterrand's decision to nationalize   (...)
  d) The **decision** of Mitterrand to nationalize is published by the press.
  e) The **decision** of the nationalization by Mitterrand is published by the press.
  f) **Mitterrand** decides to nationalize.   (?/-)
  g) The **nationalization** decided by Mitterand is published by the press.

6 a) The **press** publishes that Mitterrand decides to nationalize the banks.
  b) The **press** publishes Mitterrand's decision to nationalize the banks.
  c) The **press** publishes that Miterrand decides to nationalize the banks.
  d) The **publication** of Mitterrand's decision to nationalize the banks   (...)
  e) The **decision** of Mitterrand to nationalize the banks is published by the press.
  f) The **decision** made by Mitterrand to nationalize the banks is published by the press.
  g) The **decision** that Mitterrand has made to nationalize the banks is published by the press.
  h) **Mitterrand** decides to nationalize the banks.   (-)
  i) **Mitterrand** decides on the nationalization of the banks.   (-)
  j) **Mitterrand's** decision to nationalize the banks is published by the press.
  k) The **nationalization** of the banks decided by Mitterrand is published by the press.
  l) The **nationalization** of the banks that Mitterrand decides is published by the press.
  m) **Mitterrand** nationalizes the banks.   (-)
  n) **Mitterrand's** nationalization of the banks   (.../-)
  o) The **banks** are nationalized by Mitterrand.   (-)
  p) The **banks** nationalized by Mitterrand.   (-)

(...) *syntactically* incomplete sentence;   (-) *conceptually* incomplete sentence

Figure 11.2

	MAKE PUBLIC	DECIDE	NATIONALIZE
1 a	-	-	verb
b	-	-	noun
c	-	-	verb (passive voice)
d	-	-	verb (participle)
2 a	-	verb	verb (infinitive)
b	-	verb	noun
c	-	noun	verb (infinitive)
d	-	noun	verb (infinitive)
e	-	noun	verb (infinitive)
f	-	verb (participle)	noun
g	-	verb (passive voice)	noun
3 a	-	verb	verb (infinitive)
b	-	verb	noun
c	-	noun	verb (infinitive)
d	-	verb (participle)	noun
e	-	verb (passive voice)	noun
f	-	-	verb (participle)
4 a	verb	noun	-
b	verb	noun	-
c	verb	verb	-
d	noun	noun	-
e	noun	noun	-
f	noun	verb	-
g	verb (participle)	noun	-
h	verb (passive voice)	noun	-
5 a	verb	noun	verb (infinitive)
b	verb	verb	verb (infinitive)
c	noun	noun	verb (infinitive)
d	verb (passive voice)	noun	verb (infinitive)
e	verb (passive voice)	noun	noun
f	-	verb	verb (infinitive)
g	verb (passive voice)	verb (participle)	noun
6 a	verb	verb	verb (infinitive)
b	verb	noun	verb (infinitive)
c	verb	verb (passive voice)	verb (infintive)
d	noun	noun	verb (infinitive)
e	verb (passive voice)	noun	verb (infinitive)
f	verb (passive voice)	noun	verb (infinitive)
g	verb (passive voice)	noun	verb (infinitive)
h	-	verb	verb (infinitive)
i	-	verb	noun
j	-	noun	noun
k	verb (passive voice)	verb (participle)	noun
l	verb (passive voice)	verb	noun
m	-	-	verb
n	-	-	noun
o	-	-	verb (passive voice)
p	-	-	verb (participle)

Figure 11.3

the first case lexical items have to be shaped to fit the syntactic structure (top–down), whereas in the second case the syntactic structure has to be adapted to the data, i.e. the lexical choices drive the syntactic tree formation process (bottom–up). The grammar operates here as a filter rather than a generative device.

11.5 Conclusion

In the first part of this chapter, I have tried to explain why sentence generation is such a complex task. In the second part I have analysed why current sentence generators are inadequate to assist humans during the mapping process. Finally, I have sketched the outline of a system which should help the student express his thoughts, and, more importantly, give him an understanding of some of the variables which determine form. What has to be investigated in the future is the motivation of the choices, that is to say, under what pragmatic conditions one uses a particular linguistic form.

Notes

1. For a review, see Kempen (1986), or McKeown & Swartout in this volume.
2. We should bear in mind that languages are symbolic tools which have evolved with respect to the needs (communication) and to the particular constraints of the human cognitive system (input/output and central processing capacities). If our physical and mental equipment were different, languages would be different too. The physical and computational limitations of the symbol processor are reflected in the structure of the data as well as in the organization of the process. Put differently, the symbolic resources are dependent upon the particular constraints of the symbol-processing mechanism. If this were not the case, the information could not be processed, hence language would not be an adequate tool to communicate information under the mentioned space and time constraints.
3. Although these constraints are less severe in writing than in the spontaneous discourse, they do exist. The writer is allotted a given amount of space (pages) and time (deadline). On the other hand, the increase in expected quality (style) make up for the gained time.
4. The fact that the process is cyclic—planning (what to say) and execution (expression of content) alternate—does not necessarily entail sequential processing. As a matter of fact, speech-error data from the psycholinguistic literature (Garrett 1975; Butterworth 1980) strongly suggest that the whole process is organized as some kind of time-sharing system, where planning and execution partially overlap (see also Kempen & Hoenkamp 1982).

One could also object that content may be fully specified in written discourse. However this does not affect our basic argument, namely that natural languages ought to be flexible, because:

- written language has evolved from oral discourse
- even in written discourse, minor changes, i.e. local corrections, should be possible (deletion or inclusion of a new idea) without implying starting from scratch, i.e. destroying the whole structure.

5. Given the space (short-term memory) and time constraints (fast delivery), one may even say that the semiotic system language is a very efficient and reliable communication tool and that the user's performance is outstanding. As a matter of fact, spontaneous discourse is fast (six to eight words per second), the number of errors acceptable, and discourse, no matter how imperfect with respect to grammar, fairly instrumental or direct to achieve particular goals.

6. 'The notion of "translation" has as its consequence, if not as its goal, to solve the problem which arises for the speaker using a specific structure, and who at some point of the chain wants to connect a word which syntactically does not fit in here' (Tesnière 1959: 365).

7. It is possible that at different points in the surface structure either strategy is predominant. I would even hypothesize that structure, i.e. syntactic-driven, processing prevails towards the end of a clause.

8. Kempen & Hoenkamp's work (1982) is a notable exception. Their system is capable of modelling certain aspects of human performance. However, as they are interested in incremental sentence generation, problems like interaction of choices, or how to chunk a graph, do not arise.

9. Even though different authors (Appelt 1985; Danlos 1985; Hovy 1987) plead for an integrated approach, their systems are not designed to allow for visualizing the interaction between, for example, syntax and semantics. As far as meaning is concerned (lexical semantics), it is worthwhile noting that the process of lexicalization, i.e. the access to a mental lexicon, is very poorly modelled in current systems if at all:

In some important sense, these systems have no real knowledge of lexical semantics . . . They use fragments of linguistic structure which eventually have words as their frontiers, but they have little or no explicit knowledge of what these words mean. At best, these systems assume that each conceptual primitive corresponds to a particular unique lexical item or phrase . . . trivializing the problem of lexical semantics to the claim that the meaning of the word can be represented by the same word in upper case. [Marcus 1987: 211]

10. Similar criticisms can be found in Mann & Moore (1981) and Horacek (1987):

Many of the special demands of text processing were anticipated and accommodated in the design of the knowledge structures themselves. Second, the sentence boundaries in these systems were direct correlates of internal features of the data structures themselves. Finally, none of these systems chose the particular sentences to use in their output on the bases of quality assessment or comparisons among alternatives. [Mann & Moore 1981: 18]

In the early phase of generation several systems were capable of producing multi-sentence text, especially those based on a low-level conceptual dependency representation. The data structures that served as the basis for generation were assigned to reflect the expected sentence boundaries. This consequently predetermined the feasible word choice and the appropriate functional relations to a high degree. [Horacek 1987: 117]

11. In discovering how surface form is affected by linguistic choices, the student learns to form correct sentences, but he does not learn how to choose among different forms. In other words, he may have learnt something about grammaticality, i.e. HOW to produce well-formed sentences, but nothing about communicative adequacy, i.e. WHEN or WHY to use each of these forms. I intend at a later stage to include these choices as restrictions on the possible forms.

12. As opposed to Goldman's conceptual paraphrase generator (1975). Taking CD-graphs as input, BABEL is capable of generating paraphrases by

   (i) changing the density of lexical items, thus producing either a condensed or a decomposed version of the underlying meaning

   Bill loaned Mary a book.
   Bill gave Mary a book and he expected her to return it to him.

   (ii) changing the way of traversing the graph;
   (iii) ignoring some features of the underlying meaning (tree pruning).

13. These lexical choices actually concern only the word-stem. For example, the choice of the word *make decision* does not imply that this word will surface as a verb or a noun. This is precisely something which has yet to be determined. The fact that one has chosen this particular word means only that one does not want to use any of its conceptual alternatives, for example, *decide* or *decree*. This choice is important, as different words have different syntactic potentials; for example, not all verbs can be nominalized.

Bibliography

Appelt, D. (1985), *Planning English Sentences*, Cambridge, Cambridge University Press.

Butterworth, B. (1980), 'Evidence from pauses in speech', in B. Butterworth (ed.), *Language Production, Volume 1: Speech and Talk*, New York, Academic Press.

Danlos, L. (1985), *Génération automatique de textes en langues naturelles*, Paris, Masson.

Garrett, M. (1975), 'The analysis of sentence production', in G. Bower (ed.), *The Psychology of Learning and Motivation, Volume 9*, New York, Academic Press.

Goldman, N. (1975), 'Conceptual generation', in R. Schank (ed.), *Conceptual Information Processing*, Amsterdam, North-Holland.

Horacek, H. (1987), 'Choice of words in the generation process of a natural language interface', *Applied Artificial Intelligence*, vol. 1, Hemisphere Publishing Corporation.

Hovy, E. (1987), 'Some pragmatic decision criteria in generation', in G. Kempen (ed.) (1987).

Kempen, G. (1986), 'Language generation systems', in I. Batorie, W. Lenders & W. Putschke (eds), *Computational Linguistics: An International Handbook on Computer Oriented Language Research and Applications*, Berlin, Walter de Gruyter.

—— (ed.) (1987), *Natural Language Generation*, Dordrecht, Martinus Nijhoff.

—— Kempen, G. & Hoenkamp, E. (1982), 'Incremental sentence generation: implications for the structure', *9th COLING*, Prague.

Marcus, M. (1987), 'Generation systems hould choose their words', *TINLAP 3*.

Mann, W. & Moore, J. (1981), 'Computer generation of multiparagraph English text', *AJCL*, vol. 7, no. 1.

Tesnière, L. (1959), *Eléments de syntaxe structurale*, Klincksieck.

Index

adequacy
  pragmatic 76
  psychological 77
  typological 76
applications 5
  interactive 5
  non-interactive 6

beliefs
  hearer's 21
  mutual 45
  questioner's 25
  reader's 21
  respondent's 25

choices or decisions 2, 3
  adequacy of 187, 190
  conceptual decisions 44, 186
  evaluation and improvement 159
  linguistic decisions 44, 117, 186
    lexical 33–7, 39, 45, 188, 193
    syntactic decisions 36–7, 39, 42
  textual 186
    chunking 186, 188
communicative function 16
communicative role 16
competence
  logical 75
concept
  basic conceptual unit 176–7
  conceptual nuclei 99
constraints
  cognitive 181–2
    channel constraint 182–4
    space constraint 182, 184
    time constraint 182
    resource limitations 181
    resource management problem 182
  linguistic 120, 187–8
    grammatical constraint satisfaction 131
    lexical 120

pragmatic 113, 182–3, 187
critics 22

decisions, *see* choices
definite descriptions, *see* reference
dependency
  long distance dependencies 57
determinism 38
dialogue
  games 115
  management 113
  spoken 112–13
discontinuous constituents 67
discourse
  context 117
  goal 11
  purpose 10, 13
  roles 113
  strategies 9, 11, 13, 18, 45
direct translation 3

effect 19, 45
elaborations 31
  definition 31
  descriptions 31
  justification 31
explanation 1, 6, 7, 10, 26, 27, 29–32, 132–3, 144
  appropriate explanations 25

features
  inheritance 68
focus of attention 12, 43, 188

generation
  base generated form 58
  deep generation 3, 4, 7, 8, 45
  dialogue 113
  generational adequacy 26
  of intonation 122
  lexical-driven 190

generation (*cont.*)
  overgeneration 57–60
  paraphrase 188
  speech 122
  story generation 6
  surface generation 3, 7, 12, 32–3, 45
  syntactic 65, 64–5
  syntax-driven 190
goals 3
  communicative 112, 116
  expressive 119
  interactional 116
  multiple speaker's goals 21–2
  plan and achieve goals 114
  rhetorical 19
  speaker's 45
grammar 33, 37
  formalism 45
  functional 38, 41–2, 73
  generation grammars 37
  lexical-functional 53, 59, 63–4, 68
  non-transformational 55
  parsing 53
  procedural 41
  systemic 38, 41–2
  transformational 54–5
  unification 41–3

inference patterns 89
intended audience 15
intention 24
interrupt–resume mechanism 108
intonation contour 125–6

knowledge
  abstract 31
  base 73–4, 153
  conceptual 78
  dictionary 33, 102, *see also* lexicon
  discourse grammar 36, *see also* text
  discourse models 81, *see also* text
  domain-specific 152, 156
  perceptual 78
  phrasal 43
  problem solving knowledge 29–30
  sources 33

lexicon 68, 98
  lexical access 166–7
  lexical entry 102–4
    control unit 102
    semantic unit 102
linearization 188
logic 79
  functional 78–9
  lexical logic 88

logical syntax 79
logical system 79
predicational logic 84, 86
propositional logic 85
standard logic 79

maximum overlap principle 103–4
meta-level questions 9, 10
micro-world 114
misconceptions 15
  misattributions 15–17
  misclassifications 15–17
monologue 112

nucleus 14

ontology 79
  epistemological 80
overall structure 18
overanswering of yes–no questions 20

paragraph structure 11
parallelism 38, 172, 183
paraphrase 27, 44, 89, 188
pauses
  distribution 166
  macro-pauses 166
  micro-pauses 166
perspective 17
plan or planning 4, 9, 20–1, 30, 131–2, *see also*
      executive process
  activity 115
  cycles 166
  hierarchical 21
  ill-formed plan 25
  invalid plans 25
  lexical planning 185, *see also* lexicon/
      dictionary
  message planning 133, 137
  opportunistic 183
  planning phase 152
  plan inference 25
  prosodic form 122
  revise 115
  rhetorically annotated 38
  semantic planning 161, 185
  syntactic planning 161
  uniform planning mechanism 22
possible world semantics 21, 80
predicates
  logical 102
  rhetorical 10
  operator's 86–7
predication 78
  partial predications 85
problem-solving methods 31

procedure
    generation 103
    lexicalization 103–6, 109, 185, 188
    ordering 103, 106, 109
process
    automatic 161–4
    backtracking 38, 57, 61, 64–5, 67, 69, 71,
        119
    bottom-up 193
    controlled 162–3
    decomposition 187
    deterministic 40, 55
    different orders 185
    dual-process model 161, 166
    executive 161, 163–4, 166
    filter mechanism 59
    flexibility 161, 183–5
    flow of control 38–9, 42
    garbage-collection 59
    incremental 172, 178, 183
    independent 44
    interaction 5, 21–2, 36, 42, 44–5, 112, 161,
        186–7
    integration 44
    lexical access 163
    levels 163
    modularization
    non-deterministic 42, 141
    organization of the model 116
    separation 44
    spreading activation 163
    stages 4
        attachment 38–40
        fetching 43
        independent stages 4
        interpretation 43, 45
        phrase-structure execution 38–40
        realization 38–40
        restriction 43
    top-down 193
    transformations 55, 119, 183
    translation 184
    two-stage process 22
    unification 63, 140–1
    visualization 187
purpose 3, 30, 115

reasoning 9, 24, 73
    patterns of reasoning 79, 87
reference 23–4
    referring expression 21, 23, 172–3
    minimally specified 174
    overspecified 174–5, 177
    underspecified 174
relations
    social 19

speaker–hearer 45
representation
    abstract 27
    conceptual 81
    conceptual dependency 95
    deep-structure 37, 39, 55–7
    functional descriptions 139–40
    knowledge base 73–4
        logical component 72, 75
    knowledge representation 5, 25–7, 30
        frame-based 33
    linguistic representation 76
    logical form 33, 56, 58
    logical predicates 102
    logical representation 76
    meaning definition 89
    meaning postulates 89
    meaning representation 102, 108
    mental 53
    mental models 80
    message language 134–5
    picture theory 80–1
        actual picture 85
        hypothetical picture 85
    primitives 148, 154
    scenario 19
    separation of knowledge 27
    text 148
    trees
        discrimination-net 36, 96, 100, 108
        merging trees 97
        surface network 97, 101
        tree construction 39
    unified representation language 76
responses
    appropriate 24
    cooperative 25
restrictions
    epistemological 80
rules
    inference 79
    interpretation 79
    mapping rules 139
    phrase structure rules 56
    simplification rules 137
    structure building rules 139–40

satellites 14
schema 11
    constituency schema 11, 12, 18
    like-super schema 16
    process schema 18
    request schema 14
    templates 27, 30
    unordered 14
social background 19

social relationship 19
speech-act 22, 24, 70
speech errors
    performance errors 181, 187
    plan-internal errors 168
    non-plan internal errors 168
strategies
    discourse 9, 11, 13, 18, 45
    organizational 45
style 15, 19, 45
syntactic assembly 166

tactical component 13
text
    coherent text 8, 146, 154
    discourse plan 150
    discourse structure 9
    external structure 154, 156
    internal structure 156
    ordering patterns 43
    organization 4, 8, 13, 146

representation 148
rhetorical schemata 9
rhetorical structure theory 9, 13, 153
structured 146
text plan 154
    revision 155–6
text spans 14
topicalization 60, 70, 185, 187–8, 190
transcript analysis 15
turn-taking 115

user modelling 20, 45, 152

variable order hypothesis 162
variable priority hypothesis 62

word-based lexicon 37
word order
    free word order 64–5
    intrinsic 107, 109
    prenominal adjective ordering 175–6, 178